THE FATEFUL HISTORY OF
FANNIE MAE

THE FATEFUL HISTORY OF

FANNIE MAE

NEW DEAL BIRTH TO
MORTGAGE CRISIS FALL

JAMES R. HAGERTY

Charleston London

THE
History
PRESS

Published by The History Press
Charleston, SC 29403
www.historypress.net

Front cover, top: courtesy of the Library of Congress; *bottom*: Tamarack Village,
courtesy of Alan D. Coogan.
Back cover, upper left: by James R. Hagerty; *upper right*: courtesy of
the Library of Congress.
Back flap: by Lorraine Li-Hagerty.

First published 2012

Manufactured in the United States

ISBN 978.1.60949.769.9

Library of Congress CIP data applied for.

Contents

Acknowledgements and Thanks

This book is based on historical documents and interviews with nearly fifty former executives, directors and managers of Fannie Mae, as well as dozens of regulators, government officials, legislators, congressional staffers and bankers.

Thomas H. Stanton kindly gave advice and help with research. Kathryn McMiller, a true friend, dove deeply into files at the Nixon Presidential Library. Lisa Xing and Steve Velaski generously shared their photography. Drew Friedman and David Simonds let me reproduce their cartoons. Along with my own reporting for the *Wall Street Journal*, I drew on the work of other reporters for that newspaper and Dow Jones Newswires, including Kenneth Bacon, Patrick Barta, Jackie Calmes, John Connor, Dawn Kopecki, Joann Lublin, John McKinnon, Damian Paletta, Jacob Schlesinger, Deborah Solomon, Ruth Simon, Nick Timiraos and John Wilke. With love to my wife, Lorraine; children, Carmen and James; sister Gail; and parents, Marilyn and Jack Hagerty, who taught me my trade.

This book is dedicated to the memory of Carol Hagerty Werner.

Chapter 1

His Name Was Mudd

On the morning of Friday, September 5, 2008, Daniel Mudd, chief executive officer of Fannie Mae, arrived at the company's Georgian red brick headquarters on Wisconsin Avenue in Washington, D.C. A colleague told Mudd he had been summoned to attend a meeting at 3:00 p.m. The host would be James B. Lockhart III, director of the agency responsible for regulating Fannie. Lockhart was a powerful, though little-known, figure in Washington, with long experience as a regulator and entrepreneur. Since high school, he had been a friend of President George W. Bush, who still sometimes called him by a teenage nickname, "Juice." The other people due to attend the meeting were more imposing: Treasury Secretary Henry Paulson and Federal Reserve Chairman Ben Bernanke.

Normally, Mudd was at ease with the rich and powerful. A son of the former CBS television news anchorman Roger Mudd, he grew up in Washington and was decorated for action in Lebanon as a first lieutenant in the U.S. Marines. He later worked for General Electric in Europe and Asia under the glorious reign of CEO Jack Welch.

Mudd was proud of the work he had done since taking over as CEO of Fannie in late 2004, when an accounting scandal forced out his predecessor. He believed he had changed the company's culture to make it less arrogant and bureaucratic. Fannie had spent hundreds of millions of dollars on a restatement of its accounts to satisfy regulators. "We have a solid, successful franchise that earns billions of dollars a year by helping lenders put millions

A caricature drawn for the *Wall Street Journal* in 2006 shows Daniel Mudd under fire from critics. *Drawing by Drew Friedman.*

of working families into houses and apartments," the company had stated in a planning document for 2007 through 2011.

But 2007 didn't turn out to be a very good year, as the U.S. housing bust deepened, and 2008 was looking far worse. As an investor in home mortgages, many of them defaulting, Fannie was losing money at the rate of nearly $1 billion a month. The owners of its bonds—including central banks around the world—were getting edgy. They had the power to pull the plug on Fannie and, by extension, the U.S. housing industry.

Mudd called the Treasury and asked to speak to Secretary Paulson, a one-time college football offensive lineman and the former CEO of the Wall Street investment bank Goldman Sachs. Mudd thought he had a good working relationship with the Treasury secretary and wanted to be part of the solution—a solution that would reassure investors that Fannie had solid government backing and could survive in its current form, under its current management.

When Paulson picked up the phone, he offered Mudd no comfort. Paulson declined to explain why the meeting was being called. "Dan," Paulson later recalled saying, "if I could tell you, I wouldn't be calling the meeting."

Mudd called H. Rodgin "Rodge" Cohen, chairman of the law firm Sullivan & Cromwell. Fannie's chairman, Stephen Ashley, who was at his summer house in Vermont, got a call at around 9:00 a.m. from the company. A jet was being sent to bring him back to Washington. "My wife said, 'What's that all about?'" Ashley recalled later. "I said, 'It isn't good.'"

Mudd, Ashley and the company's general counsel, Beth Wilkinson, rode in a Fannie car to the Washington office of Sullivan & Cromwell to huddle with Cohen early that afternoon. Then the four of them walked a few blocks to the regulator's office at the corner of G and 17th Streets.

Security guards kept them in the ground-floor lobby, amid varnished blond-wood benches and a profusion of shiny green plants in white pots that gave the glass-walled waiting area the feel of a greenhouse. A *Wall Street Journal* reporter, Damian Paletta, was stationed on the sidewalk outside the lobby, punching numbers into his cellphone. Mudd was annoyed: yet again, he thought, someone had leaked bad news about Fannie to the press.

Bernanke arrived in the lobby and made awkward small talk with the Fannie executives before being escorted to the elevator. Finally, Mudd and his colleagues were invited upstairs. Inside a conference room in the regulator's office, the members of the Fannie team found themselves across the table from Lockhart, flanked by Bernanke and Paulson. Lockhart spoke first, reading from a script. His hands were trembling....

Chapter 2

An Accidental Birth

W ho wrecked the U.S. housing market? The question will stoke political debates for years, just as "Who lost China?" echoed amid a search for scapegoats after the Chinese turned to communism in the 1940s.

In explaining the housing bust, Democrats tend to blame loose regulation and Wall Street greed. Republicans point to federal programs—especially the government-backed mortgage companies Fannie Mae and Freddie Mac, responsible for funneling money into home loans and spreading homeownership. Since they began suffering catastrophic losses in 2008, Fannie and Freddie have become stick figures of hate, brandished regularly to shame those who supported government social programs of all sorts. On the campaign trail in 2008, Republican presidential candidate John McCain lashed out at Fannie and Freddie for setting off a financial crisis; they were, he said, "the match that started this forest fire."

Yet even Senator McCain could not completely escape the taint: a firm owned by one of his campaign managers was found to have lobbied for Fannie and Freddie. During Newt Gingrich's failed bid for the Republican presidential nomination in 2012, opponents gleefully tattled on his past work as a consultant for Freddie Mac, for which he collected about $1.6 million in fees.

While campaigning for president in 2008, Barack Obama described Fannie and Freddie as a "weird blend," companies with a public purpose and government backing but also with private shareholders expecting ever-rising dividends and with executives raking in Wall Street–style pay. "If these are public entities, then they've got to get out of the profit-making business," President Obama declared, "and if they're private entities, then we don't bail them out." Yet they were both public and private. And we are bailing them out.

"Bailout" has become a loaded term for a loathed policy, so it is worth being more precise. The shareholders of Fannie and Freddie were not bailed out; their shares are nearly worthless. The top executives of Fannie and Freddie were not allowed to keep their jobs, and much of their wealth was destroyed by the collapse of the companies' share prices. But the creditors—those who bought bonds and notes issued by Fannie and Freddie—are being repaid, fully and on schedule. In today's climate of political rage, any kind of bailout arouses the rancor of a public worn down by hard times.

In the heat of argument, one fact is often left out: the bailout of Fannie and Freddie is a bipartisan affair. It began under a Republican president, George W. Bush, and almost certainly would have continued no matter who won the election of 2008. It was always a bipartisan gamble. When Fannie and Freddie were resisting tougher regulation in the decades before their crash, most Republicans and nearly all Democrats in Congress sided with them.

By 2008, Fannie and Freddie had run up more than $1.7 trillion of debt to finance home loans for Americans. They borrowed much of that money overseas, largely from the central banks of China and other countries that have become America's indispensable creditors. Those creditors bought bonds from Fannie and Freddie because they assumed, rightly, that the U.S. government would stand behind Fannie and Freddie in a crisis.

Had the Treasury let Fannie and Freddie default, the U.S. government's credibility as a borrower would have crumbled. Global financial markets would have quaked. The U.S. government had no safe choice other than saving the creditors of Fannie and Freddie. When they were on the verge of failure in July 2008, the first order of business was, as President Bush is said to have put it, to "save their ass."

Because millions of mortgages backed by Fannie and Freddie have defaulted, the bailout has been immensely expensive. In the five years ending on December 31, 2011, Fannie alone reported total losses of $163.6 billion, more than double all the profits it made in the three decades through 2006. As of mid-2012, the U.S. Treasury had injected a total of about $146.5 billion of equity capital into Fannie and Freddie (net of their dividend payments to the Treasury) to keep them operating as the nation's main providers of money for home mortgages. Once all the debts are settled, it almost certainly will rank as one of the biggest corporate rescues ever by the U.S. government. The $146.5 billion bailout cost as of mid-2012 would be enough to buy more than 890,000 homes at the median U.S. price recorded in March of that year.

Our grandchildren will still be paying the costs of misguided mortgage business underwritten by Fannie and Freddie. They may wish to know how we got ourselves into this mess.

IT WAS AN ACCIDENT. President Franklin Delano Roosevelt created Fannie Mae in 1938 to help provide money for home mortgages and spur housing construction. It was a minor detail in FDR's vast New Deal—another way to create desperately needed construction jobs, something few could oppose at the time. As an obscure federal agency, Fannie did not lend money directly to home buyers. Instead, it bought mortgage loans from banks and other lenders; those purchases put money in the lenders' hands so they could make more loans, allowing more homes to be built. The goal was to give a boost to the private mortgage market, not to replace it.

After the Great Depression ended, Fannie could have been dissolved, like the Works Progress Administration, which temporarily kept the unemployed busy building roads and parks and then closed down in 1943. Instead, Fannie kept growing and evolving—an unintended long-term experiment in state-sponsored mortgage lending. The provisional became permanent. Under both Republican and Democratic administrations, Fannie eluded all attempts to take away the federal backing that allowed the company to borrow money cheaply and expand practically without limit.

Along the way, Fannie acquired a smaller clone, Freddie Mac. Together, they came to dominate the business of supplying funds for home loans and became two of the world's largest financial companies. In a nation where "socialist" is the supreme insult, Fannie, Freddie and other federal programs in recent years have financed about nine of every ten home mortgage loans.

Fannie and Freddie grew to dominance not because of any plan but through political expedience, neglect and drift. From a politician's point of view, they were magical: Congress never had to allocate a penny to pay for them and never had to include their borrowings on the federal ledger. Yet Fannie and Freddie generated vast amounts of money to propel the real estate market. The justification? The chance to buy a home would lift more Americans out of poverty. Communities and families would be stronger; people with a place of their own would be better citizens.

In essence, Fannie and Freddie were government subsidies to the housing industry. Like many subsidies, they were created to meet a specific, temporary need and then proved impossible to eliminate. That left an unacknowledged contingent liability for the U.S. taxpayers.

For seven decades, "it looked like a free lunch," Lawrence White, an economics professor at New York University, told the House Financial Services Committee in June 2009, "but we've just found out how costly this meal has been."

Fannie and Freddie flourished over the decades because their presence suited powerful people and organizations: home builders, Realtors, mortgage bankers and politicians. Along with donations from Fannie and Freddie, the politicians got plenty of opportunities to share credit for the new housing developments they financed.

This is a story of noble aspirations, low-down greed, ideological passion, political intrigue and lobbying raised to an art form—all resulting in an enormous bill for the one party never consulted during the seven-decade experiment: the U.S. taxpayer.

What went wrong? It was not the greed, incompetence or evil of any one person, clique or political party—though certainly there were greed, incompetence and delusions aplenty. No, it was that, by accident, the government created an entity able to mutate and perpetuate itself until it became so enormous and so entangled in the global financial fabric that the errors of its management, coinciding with a steep fall in house prices, could produce a financial calamity. The nature of the beast made it almost certain to fail.

IT HAS NEVER BEEN difficult for American politicians to decide whether to support homeownership. Until the Great Depression, however, federal support for the housing industry was limited.

In 1892, Congress allotted $20,000 for a Labor Department study of urban slums, but legislative efforts to improve housing standards were left to states and cities. Social reformers, such as Lawrence Veiller of New York, fretted about renters crammed into tenements. "Where a man has a home of his own he has every incentive to be economical and thrifty, to take his part in the duties of citizenship....Democracy was not predicated upon a country made up of tenement dwellers," he wrote in 1910.

An Accidental Birth

When the federal income tax was created in 1913, Congress enacted a deduction for interest paid on home mortgages, giving well-heeled Americans another reason to buy rather than rent.

Near the end of World War I, the Labor Department briefly operated the U.S. Housing Corporation to build housing for people making war materials. Even on a small scale, this government intervention was controversial. The National Association of Real Estate Boards, a trade group for real estate brokers, opposed it. The government discontinued the program in 1919. In 1922, the Real Estate Boards reported that "the danger of municipal or governmental housing seems to have nearly passed."

The Republican administrations of the 1920s provided moral support for Americans yearning to buy homes. In the early 1920s, the Commerce Department, then headed by Herbert Hoover, published an "Own Your Own Home" pamphlet to support local campaigns by home builders, real estate brokers and architects.

In the 1930s, the government moved much more deeply into housing as it struggled against the Great Depression. By 1934, unemployment had risen to around a quarter of the workforce. Many people still working were on reduced wages. Thousands of banks were failing. Around half of all home mortgage debt was in default by 1933, according to one official estimate. Dislodged from their homes by foreclosing banks, stunned Americans crowded in with relatives or lived in shantytowns known as Hoovervilles in derision of President Hoover.

As the new president, Franklin Roosevelt, searched for remedies after his election in 1932, he became known as the "great experimenter." Fannie Mae was one of his lesser-noted experiments. The Roosevelt administration did not set out to take over the mortgage market. Instead, it was trying to revive housing construction, one sure way to create jobs. Housing starts had dropped to about ninety-three thousand units in 1933, about a tenth of the peak levels of the mid-1920s.

Among the Roosevelt administration's tools were two new financial institutions created by legislation signed by President Hoover in 1932. One was the Federal Home Loan Bank System. The twelve regional Federal Home Loan Banks sold bonds and used the proceeds to make loans, called "advances," to savings and loan (S&L) institutions. Funding from the home loan banks allowed the S&Ls to make more mortgage loans.

The second institution was the Reconstruction Finance Corporation, or RFC, which also made loans to financial institutions. President

A man bides his time in a Portland, Oregon shantytown of the sort known during the Depression as a Hooverville. *Courtesy of the Library of Congress.*

Hoover wanted this temporary government corporation to provide funding to financial institutions serving commercial, agricultural and residential borrowers.

President Roosevelt went much further. In 1933, the administration sought and obtained legislation creating the Home Owners' Loan Corporation, or HOLC, to refinance defaulted home mortgages and avert foreclosures. The HOLC helped over one million borrowers to refinance between August 1933 and June 1936. This agency managed to show a slight profit when the housing market recovered and the corporation was wound up in 1951.

Building on Hoover administration plans, the Roosevelt White House turned the RFC into a vital part of the New Deal. Headed by Jesse Jones, an entrepreneur from Houston, the RFC began lending large amounts to banks, trust companies, insurers, thrift institutions, mortgage companies, credit unions, agriculture-financing institutions, railroads and other businesses and public agencies.

The Roosevelt administration also worked with Congress to enact the Housing Act of 1934, creating the Federal Housing Administration, or FHA, offering insurance to lenders against defaults on home mortgages. The idea was to make mortgage lending less risky for lenders so mortgages would be more widely available. Before the FHA, mortgages normally had to be repaid after just three to five years. These loans were called balloon mortgages. Borrowers paid only the interest during the term of the loan. The full principal was due at the end of the three- or five-year term. For those who couldn't pay off the loan or refinance it, foreclosure loomed. The FHA insurance program helped make possible mortgages of up to thirty years.

Creating this FHA mortgage insurance was not considered enough. To heal the housing market, the government wanted to ensure that plenty of money was available for making FHA-insured loans, beyond what local banks could gather in deposits. So the legislation provided a means for private investors to create "national mortgage associations" to buy and sell FHA-insured mortgages. These private associations were to borrow money, by issuing bonds, to pay for the mortgages.

The government hoped private companies would eagerly apply for national mortgage association charters and set up shop around the nation. One problem was that the savings and loan industry disliked the idea. The S&Ls already had funding for mortgages through the Federal Home Loan Banks. The mortgage associations would help the S&Ls' rivals, mortgage banks, which didn't have access to the Federal Home Loan Banks.

Prodded by the S&Ls, Congress adjusted the plan for national mortgage associations in ways that made them less appealing to any investors who might be tempted to set one up. Congress eliminated a proposed exemption from income taxes. The borrowing authority of each association was limited to ten times capital, rather than fifteen times as originally proposed. Later amendments in 1935 loosened some of the restrictions on the associations— for example, by increasing permitted leverage to twelve times capital. Amendments in 1938 made further concessions, permitting leverage up to twenty times.

President Hoover escorting his successor, Franklin D. Roosevelt, to the Capitol in 1933.
Courtesy of the Library of Congress.

Even with the amendments, the proposition proved unappealing to private investors. No private mortgage association was ever formed. "Times were so pessimistic that no one would put up money for common stock in such an enterprise," Jones, chairman of the RFC, wrote in his memoir. "We wanted private investors to own the business, to do the work and make a fair profit. But we couldn't induce anyone to try it."

What private investors wouldn't do, the government did. At the urging of the Roosevelt administration, the government-owned RFC took on the additional role of buying FHA-insured loans. On February 10, 1938, Jones announced that the RFC—under provisions of the National Housing Act—had chartered the National Mortgage Association of Washington as a subsidiary of the RFC. On April 11, the name of this new entity was changed to the Federal National Mortgage Association, or FNMA, whose initials eventually suggested the folksy nickname of Fannie Mae. This new agency's role was to use borrowed money to buy FHA loans from lenders. Fannie's initial borrowing limit was $220 million, or twenty times its capital. The first president of the agency was an RFC official, Sam Husbands. The birth of Fannie Mae was not

President Franklin Roosevelt signing papers to create the Federal National Mortgage Association in February 1938. *Courtesy of Fannie Mae.*

heralded as major news; the *Wall Street Journal* devoted eight sentences to the story on page two. In its first year, Fannie bought 26,276 mortgages and started foreclosures on 25 of them.

The creation of this agency "was a stopgap measure," James Johnson, a future chairman of Fannie, would write in his 1996 book *Showing America a New Way Home.* He added, "This improvisation had an unintended, if predictable, side effect: now potential investors were reluctant to fund private mortgage associations because of competition from the RFC." The federal government was becoming entrenched in a business that Congress had intended for private investors.

The sort of improvisation that created Fannie was not new. For centuries, governments had chartered companies to do things that otherwise might have gone undone. These companies have included the East India Company, which did the English kings' bidding in India, and the Hudson's Bay Co., which organized the fur trade in North America. The results have not always matched the original intentions. As the economist Adam Smith wrote in *The Wealth of Nations,* published in 1776, "These companies, though they may, perhaps, have been useful for the first introduction of some branches of commerce, by making at their own expense an experiment which the state might not think it prudent to make, have in the long run proved, universally, either burdensome or useless."

THE U.S. GOVERNMENT WAS moving into housing in another, more obvious way—one that, unlike Fannie, would generate public debate. In January 1937, the newly reelected President Roosevelt declared that a third of the nation was "ill-housed." His support helped push forward legislative efforts to allocate federal money to help local housing authorities build low-rent housing for the poor.

Many in the real estate industry feared a government takeover of their realm. "Housing should remain a matter of private enterprise and private ownership," declared Walter Schmidt, president of the National Association of Real Estate Boards. He added, "There is sound logic in the continuance of the practice under which those who have initiative and the will to save acquire better living facilities and yield their former quarters at modest rents to the group below."

Despite such qualms, Congress in mid-1937 overwhelmingly approved the Wagner-Steagall Housing Act to create the U.S. Housing Authority, a forerunner of today's Department of Housing and Urban Development. The federal government was now firmly in the business of providing homes for the poor, via funding for local housing authorities. The people running those local authorities, powerful sources of patronage and natural advocates for a larger federal role in housing, eventually would provide another layer of political support for Fannie.

Chapter 3

The War Eisenhower Lost

Though barely noticed by most Americans, Fannie grew quickly until the U.S. entry into World War II. The agency's business then slowed during the war, when the nation was too busy making weapons to build many houses. The total value of mortgages owned by Fannie dwindled from about $211.0 million at the end of 1942 to $4.4 million five years later. Mortgages were being sold to other investors or paid off faster than Fannie was buying them.

But it was clear that the end of the war would mean surging demand for homes from returning soldiers. In 1944, Congress enacted the Serviceman's Readjustment Act, or GI Bill of Rights. It included provisions for the Veterans Administration to guarantee loans for veterans who were buying or improving houses.

Then came a four-year legislative battle over the federal government's involvement in housing the poor. Home builders and real estate brokers generally supported federal subsidies for mortgage credit via the FHA, Fannie and the Federal Home Loan Banks. But the builders and brokers vigorously opposed the creation of more public housing, which they depicted as a dangerous government intrusion into free enterprise. On the other side of the debate, organized labor lined up with public housing authorities, veterans' groups and big-city mayors to support an expanded federal role in subsidized housing. They argued that private enterprise was not building enough affordable housing for the poor.

Senator Robert Taft, a Republican from Ohio, held hearings and supported a new push for public housing. "I believe that the government

Senator Robert Taft (center), an Ohio Republican, shown in early 1940, had a big role in pushing through the 1949 housing act. *Courtesy of the Library of Congress.*

must see that every family has a minimum standard of decent shelter along with subsistence, medical care and education," he wrote in 1946. Congress was deeply split on housing policies, but Taft and his allies kept pushing for legislation.

Democratic victories in the 1948 election broke the impasse. After a tense debate in the House, where Representative George Dondero of Michigan decried what he called "the first fatal step toward national socialism," Congress finally approved the Housing Act of 1949. President Harry Truman signed it. The law extended the government's role in redeveloping slums and assuring the availability of rental housing for the poor. It called for "the realization as soon as feasible of the goal of a decent home and a suitable living environment for every American family, thus contributing to the development and redevelopment of communities and to the advancement of the growth, wealth and security of the nation."

Many American homes were still primitive. The 1950 Census found that 29 percent of American homes lacked flush toilets. Now it was official federal government policy to ensure that everyone had a healthful place to live.

FANNIE WAS STILL ONLY a small part of that policy. In 1948, Congress adopted legislation formally chartering Fannie. Among other things, the company gained authority to purchase VA mortgages, along with FHA ones.

After the wartime lull, Fannie's loan investments rebounded as surging demand for housing spurred construction, especially in the suburbs. For home builders, Fannie was becoming a financial lifeline. Builders often relied on an advance commitment from Fannie to purchase a mortgage at a specified interest rate once construction of a home was completed and FHA insurance secured. By 1953, Fannie's portfolio totaled $2.5 billion, up from $4.4 million at the low point in 1947.

Fannie was finally big enough to stir up some controversy. Some critics accused Fannie of bursting out of its legal confines. The agency's advance commitments to buy mortgages, argued Richard W. Bartke, a legal scholar at Northwestern University, meant that the private mortgage bankers were merely acting as middlemen, taking no real risk. "Fannie Mae was in effect the lender," Bartke wrote.

SOME HOME BUILDERS AND mortgage lenders argued that Fannie had grown too big and warned of the risk of "socialization" of the mortgage business. In early 1950, there was talk among builders and bankers of creating privately owned entities to take over at least part of Fannie's role in buying mortgages—an idea that later fizzled out. R.O. Deming Jr., president of the Mortgage Bankers Association, told the *Washington Post* that he did not wish to see Fannie eliminated. But, he said, the agency should revert to being a standby source of money when other sources dried up, *not* a constant provider.

IN A 1950 REORGANIZATION, Fannie was transferred from the RFC to the Housing and Home Finance Agency, which also administered the FHA program. The goal was to increase coordination of government housing programs. The early heads of Fannie had been RFC officials, usually serving just a year or two in that post. President Truman in 1950 appointed J. Stanley Baughman as president of Fannie. Baughman, a World War I veteran and native of Pittsburgh, had spent most of his career as civil servant at the federal Home Owners' Loan Corporation. He remained president of Fannie until he retired in 1966.

Fending off occasional questions about federal meddling in private business, the low-key and diplomatic Baughman ensured that Fannie made itself useful, notably by helping to finance the postwar housing boom and homes near remote military bases. At a Senate Banking Committee hearing in February 1952, Senator J. Allen Frear Jr. reminded his colleagues that Fannie was "an extremely profitable organization." The Delaware Democrat added, "They [Fannie and Freddie] do not cost the government any money."

BY 1952, THE DEMOCRATS' two decades in control of the White House were ending. Now came an occasion to rethink the hodgepodge of housing programs created over the past two decades. General Dwight Eisenhower, preparing for his successful run for president, sought housing-policy advice from Miles Colean, an economist and consultant to mortgage lenders. In a memo to Eisenhower, Colean noted that the profusion of government interventions in housing had been "improvised in a progression of crises." The federal intervention lacked "a recognizable settled policy," and "no limit to the expansion of the federal jurisdiction is discernible."

Could housing now be left purely to private business? "The federal government is now too deeply involved to withdraw," Colean wrote. But the government still could "establish a consistent policy by which its future activity may be guided and limited."

In mortgages, Colean foresaw a smaller government role: "The federal policy should be one of aiding to stabilize the flow and equalize the distribution of private funds. It should not be one of exercising direct and detailed influence on the building market, or of entering the lending market directly or indirectly with government funds, or of attempting to regulate the rate of interest by arbitrary devices."

Colean and others wanted more of a free-market approach. "The only way that an adequate supply of mortgage money can be assured is to permit mortgage borrowers to compete freely for funds with other borrowers," he wrote. If interest rates and loan terms were set by government officials, "this kind of credit system becomes a political instrument of the powerful and dangerous sort."

To avert this danger, Fannie should be transformed from a federal agency to "a federally chartered institution," Colean wrote. The capital would come not from the government but from private lending institutions. Still, the White House would select the board of directors.

AFTER TAKING OFFICE IN 1953, President Eisenhower followed through with an effort to reconfigure housing policy. He signaled a change of marching orders by selecting Albert Cole as administrator of the Housing and Home Finance Agency. Cole, a Republican from Kansas, as a U.S. representative had voted against the Housing Act of 1949 with its expansion of the federal role in housing. Senator Hubert Humphrey declared that putting Cole in charge of the housing agency was "like putting a fox in the chicken coop." Yet this fox proved sympathetic to housing programs and fought against an early attempt to slash funding for public housing.

Cole later recalled ambiguous marching orders from President Eisenhower: "We don't have a housing program. But more and better housing is a very important part of the plans this administration wants to develop." Cole spent much of 1953 traveling around the country to gather information and views. Back in Washington, he was relieved at what he found in the Housing and Home Finance Agency created by the preceding Democratic administrations: "The operations were quite efficient and the staff excellent."

In September 1953, President Eisenhower created the Advisory Committee on Government Housing Policies and Programs, headed by Cole. Among other things, this committee concluded three months later that the nation's "secondary market facility"—one of the main functions of Fannie, the purchasing of home loans— "should be privately financed and should operate without expense to

As a senator, Hubert Humphrey worried that President Eisenhower's housing chief would not be sufficiently supportive of a federal role in improving accommodations for the poor. *Courtesy of the Library of Congress.*

the federal government." President Eisenhower's strategy was clear: get the government out of the mortgage-buying business. His tactics fell short.

The president's message to Congress in January 1954 stated that Fannie should be reorganized to require users of the company's services—mortgage lenders selling loans to Fannie—to "invest funds on a basis which would eventually permit the full retirement of government funds from secondary mortgage market operations. The federal government should be enabled to purchase the initial stock of the reorganized association, but private capital funds supplied by users of the facility should be built up to speed the retirement of the government's investment."

The Housing Act of 1954 reflected the president's proposal. It specified that Fannie's purchases of mortgages "shall be financed by private capital to the maximum extent feasible."

First, some tidying up was needed. The legislation designated the administrator of the Housing and Home Finance Agency, then Cole, as chairman of Fannie and gave him authority to appoint officers and directors. "Contrary to the accepted custom of new administrations in asking for resignations from holders of political appointments, I retained the officers" of Fannie, Cole later wrote.

The legislation also carved up Fannie. Two parts of the agency were to remain part of the government: "special assistance" for mortgage programs deemed to be in the public interest that would be difficult to finance in the private sector; and the management and liquidation of mortgages acquired before 1954. What remained of Fannie, the "secondary market operations," was put on a vague course toward becoming a private company. These operations involved the buying and selling of mortgages to ensure that enough money was available to support an efficient national market for home loans insured by the FHA and the VA.

Mortgage banks selling loans to Fannie now would be required to buy small amounts of common stock in the agency. The Treasury retained control through its holdings of preferred stock in Fannie. But the law envisioned that mortgage banks and other investors eventually would acquire the Treasury's stake, turning Fannie into a private company "as rapidly as [Fannie] shall deem feasible." The rub was that there was no deadline for this transformation and no legal mechanism to ensure it happened. So, until much later, it didn't happen. Mortgage banks and others acquired common stock but only in small amounts; the Treasury enlarged its stake during times of tight credit, when Congress wanted more money to flow into housing.

President Eisenhower signed legislation in 1954 setting Fannie Mae on a vague course toward private ownership. *Courtesy of Fannie Mae.*

Fannie's funding helped build suburbs like Levittown on Long Island, New York, whose shopping center is shown in 1957. *Courtesy of the Library of Congress.*

The new charter for Fannie specified that the agency was to provide only "supplementary assistance" to the mortgage market. Fannie was to buy and sell mortgages "only at such prices and on such terms as will reasonably prevent excessive use of the corporation's facilities." The idea was that Fannie shouldn't bid so aggressively for mortgages as to deter private investors from competing for that business.

At a Senate banking subcommittee in 1956, Fannie President Baughman explained to Senator John Sparkman that Fannie, now partly funded by private investors and no longer purely a federal agency, should not "attempt to stabilize or regulate the prices of mortgages all over the United States." The Alabama Democrat replied, "Well, I wonder then if we made a mistake by changing it."

POLICY MAKERS AND CONGRESS still found Fannie to be a handy instrument. In 1958, through the Emergency Housing Act introduced by Senator Sparkman, Congress allocated $1 billion of additional mortgage-purchasing authority to Fannie as a way to spur housing during a recession. Eisenhower signed the bill while grumbling about its "burden on the federal purse." Fannie's mortgage purchases surged in 1959.

"When money gets tight, as it is now, we expect mortgage lenders to turn to us," Fannie President Baughman told the *Wall Street Journal* in late 1959. "That's what we're here for."

Fannie was "a government gal with one of the most alluring bankrolls in town," the *Wall Street Journal* remarked. The "government gal" was a fixture of the housing industry by now. Robert E. Scott, an Elizabeth, New Jersey real estate investor, put it this way at a Senate hearing on housing in December 1958: "There is no longer any question that the federal government can and must play a vital role in the field of mortgage finance if private enterprise is to attain its maximum potential in meeting the housing needs and aspirations of all of our people."

Baughman, who was balding and resembled a kindly professor behind his owlish glasses, encouraged the idea that the agency was, as he put it, an "invisible hand" helping Americans buy homes. When he retired in 1966, the National Association of Home Builders inducted him into its Housing Hall of Fame. As the builders presented him with a silver bowl, an organist played "Mr. Wonderful."

Chapter 4

A Patronage Pudding

In the tumultuous 1960s, amid war, assassinations, riots and civil rights marches, the time was not right for a review of anything so arcane as federal aid to the mortgage market. If not for a budgetary crisis, the subject might not have arisen.

President Lyndon Johnson, struggling to finance both the war in Vietnam and his Great Society crusade against poverty, fought with Congress about the rising federal debt. In the mid-1960s, the administration had resorted to a controversial budgetary maneuver: Fannie and other federal agencies put together large "pools" of individual loans made by the government to finance housing, tuition and other things. The agencies then sold "certificates of participation" in those loans to investors. The investors in effect were lending money to the government to be repaid mainly with funds generated by the interest and principal payments from borrowers who had received loans from the government.

The sale of these participations was treated as an offset to spending in the budget, lowering the reported deficit by billions of dollars. Republicans and other critics argued that the administration was using the sales of participations to conceal the true level of government spending and borrowing.

In an attempt to stop the bickering, President Johnson formed the President's Commission on Budget Concepts to propose better ways to account for the government's spending and obligations. The commission recommended in 1967 that the debts of agencies such as Fannie be included in the federal budget under a new type of summary statement. In the case of Fannie, that would swell the budget by an estimated $2.5 billion, an alarming amount in those days.

A convenient solution was at hand: the original intent of the 1954 housing act was to transform Fannie into a private company. The administration seized on that nearly forgotten bit of legislative history.

The White House appointed a mortgage finance task force—including representatives of the Bureau of the Budget, Department of Housing and Urban Development (known as HUD, the successor to the Housing and Home Finance Agency), the Treasury and the Federal Reserve Board—in September 1967. A plan was worked out by early December and submitted to Congress in February 1968. Housing officials were eager for a quick solution because they feared the growing federal deficit would push up interest rates and deter construction.

The main parties in the debate over how to extract Fannie from the federal ledger were officials of HUD and the Bureau of the Budget, along with Raymond Lapin, the new president of Fannie. The idea was to retain government control or at least heavy influence, even though the government would no longer own any of the shares. Another priority was to devise a plan that could be sold to interested lobbies, notably the home builders. The builders, an administration memo said, "will need to be convinced that their interests will be adequately protected." As for another powerful lobbying group, the memo added, "Realtors already, on the other hand, favor a FNMA [Fannie Mae] independent of HUD and its muddle-headed bias in favor of new construction; they would go for a weak regulatory role."

Another consideration was to avoid proposals that might stir up political debate in Congress. In any such debate, the memo warned, "the gratuitous opportunities for mischief are legion." There was no mention of the risk that the government was creating an untenable hybrid of the public and private spheres and leaving a contingent liability for taxpayers.

The Johnson administration was preoccupied with matters of much greater public interest, including Vietnam and the 1968 elections. Officials could hardly have imagined that within four decades Fannie would transform itself from an obscure federal agency into a financial colossus with nearly $1 trillion of debt. The debate over Fannie's future was left to subordinates. There was little public discussion of a topic too technical to engage voters.

From the initial administration discussions, two approaches emerged. One, pushed by HUD, involved selling Fannie to private shareholders but retaining a government-appointed board of directors, headed by the HUD secretary. HUD feared giving too much power to shareholders, whose interests in profits and dividends might diverge from government policy. The government would lose "powers to take the initiative" at times when "housing and various financial markets are under stress," an administration memo stated.

The Bureau of the Budget, however, favored a new "private" board for Fannie. This plan included "strong federal regulatory machinery to insure [*sic*] national interest management," according to an administration memo.

The formal recommendation for a spinoff of Fannie from government ownership came from Charles Zwick, assistant director of the budget bureau; James Duesenberry, a member of the president's Council of Economic Advisers; and Fred Bohen, another administration official. In a December 2, 1967 memo to Joseph A. Califano Jr., then a special assistant to the president, they called for removing Fannie's secondary-market operations (the business of buying mortgages from lenders) from the federal budget "and converting it into a private 'for-profit' institution, with the proviso that it not discriminate against subsidized paper," mortgages backed by the FHA and other government agencies. The memo said this approach was "consistent with legislative history and intent."

Home builders would likely resist the plan on the ground that a private, profit-seeking Fannie might mean "slightly" higher mortgage costs, the memo said. But, it added, "we believe that it can be sold to the homebuilders when packaged with a large, long-term program of subsidized housing that provides builders with guaranteed markets and profits." The transformation of Fannie would be only a detail in a major legislative act providing more federal support for housing and urban renewal.

The three officials rejected a proposal to replace Fannie with a new federal "housing bank" to finance subsidized housing. They argued that such a bank wouldn't be able to do that job better than a private Fannie. Creating a bank also would require spending $100 million to $300 million of federal money to provide capital. Though it might be legally possible to keep loans made by such a bank off the federal budget, the memo said, "creation of a bank outside the budget would invite new attacks of budget gimmickry."

Robert Weaver, secretary of HUD, sent his own memo to Califano on December 15, 1967, and also opposed creation of a bank to take over Fannie's role. Fannie already had the ability to support the mortgage market in times of stress, Weaver said, and a new bank might have trouble raising money at a reasonable cost during periods of tight credit. Besides, Weaver wrote, trying to create a bank could lead to "disastrous political consequences." Among them: "The homebuilders would react violently in opposition."

Though the principle of turning Fannie into a private company was now accepted by HUD and the budget bureau, the two bodies bickered in the early days of 1968 about how to achieve this sleight of hand. Zwick, the assistant director of the budget bureau, complained in a January 5, 1968 memo to Califano that HUD Secretary Weaver wanted to keep Fannie "completely staffed and operated by government employees" and "completely under government control." Zwick concluded, "This proposal is so bizarre that the President could not possibly recommend it. As HUD is digging in its heels, you must have a meeting as soon as possible with Weaver."

Weaver backed down. The same day, Lapin, Fannie's president, who effectively worked for HUD, sent a memo to Weaver proposing that Fannie employees would cease to be civil servants. Lapin still hoped the president of the company and the entire board would be appointed by the White House—an idea that didn't make it into the final legislation.

Lapin proposed that stock in the company be kept in the hands of the mortgage lenders who sold loans to Fannie rather than letting them sell it to other investors. "As long as the common stock is transferable, it will be sold to parties who are interested in maximizing profits and are not committed to the well-being of the mortgage market," Lapin wrote. That idea also went nowhere, and Fannie stock eventually was offered to all sorts of investors, who indeed were mainly interested in getting a good return for their money while benefiting from a perceived government guarantee.

In his memo, Lapin also expressed an aim that did endure in Washington and grew increasingly awkward: "The new private corporation must remain publicly oriented despite its private ownership."

Congress took up the administration's plan as a small part of the Housing and Urban Development Act of 1968. Part of the old Fannie remained within the government as the Government National Mortgage Association, or GNMA, inevitably dubbed Ginnie Mae. Ginnie's role was to guarantee payments on a new type of security backed by pools of FHA and VA mortgages. Thus was born what became over the next several decades a mammoth market for mortgage-backed securities.

The rest of Fannie was to become a corporation owned entirely by private shareholders. The board would be composed of fifteen members—ten elected by shareholders and five by the White House.

HUD Secretary Weaver told Congress that the desire to avoid a budgetary burden was a major reason for the administration's decision to remove

Fannie from the government ledger. The budget issue "is not the only reason" for taking Fannie out of the government, Carl A.S. Coan Sr., staff director for the housing subcommittee of the Senate Banking Committee, explained at an executive session of that subcommittee on April 9, 1968, but it "may be the impelling reason why we do it now." Coan's son, Carl A.S. Coan Jr., remembered the budget squeeze as the only reason for taking Fannie off the government books, despite "high-sounding statements" to justify it. The younger Coan, who was then an assistant general counsel at HUD, later told me he didn't recall any concerns raised of possible future conflicts between Fannie's continued political role in supporting the housing market and the desire of its shareholders for maximum profits.

Home builders raised questions about whether the new Fannie would buy mortgages even in hard times. Senator Sparkman, chairman of the Senate subcommittee, expressed concern about getting the right balance between regulation and autonomy. "If you are going to have a private industry, it ought to have certainly a high degree of private control," he said at a subcommittee meeting. "But, on the other hand, since this is dealing with matters and programs for which the government has a vested interest, and a vital interest, certainly there ought to be a close connection between the

President Johnson signing legislation that turned Fannie into an odd sort-of-private company on August 1, 1968. *Courtesy of Fannie Mae.*

government [and Fannie]. We ought not to divorce it completely. This is just my loose thinking."

Califano told me in a 2009 interview that Fannie in its new incarnation was seen as a way to attract private funds that otherwise wouldn't have gone to housing. "It was like a hive that attracted the private-money bees," Califano said. The Johnson administration saw no contradiction between Fannie's duties to shareholders and the public role it was to play in promoting homeownership. "We didn't see a conflict," he said. "We thought this was brilliantly leveraging federal power" to draw more money into housing without increasing the budget.

Congress approved the housing act, and President Johnson signed it on August 1, 1968.

The legislation gave Fannie huge advantages over other private companies:

- The U.S. Treasury could buy up to $2.25 billion of its debt securities if Fannie ever needed financial support.
- Fannie was exempt from state and local income taxes.
- The company didn't have to pay registration fees to the Securities and Exchange Commission (SEC) when it issued securities, as other corporations did. It was exempt from SEC financial-reporting and disclosure rules.
- Federally regulated banks had no limits on the amount of their funds that could be invested in Fannie debt, regarded as being nearly as safe as Treasury securities.

Fannie's biggest advantage was that investors would continue to see it as virtually an arm of the government. That meant Fannie could borrow money cheaply—at interest rates almost as low as those paid by the U.S. Treasury—because investors assumed Uncle Sam would make good on those debts if Fannie could not. The Johnson administration and Congress fudged the issue of who was responsible for the risks in Fannie's financing of mortgages. In reality, the risks of calamity were still with U.S. taxpayers. The profits would flow to private investors.

FANNIE BEGAN A TRANSITION to private ownership, achieved on May 21, 1970. To complete the process, Fannie raised money by selling subordinated debentures and used the proceeds to pay $164 million to the Treasury in exchange for the government's preferred stock. Fannie paid an added $52 million to the Treasury for the government's share of Fannie's retained earnings.

"The result of this forced birth was a strange creature indeed," a HUD report to Congress noted eighteen years later. Private? Public? No one could really say for sure. In the bond market, traders would still refer to Fannie bonds as "agency debt," a term implying the support of Uncle Sam.

ARRANGEMENTS HAD TO BE made to run Fannie during its transition from public to (sort of) private. In a memo on August 1, 1968, Califano recommended to President Johnson that Fannie's president, Lapin, should keep that job during the transition. Money was at stake. "If this appointment can be made immediately, it will probably save some $200 million in the budget by having the private corporation, rather than the public Fannie May [sic], sell bonds in September," Califano advised. He added that Lapin was "well respected in the financial community" and "I have found him to be first rate." The president reappointed him.

Lapin, who had originally been appointed to head Fannie by President Johnson in June 1967 at an annual salary of $26,000, saw "our chance to take Fannie Mae and make it into something that works," recalled Lorraine Legg, who was his assistant at the company in the late 1960s. Lapin had been frustrated by Fannie's dependence on shifting government-budget priorities. Fannie had sometimes run out of money to buy more mortgages just when its services were most needed, Lapin used to say, and so was "like a fire department that always has water except when there is a fire." Now Fannie could borrow on its own.

BEFORE THE TWO-YEAR TRANSITION to private ownership was completed, the 1968 presidential election brought in the administration of Richard Nixon. As he moved into the White House in early 1969, Fannie was moving out of the federal bureaucracy. Yet Nixon's aides thought there might be one last chance for the White House to put a friend in the top job at Fannie.

Lapin, a California mortgage banker and a prominent Democrat, fancied himself well qualified to remain in that post. He had earned a master's degree in business from the University of Chicago. After serving as a captain in the U.S. Army during World War II, he worked in the research department of the Federal Reserve Bank of Chicago. In 1954, he formed a one-man company,

Raymond Lapin was appointed president of Fannie by President Johnson—and then booted out by President Nixon. *Courtesy of Fannie Mae.*

Bankers Mortgage Co. of California, with initial capital of about $25,000. A decade later, Bankers Mortgage was one of the largest mortgage banks in the United States. Lapin sold it in 1964 to Transamerica Corp.

Like many who have succeeded in business, Lapin figured he was equally qualified to deal with public policy. He contributed to the successful campaign of Edmund Brown, who defeated Nixon to become governor of California in 1962. In 1966, Lapin became commissioner of the California State Economic Development Agency. A year later, President Johnson put him in charge of Fannie.

When Lapin arrived, Fannie was still based inside a HUD building. He moved the company in the fall of 1969 to an office building on 15th Street NW near the *Washington Post* offices and the Madison Hotel. (Nixon declined an invitation to appear at a dedication ceremony for the new offices.) Lapin also began hiring people from outside the civil service.

"Ray was a warm kind of teddy bear, but smart and tough," said John Kuhnle, who worked for him briefly as a speechwriter and executive assistant in 1969. Legg, his assistant, remembered Lapin as kind but impatient with people who were not "sufficiently mentally agile."

Almost immediately after President Nixon took the oath of office in January 1969, Lapin clashed with the new Republican leaders at HUD, especially Sherman Unger, a lawyer from Cincinnati who served as general counsel of that department. By mid-February 1969, less than four weeks after Nixon's inauguration, White House aides were discussing the "removal" of Lapin, according to documents at the Nixon Presidential Library. Handwritten notes from Egil "Bud" Krogh, then a twenty-nine-year-old White House lawyer (and later jailed for his role in the Watergate scandal), described Lapin as an "ardent Dem; ardent empire builder; autonomous." Apparently taking notes at a meeting of Nixon aides, Krogh scrawled, "HUD needs to get control of Fannie Mae as quickly as possible."

A Patronage Pudding

One attraction was that there was "much patronage," as Krogh put it, in the form of Fannie's awards of foreclosure work to lawyers. Those legal fees averaged about $1 million per year, Krogh noted. Harry Dent, a White House political aide, already had heard from Republican lawyers in his home state of South Carolina; they were unhappy that a Democrat was getting Fannie's foreclosure work there even though the Republicans held the White House. "I can't explain it," Dent fumed in a memo. Dent asked HUD's Unger to get a list of all lawyers receiving fees from Fannie for foreclosure work.

Unger responded in a March 20, 1969 memo that Lapin "has seen fit to be non-cooperative in the matter and is not transferring the work to Republican lawyers (as you know, FNMA is quasi-private and we have no direct authority over this matter)." Unger added, "We have made this matter an item of first priority and hope to resolve the conflict as soon as possible."

Another dispute between the Nixon administration and Lapin involved allegations that he had used company postage stamps to send letters supporting a Democratic congressman, according to Legg. She told me that Lapin wasn't aware that Fannie's "franking," or postage, machine had been used. "He never got involved in those kind of details," she said. Another person who worked at Fannie at the time recalled that Lapin's political letters were sent out on Fannie stationery.

Lapin and the White House skirmished for months. Then, in a two-sentence letter dated November 26, 1969, Nixon fired Lapin without spelling out the reasons: "You are hereby removed for good cause from the office of president of the Federal National Mortgage Association. This action is taken because, in my judgment, the policies and practices pursued by you in that office are inconsistent with the objectives of applicable law and with the standards expected of officials holding positions of trust and confidence under the laws of the United States."

The White House press secretary, Ron Ziegler, told reporters that Nixon had acted on the "unanimous recommendation" of Fannie's directors and HUD Secretary George Romney. A letter from Romney to the president said the working relationship between HUD and Fannie "has ceased and cannot be reestablished" with Lapin in office.

Though Fannie was on its way out of the federal government's hands, it was "especially important...during the transition period that HUD maintain harmony" with Fannie, William Timmons, a deputy assistant to Nixon, explained in a letter to Representative Dan Kuykendall of Tennessee. That was impossible, Timmons wrote, because of Lapin's "lack of cooperation" with Secretary Romney. Nixon administration sources told the *Washington Post* that Lapin had been making "unilateral" decisions without agreement from the board or HUD.

Lapin called a press conference and thundered that Congress had intended for Fannie to become a private company, "not a patronage pudding." He described his dismissal as a "lawless exercise of raw power." When reporters asked whether he knew which policies and practices Nixon was referring to in his letter, Lapin said, "I'm dying to know what the hell he's talking about. I don't have the slightest idea." As for Romney, "he wants someone here who takes orders from him," Lapin said. He told reporters that HUD had offered him a deal: if he would leave quietly, he would get the "traditional accolades" given to departing officials.

Lapin argued that the White House was required by law to show "good cause" to fire him. "I am entitled...to written notice of the charges against me, if any, and a fair opportunity to respond to them. The letter from the President affords me neither of these crucial Constitutional rights." He added, "We do have laws in this land. Even the President is subject to the law."

At the press conference, a reporter asked Lapin whether he would be back at the Fannie office the next day. "You're damn right I will," Lapin replied.

Representative Robert Leggett of California sent a note to the White House saying he was "shocked at your action to remove a great American and excellent banker." Senator Sparkman of Alabama telephoned the White House on December 8 and outlined a proposed compromise, backed by Lapin: he would accept that he was no longer president of Fannie and drop all legal challenges but remain chairman (with no executive duties) until the next shareholder meeting in May, according to a memo on file at the Nixon library. It is unclear whether the White House considered such a deal.

In mid-December, Lapin traveled to New York and met with securities analysts in an apparent effort to drum up support from shareholders. He again complained about how the Nixon administration had treated him, according to a *New York Times* account.

"You seem to be hinting that this has become a political football," one analyst said.

"Hinting, hell!" retorted Lapin. "I'm *telling* you."

Senator Sparkman called the dismissal "unwarranted, unwise and probably illegal." He said the "crucial needs of our housing industry and of the millions of Americans who hope to own their own homes shouldn't be interfered with by short-sighted, politically motivated attempts to tamper with Fannie Mae."

Lapin filed a suit in federal court but was denied an injunction to block his ouster. At one point, according to Lapin's son John, the electricity was shut off in Lapin's offices; he suspected that was arranged as another way to apply pressure. Kuhnle, the speechwriter for Lapin, recalled that both electricity and phone services were cut off at some point during the standoff.

Finally, Lapin backed down. In January 1970, Nixon installed as president of Fannie an old friend, Allan Oakley Hunter, a real estate lawyer from Fresno, California.

After the ouster of Lapin, White House officials discussed whether the Fannie board could be tilted further toward the Republican persuasion. A March 16, 1970 White House memo from Henry C. Cashen II to Peter Flanigan noted that Philip Brownstein, then a member of Fannie's board, "is an active Democrat...and only tacitly went along with the Lapin situation. If there were a discreet way to replace him with a Republican with strong recognition in the mortgage and finance areas, I would recommend doing so. However, we have had enough public problems with FNMA and Lapin, and if this would add credence to Lapin's statements that the President intends to make FNMA completely

President Nixon signing legislation authorizing Fannie to purchase conventional mortgages in 1970. *Courtesy of Fannie Mae.*

political, then I would recommend continuing Brownstein as a candidate" to remain on the board. The idea fizzled; Brownstein stayed on the board until 1972.

Lapin went on to other mortgage ventures. Documents unearthed in 1973 during the Senate's Watergate investigation showed that he was among scores of politicians, celebrities, journalists and businesspeople listed by the White House as "enemies" of Nixon. Though Lapin never achieved his aim of returning to his old post at Fannie, he won a consolation prize: President Jimmy Carter appointed him to Fannie's board in the late 1970s.

Fannie was launched as a shareholder-owned company. Still, the firing of Ray Lapin showed it had not escaped the political realm.

Chapter 5

Flowers, Candy and Compromise

Allan Oakley Hunter, known to friends by his middle name, was tall and affable. He grew up in Fresno and earned his law degree at the University of California, Berkeley in 1940 and then worked as an FBI agent, spending some of his time in Argentina and Brazil. During World War II, he served with the Office of Strategic Services intelligence agency in France and Germany. Back in Fresno as a young lawyer, he got involved in politics and met Nixon. In 1950, he accepted a long-shot Republican nomination and ended up winning a seat in the U.S. House of Representatives, representing the Fresno area. After two terms, he lost the 1954 election.

The Eisenhower administration gave Hunter a soft place to fall. He worked for two years as general counsel for the Housing and Home Finance Agency, which later became the Department of Housing and Urban Development, or HUD. Then he settled down to practice real estate law in Fresno. He and his wife, Geene, had four children.

When Nixon was elected president in November 1968, Hunter saw a chance to return to a more glamorous life in Washington. He pressed his case in a chatty letter to Rose Mary Woods, President Nixon's secretary, shortly after the election. Hunter told her he would be happy "to lend a hand" at HUD for the new administration. "I guess you would say my special field is housing and urban development," he wrote. "Al Cole and I ran the Housing and Home Finance Agency...during the Eisenhower administration....There are very few Republicans in the [housing] field and even fewer who RN would care to be with in a lifeboat on the open sea." Hunter closed with a personal touch: "Stay healthy. You are photographing well. Geene sends her best."

Once installed at Fannie, he thanked Nixon in a March 2, 1970 letter: "I would never rest peacefully if I did not participate actively in some way in your administration. As far as I am concerned, there is only one President in my lifetime, and the desire and conviction that you would ultimately occupy that position has been with me since we first met on Lincoln's birthday in Fresno in 1950." The president replied nine days later: "We have been together in a number of battles since then and I will always be grateful for the friendship and encouragement you and Geene have given to us."

Hunter tried to run Fannie in a low-key way to avoid attracting critical attention from Capitol Hill. When his staff proposed an advertising campaign to help the public better understand Fannie's role, Hunter nixed it. (There *was* a small branding issue: he later found, during a visit to Chicago, that some people confused his company with Fannie May, a candy maker.)

Hunter kept salaries fairly low, though above civil-service levels. Rather than using giant banks and Wall Street firms as the benchmark, as was the case later, Hunter took compensation cues from the World Bank and the Federal Reserve Bank of New York, among others.

There was still some confusion over the exact legal status of Fannie. In July 1970, the HUD's general counsel, Sherman Unger, sought clarification on whether directors of Fannie were subject to the conflict-of-interest rules that applied to federal bureaucrats and officers of government-owned corporations. William Rehnquist, then assistant attorney general at the Justice Department (later chief justice of the Supreme Court), wrote a scholarly eight-page letter concluding that Fannie shouldn't be considered a government agency or corporation. "Needless to say," he added, "this conclusion does not in any way indicate that there are no ethical or legal restraints on the directors" of Fannie Mae.

The business model was simple. Fannie raised money by selling bonds. The company then used the proceeds to buy mortgage loans shortly after they were made by mortgage bankers. It received the payments on those loans. Profits came from the difference between Fannie's low borrowing costs and the higher ones paid by homeowners. Fannie also profited by selling "commitments," contracts that gave mortgage banks the right to sell loans to Fannie on specified terms within a set period.

As long as few homeowners defaulted and interest rates were fairly stable, it was a fabulous business. It was precarious because Fannie relied on short-term borrowings to finance holdings of long-term mortgages. A sudden rise

Oakley Hunter celebrates the public listing of Fannie's stock in 1970. *Courtesy of Fannie Mae.*

in short-term interest rates could push the company's borrowing costs above the yield on its mortgage investments. That happened in early 1970 when total borrowing costs briefly averaged 1 percentage point more than the average yield on mortgages.

Hunter initially reported to a non-executive chairman, the retired General Lucius Clay, who had overseen the Berlin Airlift. Later, Hunter became chairman as well as president. Fannie's executive vice-president for management and operations for most of the 1970s was Lester Condon, who, like Hunter, was a former FBI agent. Condon also had been an assistant secretary of HUD.

Hunter's other executive vice-president was Robert Bennett, who joined the company in 1972 as chief financial officer. Bennett, a native of Long Island, served in the U.S. Navy during World War II, graduated from Harvard and worked on Wall Street and at a mining company before a friend told him that Fannie was looking for a CFO.

Hunter and his crew tried hard to keep mortgage banks happy. Fannie's loan purchases were a reliable source of cash for the mortgage banks, allowing them to make more loans and earn more fees for arranging them. Even so, there was a growing belief in Congress and the housing industry that Fannie alone could not provide enough money to keep the housing market humming. In periods of tight credit, notably in 1969, interest rates on mortgages shot upward; residential construction slumped, leading to talk of a "housing crisis."

The S&Ls, which had long opposed Fannie's growing role in mortgages, now saw advantages in having a powerful, government-backed provider of funding, partly because Americans had become less inclined to put their savings into the low-yielding passbook accounts that had long provided money for home loans. Congress began drafting legislation that became the Emergency Home Finance Act of 1970. This act created the Federal Home Loan Mortgage Corp., or Freddie Mac, as a provider of funding that, initially, would pay particular attention to the S&Ls' needs.

IN THE SAME LEGISLATION, Congress allowed Fannie to buy "conventional" mortgages as well as loans insured by the FHA and VA. In the mortgage world, "conventional" means a loan that is not insured by a government agency like the FHA. The idea of letting Fannie buy conventional loans, pushed by Senator Sparkman as well as much of the housing industry, sailed through Congress despite reservations expressed by the Federal Reserve. Though little discussed at the time, it proved to be a momentous change. Eventually, both Fannie and Freddie focused almost entirely on conventional mortgages and set the standards for these loans, the type used by most Americans to buy homes. Fannie had burst out of its niche and was now authorized to finance the homes of mainstream America—a vast market that would soon grow into the trillions of dollars of loans granted annually. When he signed the act in July 1970, Nixon praised Senator Sparkman for his initiative and declared that the new law would "alleviate the nation's critical housing shortage."

As the scale of the business grew, Fannie was becoming a voracious borrower, not just in the United States but around the world. Hunter made a trip to Saudi Arabia to court investors who needed places to invest the vast proceeds of oil sales. On other trips, Fannie executives courted investors across Europe and Asia.

It wasn't all work. On Wednesday evenings, Hunter and a dozen other officers met for cocktails, "a couple of pops," as one later recalled. Hunter was known as a bon vivant. At one party hosted by Fannie in the 1970s,

Fake Fannie money was used to bid for prizes at a staff party in the 1970s. *Courtesy of Robert Bennett.*

guests were given mock dollar bills marked "Fannie Money," featuring a comical drawing of a woman with freakishly large breasts and the slogan "Nobody Pours It Like Fannie Mae." One of the guests recalled that the currency was used to bid for prizes. Hunter's turbulent love life enlivened Washington gossip: while at Fannie, he divorced his first wife, Geene, only to remarry her a few years later and then split up again.

Sheldon Lubar, a mortgage banker who served as a director of Fannie in the mid-1970s, told me he initially was skeptical of Hunter and his team but soon concluded that they were "capable." Hunter's judgment was sound, Lubar found, and "he wasn't a showboat."

Others were not so sure. Despite Hunter's general policy of keeping a low profile, he decided the company needed a grander headquarters than the rented space it occupied in downtown Washington. There was debate between two choices. One was the site of a former creamery near the Georgetown district that could be converted into offices. The second was a three-story red brick building on Wisconsin Avenue, built in the colonial style of the governor's palace in Williamsburg, Virginia. The Wisconsin Avenue building had previously housed an insurance company. Bennett, the chief financial officer, considered the Wisconsin Avenue building impractical and believed it would be too expensive to convert the "rabbit warren" of offices inside.

But Hunter chose the Wisconsin Avenue building. "He bought his Taj Mahal," commented Carl A.S. Coan Jr., who served as an assistant general counsel at HUD in the 1960s and later as a lobbyist for the National Association of Home Builders. Bennett, the CFO, mocked the new headquarters as "Versailles West." In what he considered another extravagance, Bennett was sent out with a decorator to choose posh furniture for his office; he also recalled a "very attractive woman" hired by Hunter as an "art consultant" for the new headquarters. Lawrence Simons, then a senior HUD official, quipped, "It's what Versailles would have looked like if the French king had more money."

Another onlooker who disapproved was Paul Volcker, later to become chairman of the Federal Reserve Board. In the 1970s, Volcker was undersecretary of the Treasury for monetary affairs and a presidential appointee to the Fannie board. "My whole mentality was: What do they need a fancy building for?" Volcker told me in an interview in 2011.

Though Fannie was no longer a government agency, Volcker said, he didn't believe it should act exactly like a private company: "It was never in my mind that they were supposed to maximize profits." He favored keeping salaries at modest, public-service levels and focusing the business on its public-policy role. "I was probably an irritant to them," he said. "They were probably glad to get rid of me as a director."

Volcker's position at the Treasury also put him in charge of regulating Fannie's debt issuance, making sure that the timing of Fannie borrowings did not conflict with sales of Treasury bonds. He recalled rejecting a request by Fannie executives for permission to borrow in the commercial paper market, a move that could leave the company even more reliant on short-term debt.

HUNTER DID NOT HIDE his Republican ties; he sent a note to Rose Mary Woods in the White House in May 1970 to remind her of his desire for an autographed picture of the president. In general, though, Fannie tried to stay out of politics. Gordon Nelson, who was Fannie's spokesman, recalled Hunter saying that Fannie wasn't political and shouldn't be seen that way. There was only one staff lobbyist employed by Fannie, Andrew Ignatius Hickey Jr., a vice-president who served as a liaison with Congress. "We walk a tightrope between the public purpose and the stockholders," Hunter often said, according to another former colleague. Eventually, Hunter fell off that wire.

Groups favoring better housing for the poor complained that Fannie's underwriting standards—the terms and conditions set for loans—were too strict, shutting out too many people. Some considered the company partly to blame for the tendency of mortgage money to flow to new suburbs rather than inner-city neighborhoods. Fannie tried to show it was serving the public. In 1973, it held a forum at the sumptuous Airlie conference center in Virginia for builders, bankers and others to ruminate over ways to help people with too much income to qualify for public housing but too little "to buy decent homes in suitable environments."

That kind of effort wasn't enough for some in Congress. In late 1976, Senator William Proxmire, chairman of the Senate Banking Committee, held a hearing on Fannie's operations and criticized HUD for neglecting its role in supervising the company. HUD's neglect, the Wisconsin Democrat said, was "leaving this massive corporation to conduct its affairs in any manner it sees fit."

When President Carter took office in 1977, he appointed Patricia Roberts Harris as secretary of HUD. Harris, the daughter of a railroad dining-car waiter, had risen to become dean of Howard University's law school. She did not intend to neglect Fannie. She did not share Hunter's vision of Fannie's role and responsibilities. She wanted the company to act less like a private company and more like an instrument of her policy, ensuring that mortgage money flowed to poor people and to inner cities. Harris began a campaign to force Fannie to meet minimum levels of support for these goals.

Hunter thought some of the types of loans Harris wanted Fannie to back were too risky. Fannie's risks already were considerable, as would be shown by heavy losses in the early 1980s. Hunter sometimes described Fannie—with its reliance on short-term borrowings to finance long-term mortgages—as "the world's largest floating crap game."

In 1977, Senator Proxmire and Senator Alan Cranston, a California Democrat, introduced legislation, supported by the Carter administration, to increase the number of directors that the White House could appoint to Fannie's board from five to nine. (The result would have been nine directors appointed by the White House and ten representing shareholders—increasing the likelihood of squabbles and deadlock.) Senator Cranston cited the "growing concern about [Fannie's] performance, and particularly its apparent image of itself as a normal private corporation." He wanted Fannie to "develop an attitude which is more inclined toward serving the public interest...and less inclined toward defending its corporate prerogatives."

To pressure Hunter, Harris and other HUD officials dragged their feet when Fannie sought permission to start new mortgage programs. The delays infuriated Fannie executives. John Meehan, a Fannie executive at the time, told me later that HUD for a time wanted to force Fannie to get HUD approval a month in advance for the terms of any borrowing. That would have created huge problems, given day-to-day changes in the bond market's appetite for new debt. "We had to circle the wagons," Meehan said.

HUD Secretary Harris tried to go further and fire Hunter. After all, President Nixon had fired Lapin. But Harris found that, unlike the Nixon White House, she had no legal power to hire or fire Fannie executives. (Nixon had acted before Fannie was officially transformed into a private company.)

The courtly Hunter bought flowers and candy for Harris and tried to deliver them to her office personally, according to one of his colleagues; she refused to see him. Another colleague recalled that Hunter sent her a heart-shaped box of Fannie May candy on Valentine's Day; she returned it with a good-humored note, saying that if she ate it she would be as fat as Fannie Mae's profits.

The Proxmire-Cranston bill died in committee after Fannie rallied its friends in Congress. HUD and Fannie eventually reached a compromise under which the department would set goals for Fannie's financing of housing for low- and moderate-income people if the company's purchases of such loans fell below 30 percent of total investments. Hunter called that plan "an acceptable regulatory framework within which [Fannie] can continue to operate legally, effectively and profitably." Fannie officials believed they were promising to do only what they would have done anyway. Even so, a precedent had been set for HUD to impose quotas.

Fannie's compromise with the Carter administration was only a truce. Pressure from politicians for Fannie to do more for the poor would never go away. From then on, a large part of the job of any Fannie president or CEO would be to persuade Congress that the company was expanding homeownership opportunities for the poor. In April 1978, Fannie produced a twenty-four-page report in an attempt to defend its record and demonstrate that it was not simply trying to enrich shareholders and executives. For instance, Fannie had foregone $83 million of income in purchasing FHA-subsidized loans for apartment buildings "at the lower end of the market price range" from 1969 through 1977, the report said. Fannie also provided funding for housing research. The company held conferences and created task forces to study ways to funnel mortgage credit to decaying inner-city neighborhoods and to improve the design of homes and neighborhoods. It funded a public-service film, *A Place of Your Own*, to teach people how to buy a home.

Fannie was discovering the value of friends in local government. In the same April 1978 report, the company quoted a letter it received in June 1977 from Mayor Kenneth Gibson of Newark: "As President of the

U.S. Conference of Mayors, I have long been an active advocate for the strong support of Fannie Mae at the federal level. While recent criticisms have been directed at Fannie Mae for 'alleged' non-involvement in the inner city, I can only affirm that Fannie Mae has played a major, if not indispensable, role in financing the revitalization of our once deteriorated residential areas."

The report pointed to a difficulty in assessing what Congress should expect: Fannie was "a one-of-a-kind corporation with a unique set of responsibilities. Accordingly, there is no clear precedent, and certainly no precise standard, for measuring how much public service effort is appropriate in the aggregate—and here we believe honest differences of opinion are inevitable."

This battle with the Carter administration left scars. Fannie executives felt they had to be ready at all times to defend the company from meddling by Congress, bureaucrats or rivals in housing finance.

As Hunter's era at Fannie neared its end, financial worries also surfaced. In October 1979, the Federal Reserve, now led by Volcker, declared war on inflation. Nixon's wage-and-price controls hadn't worked. Nor had President Gerald Ford's Whip Inflation Now buttons. Volcker was imposing tougher medicine: double-digit interest rates.

This surge in interest rates was a problem for anyone who had to borrow money to finance holdings of long-term investments, such as mortgages. Suddenly, the cost of borrowing exceeded the interest earned on the mortgages, creating losses for Fannie and thousands of savings and loan institutions.

Another problem was that in the late 1970s, Fannie had begun selling commitments to buy mortgages at predetermined rates as much as two years in advance, up from the normal period of ninety days. When interest rates rose, Fannie had to keep buying loans with below-market rates, increasing its losses.

A 1972 portrait of Oakley Hunter, a Nixon backer who became president of Fannie. *Courtesy of Fannie Mae.*

The decision to sell these long-term commitments was "a fundamental blunder," Bennett, the chief financial officer under Hunter, told me in 2009. "I didn't foresee it better than anyone else."

Bennett and James Murray, then general counsel, tried to persuade Hunter to renege on the commitments, citing the unforeseen change in circumstances caused by the Fed's decision to jack interest rates up to double-digit levels. Murray thought the mortgage bankers, who were making a windfall on the commitments, were unlikely to prevail if they sued Fannie. But, he said, Hunter refused to renege, saying Fannie needed to retain the mortgage bankers' support.

"It was tense," recalled Steve Frank, then in the controller's department. He made calculations about how many more months Fannie could stay solvent at the current rate of losses.

Meanwhile, Hunter had heart problems and would soon need surgery. The board began to worry about who would succeed him. Bennett advised Hunter to choose someone else as president and remain chairman for a time. Bennett himself hoped to become president. Hunter dithered until the board hired a recruitment firm, Russell Reynolds, to find someone to take over as both chairman and president.

On September 10, 1980, the *Wall Street Journal* reported that Fannie was looking for a successor to Hunter:

> *The search for a new president is rekindling a decade-old debate about whether Fannie Mae should be more like a private corporation or a government agency. One camp, which includes many of the private stockholders, wants to move Fannie Mae far from direct government control. Another faction would like to see the company run more as an arm of the government, allocating mortgage capital to accomplish social ends.*

Some people in the Carter administration backed Lawrence Simons, a home builder from Staten Island who then was federal housing administrator at HUD. But Fannie's board chose David O. Maxwell, a former HUD official, to succeed Hunter. Maxwell's initial salary of $225,000 a year—well above the $184,000 earned by Hunter—caused a stir. The *New York Times* noted that the president of the United States earned "only $200,000."

Hunter could leave with grace. "I feel comfortable leaving now because we are not under [political] attack," he told the *Times*. "We do have financial problems, but no one is after my scalp."

Chapter 6

Fatal Course

When he took command as chairman and chief executive officer in May 1981, David Maxwell's assignment was straightforward: save the company.

Fannie was no longer an obscure little agency. It was the nation's fifth-largest company in terms of assets and held about 5.00 percent of U.S. home mortgages outstanding. It was losing huge amounts of money. For a spell in the early 1980s, losses exceeded $1 million a day. Fannie's borrowing costs had soared far above the income it received on its holdings of mortgage loans, most of which had been made when interest rates were low. In 1981, the average yield on mortgages owned by Fannie was 9.45 percent, below the 10.81 percent average interest cost on its debt.

"Basically, Fannie Mae was the nation's largest insolvent thrift," Susan Woodward, who was HUD's chief economist in the late 1980s, told me. "What the government did about [this problem] mostly was to cross their fingers and pray for lower interest rates."

After a small profit of $14 million in 1980, Fannie reported losses of about $190 million for 1981 and $105 million in 1982. Sales of mortgages allowed the company to show a profit of $76 million in 1983, but it relapsed into a $57 million loss for 1984. In 1981, the market value of Fannie's liabilities exceeded its assets by $11 billion, according to a June 1987 HUD report.

Maxwell was confident he could set things right. The son of a prominent Philadelphia lawyer, he had attended Yale University, where he was on the tennis team. His father wanted him to be a lawyer. Partly for that reason and partly because, as he later put it, "I didn't know what I wanted to do," he went to Harvard Law School and got a degree there. After serving in the U.S. Navy, he practiced law from 1959 to 1966.

In 1960, at the age of thirty, Maxwell ran for Congress as a sacrificial-lamb Republican in a heavily Democratic district in the Philadelphia area. "I got creamed," he said later. His political career wasn't over, though. In 1966, he helped lead Raymond Shafer's successful campaign to become governor of Pennsylvania. Governor Shafer appointed Maxwell as state insurance commissioner and later budget director.

Then Maxwell went to Washington, appointed by the Nixon administration to be general counsel of HUD, where he remained until January 1973.

Ticor of Los Angeles, a title insurance company where Maxwell had an acquaintance, asked him to move there to set up a mortgage-insurance subsidiary. He stayed at Ticor until he was recruited to join Fannie.

Maxwell found that Fannie was still run in some respects like a government agency. The tone soon changed. Maxwell rode around Washington in the back seat of a limousine. He always wore a well-tailored suit. Soon, the company's critics and the press were twittering about his $225,000-a-year salary. Maxwell said Fannie had to pay the market rate for top talent.

One of Maxwell's early hires at Fannie was Douglas Bibby, previously an executive recruiter at Russell Reynolds. Bibby became senior vice-president for corporate affairs, including public relations, advertising and investor relations. Bibby later recalled that he admired Maxwell for his intelligence, grace, competitiveness (both in business and in tennis) and general "unwillingness to accept mediocrity."

One thing Maxwell would not tolerate was a split infinitive. He wanted his speeches to be written in a fussily polished way, making them ready for publication. But Maxwell was a stiff speaker. Bibby found a speaking coach for Maxwell (and for other Fannie executives, so it wouldn't look as if only the boss had a problem).

Sometimes Maxwell lost his temper with subordinates. A day after such an outburst, the victim might find a graceful handwritten note of apology from Maxwell.

When Oakley Hunter, his predecessor, publicly criticized some of Maxwell's actions in an article in *Regardie's Magazine*, Maxwell was furious and ordered that Hunter's portrait be taken down from a wall in Fannie's headquarters. A few days later, realizing he had been petty, Maxwell relented. The portrait returned to its former spot.

Maxwell didn't tolerate blather. One subordinate recalled being instructed by Maxwell to explain a certain issue "in 25 words or less."

The need for action was urgent. Fannie at that point owned about $57 billion of mortgages, and most were yielding less than the company's borrowing costs. Some executives referred to this mass of money-losing assets as "a block of granite" or "the bag of dead cats."

As one way to generate more profitable business, Fannie followed Freddie's lead into the new business of mortgage securities—interest-paying instruments backed by the flows of money from thousands of individual home mortgages. Fannie and Freddie earned fees for their guarantees on these securities—essentially promises to pay for any losses from defaults by the mortgage borrowers.

The "securitization" of mortgages, dating from the early 1970s, was changing the home-loan business. These securities allowed a huge range of investors worldwide to buy mortgages in a form that made them easier to trade and value. Lenders became less dependent on selling loans to individual buyers, such as banks, insurers or pension funds, because they now had the alternative of selling them in large numbers to packagers of mortgage securities, including Fannie and Freddie. It was becoming less of a relationship business—involving the wining and dining of individual loan investors—and more of a high-volume transactional business. That brought money-saving efficiencies but also, eventually, the potential for abuse as distant buyers of the securities sometimes had little idea of what they were buying.

Maxwell also put more emphasis on marketing Fannie's services. He hired people to go out and find customers, particularly among savings and loan institutions, which had mainly used Freddie.

ONE OF THE FEW senior people from the Hunter days to remain in place was John Meehan, an ex-marine from Brooklyn who had done combat duty in Vietnam. After trading bonds for Chase Manhattan and Goldman Sachs, Meehan joined Fannie in 1975 and eventually became treasurer. He was the face of Fannie on Wall Street. He decided when and how to raise money in the bond markets.

When Maxwell arrived, he frequently challenged Meehan's views, whether the two were alone or in front of others, Meehan recalled. At times, he said, Maxwell "ticked me off." Meehan nearly quit. Then Maxwell started showing more confidence in him. Meehan stayed until 1985, when he went back to work on Wall Street. He was proud of helping steer Fannie through its crisis. "We never went to the Treasury for a penny," he said. Meehan credited Maxwell with bringing in better "players" to run Fannie: "He wanted to win the pennant."

The most important recruit of Maxwell's early years at Fannie—in terms of its long-run effects on the company—was a tall, slender, athletic Californian, J. Timothy Howard. One of three sons of a lawyer, Howard spent his early years in Palmdale, an inland town in Southern California. When he was ten, his father died in a car accident. His mother supported her three boys with a secretarial job.

Howard started out majoring in English at the College of William and Mary in Virginia and then transferred to the University of California, Los Angeles, where he earned a bachelor's degree in English and economics and a master's in economics. After graduating, he spent a couple of years in France and Spain. Then he fetched up in Mexico and helped set up a company that exported dried fruit. Finally, he moved to San Francisco and began work as an economist, first at Chase Econometric Associates and then at Wells Fargo Bank. In this latter job, though still only in his early thirties, the confident and well-spoken Howard began to get calls from reporters for the *Wall Street Journal* and the *New York Times*, who quoted his comments on Federal Reserve interest-rate policy.

In 1982, Howard got a call from Fannie's chief economist, Peter Treadway, who planned to leave the firm and was charged with finding a successor. Howard took the job. He found Fannie an "energized" place to work and liked Maxwell, who "certainly didn't tolerate sloppy thinking."

Soon he was working on the arcane science of trying to match the terms of the company's borrowings as closely as possible with those of its mortgage investments to avoid another trap in which it was funding long-term mortgages with short-term money.

This matching of borrowing costs and interest income is tricky because the duration of mortgage loans—the amount of time before they will be paid off—is hard to predict. If interest rates drop sharply, many borrowers will refinance into new, cheaper loans, paying off their old loans in the process. Thus, mortgages suddenly become short-term investments, liable to be paid off quickly. If interest rates go way up, mortgages suddenly have a longer duration; it doesn't make sense to refinance, so people pay off mortgages early only if they are moving to new houses.

Through the 1980s, Howard took on more and more duties. He became senior vice-president of economics and planning. He headed a committee that decided the terms Fannie should offer each week when it held auctions of its commitments to buy mortgages. In September 1987, he became an executive vice-president, with responsibility for strategic planning.

He concluded that the company's process for managing interest-rate risks was too informal. No one was in charge of matching the borrowing costs to the mortgage purchases. He told Maxwell that one person should oversee the mortgage holdings. Maxwell agreed. So in December 1987, Howard became executive vice-president, asset management. Now he was in charge of acquiring mortgages, funding them and hedging the risk.

In 1990, he became chief financial officer. It was an unusually broad span of responsibility, including strategic planning, purchases of mortgages, fundraising and management of the portfolio. "I was on every committee of importance in the company," he later recalled.

MAXWELL ALSO REACHED OUT to old friends. One of his former college roommates, Joseph Califano, had served as U.S. secretary of Health, Education and Welfare under the Carter administration and was involved in the LBJ maneuver that took Fannie off the government books. In the 1980s, under Maxwell, Califano became an outside legal counsel for Fannie.

In Maxwell's early years at Fannie, the business was in such bad shape that he didn't dare speak about it in public. He and other top officials regularly adjusted a chart called "months to go." It kept track of how many months the company's capital would last at the current rate of losses.

But Maxwell could speak frankly in private with Volcker, the chairman of the Fed. During breakfast meetings, Maxwell later recalled, they talked about Fannie, housing and the economy. At one point, Volcker called to ask about rumors from New York that Fannie was struggling to make its debt payments. Maxwell assured him that was not the case.

MAXWELL ADOPTED A STRATEGY of growing the company's way out of trouble. To offset the drag of low-yielding mortgages on its books, Fannie bought large amounts of higher-yielding home loans, including loans with adjustable rates. Mortgage holdings grew to $94 billion in 1986 from $56 billion in 1980. Fannie got an increasing stream of fees for guaranteeing payments on mortgage securities.

Fannie also got a little help from the Reagan administration, despite its ideological aversion to government-sponsored enterprises. In June 1981,

Ronald Reagan's first year in the White House, his administration created the President's Commission on Housing to review housing policies. The chairman, William F. McKenna, was a Yale-trained lawyer who had been involved in federal housing and mortgage policy for four decades as a regulator, congressional aide and adviser to S&Ls. The other twenty-nine members included lawyers, real estate developers and brokers, builders, investment bankers and mortgage lenders.

These worthies created a "blueprint for a housing system" in the form of a 278-page report issued in April 1982. In tune with the president's political beliefs, the report affirmed "that the genius of the market economy, freed of the distortions forced by government housing policies and regulations that swung erratically from loving to hostile, can provide for housing far better than federal programs. The 1970s taught not only the limits of the good that can be done by government action, but also the depths of harm that can be wrought by ill-thought or ill-coordinated government policy." This blueprint devoted only a few muddled pages to Fannie and Freddie, which were on their way to becoming one of the biggest federal interventions ever into the genius of the market economy.

In the long term, the commission wanted Fannie and Freddie to be "private corporations that retain limited benefits arising from Congressionally mandated commitments to housing." Fannie and Freddie had "the size, reputation and ability to serve as guarantors" of mortgage securities. But they "should not have such unfair competitive advantages over other private institutions that market inefficiencies develop," the report said.

Exactly how these unfair advantages might disappear was left vague. Eventually, the report suggested, Fannie's ability to borrow from the Treasury might be phased out, along with the "agency status" of Fannie's debt, which allowed the company to borrow money almost as if it were still a government agency. Agency status was not primarily a matter of law, however, but rather of investors' firm belief that Uncle Sam would stand behind Fannie and prevent the company from defaulting. The commission did not explain how Fannie would be a congressionally chartered instrument of housing policy and yet also operate as a purely private company.

In any case—conveniently for commission members, who probably could never have agreed on the details of any ambitious reform—radical change was not contemplated for the present. Because Fannie was then in a weak financial state, the commission advised against any abrupt withdrawal of federal support. The company's "beneficial federal linkages should not be altered until [Fannie] returns to a positive profit position," the report said.

In line with the Reagan spirit of deregulation, the commission favored an immediate elimination of HUD's regulatory authority over Fannie. HUD regulation had "seriously limited" the company's flexibility in the late 1970s, according to the commission's report. The report did not specify how or whether Fannie would be regulated if HUD's authority were withdrawn, though it suggested some kind of HUD "oversight role" should continue. The commission delivered its report to the White House, disbanded and vanished from the public-policy discussion with barely a trace.

The Reagan administration might have been expected to abolish Fannie as a relic of the New Deal and the now-scorned habit of federal manipulation of the economy. Instead, President Reagan's appointees helped sustain the company through a difficult patch. The economy was fragile. The housing market was wobbly. Bold reform could wait for a better day.

As Fannie's losses ate into its capital, HUD in 1982 allowed the company to raise its borrowings to thirty times capital from twenty-five times. Around the same time, Congress passed legislation, backed by the Reagan administration, giving Fannie a tax break. The legislation allowed Fannie to "carry back" losses to recapture money previously paid in federal taxes over the prior ten years. In December 1981, a Treasury official estimated that the tax break would cost $200 million in lost federal tax revenue.

Maxwell told the House Ways and Means Committee that the tax break would help Fannie reduce borrowing costs. If it didn't get the break, higher borrowing costs would be passed along to home buyers, he said.

THE LOSSES FANNIE SUFFERED in the first half of the 1980s were mostly due to high interest rates. But some of the losses came from a surge in foreclosures on loans owned by Fannie. Maxwell's strategy of growing the company out of trouble meant buying riskier loans. Foreclosure losses as a percentage of Fannie's portfolio nearly tripled to 1.16 percent in 1986 from 0.42 percent in 1981.

Some employees grumbled that Fannie was paying "cash for trash." The company loosened its standards by accepting loans made to borrowers with higher debt in relation to income, for instance. It stopped requiring lenders to use Fannie-approved appraisers to estimate home values. So that it could buy loans faster, Fannie quit examining each loan it bought and delegated more authority to lenders to ensure that the loans met Fannie's standards.

Fannie also bought adjustable-rate mortgage loans that came with "teaser rates," artificially low introductory interest charges that would rise after a year or so. Some borrowers could afford the initial low monthly costs but struggled once payments adjusted to the full rate. It was not until 1987 that Fannie required lenders to ensure that borrowers were able to cope with payments at the full rate, not just the teaser rate (a lesson the mortgage industry would forget during the next boom).

When borrowers defaulted, Fannie ended up acquiring their homes through foreclosure and then had to sell those homes. The houses often fetched much less than the loan balance due, creating a loss for Fannie. By late 1984, Fannie owned about 5,400 foreclosed homes that it was trying to sell, compared with a typical level of 100 or so a few years earlier.

In response to these foreclosure losses, Fannie tightened its credit standards and intensified scrutiny of the loans it purchased to make sure lenders had followed the required standards. If loans did not meet those standards, the lenders could be forced to buy them back.

These measures helped, but Fannie's rebound was mainly due to forces beyond the company's control—a recovery in the economy and a drop in interest rates in the mid-1980s. Fannie could then absorb foreclosure losses because the interest earned on its mortgage holdings once again comfortably exceeded borrowing costs. Soon Fannie was making almost embarrassingly large profits. The company's return on equity soared to 33.8 percent in 1990 from 9.6 percent in 1986.

Even so, the brush with insolvency in the early 1980s stirred longer-term concerns. A 1985 report by the U.S. General Accounting Office (GAO) concluded that Fannie's business was "inherently risky" and exposed the federal government to the risk that it would be compelled to bail out the company. HUD had "fallen short" as Fannie's regulator, the report said. There was no one at HUD whose full-time job was to oversee the company, by then the nation's second-largest borrower after the U.S. Treasury. HUD had failed to submit required reports to Congress on Fannie's activities or to analyze the financial risks the company posed to the government.

Indeed, "HUD officials responsible for oversight and regulation are unsure of the nature of their role" and did not believe they had the expertise to perform some tasks that would be expected of a financial regulator, such as monitoring Fannie's interest-rate risks, the report said. As Fannie increased its holdings of mortgages, the potential for losses was growing.

Congress needed to act, the GAO said. It recommended legislation to set up "a permanent oversight function" at HUD or elsewhere in the government to monitor Fannie, evaluate how it was doing in its public-policy role and report periodically to Congress. Congress did act—but not until seven years later, in 1992, and then only feebly.

Maxwell was not eager for more regulation. "Above all," he told the GAO in a letter dated April 5, 1985, "Fannie Mae must have the ability to respond flexibly and quickly to the evolving demands of the marketplace," and since Fannie's stock was traded on the New York Stock Exchange, the company's actions were "subject to scrutiny in the market place." In the market, however, investors were relying more on government backing than on the wisdom of Fannie's executives.

THOUGH HE MANAGED TO return the company to profitability, Maxwell wasn't so successful in finding and keeping the right No. 2 executive. During his ten years at Fannie, five presidents served under him. The first, James Murray, was a holdover from the Hunter era. Maxwell considered him unsuited for the task.

Then came Bob Mylod, a mortgage banker from Detroit. Maxwell thought Mylod was perfectly suited for the job of president. Mylod, however, wanted to run his own show and soon moved on. He later served as chairman of Michigan National Corp., a banking company.

Next up: Mark Riedy. An economist, he had previously worked as executive vice-president of the Mortgage Bankers Association (MBA). As part of his MBA duties, Riedy later recalled, he occasionally had lunch with Maxwell to discuss mortgage industry issues. "Absolutely out of the blue," Riedy told me, Maxwell one day in 1984 asked him if he would like to be president of Fannie. "I said sure."

Working with Maxwell "was exciting because he was a very bright guy," Riedy said. It was also difficult because the two never agreed on who should do what. They couldn't even agree on office décor. Riedy recalled decorating his office at Fannie with framed posters of the Monopoly game cards for Boardwalk and Park Place—a suitable real estate theme, he thought. Maxwell told him to take the brightly colored posters down. "He just didn't think it was elegant enough," Riedy said.

After about eighteen months, the two finally had a frank talk about how things were going. Fannie soon announced that Riedy was leaving "to explore other career opportunities." An article in the *Wall Street Journal* gave this account of some of the friction: "Friends said that Riedy particularly chafed at recent restrictions that Maxwell imposed on his public speechmaking, selection of subordinates and use of corporate perks, such as a chauffeur-driven limousine and expense account."

Around that time, a high-flying banker was available. Frank Cahouet had served as chief financial officer of one California-based banking company, Security Pacific Corp., and as CEO of another, Crocker National Corp. When Wells Fargo acquired Crocker in 1986, Cahouet was ready for a new job. In an interview in 2009, Cahouet told me that Carla Hills, a Fannie director in the 1980s, helped recruit him as president.

Cahouet, the son of a lawyer, grew up near Boston and attended Harvard. He became an executive known for his ability to heal ailing banks. The plan at Fannie when he arrived in September 1986, he told me more than two decades later, was for him to succeed Maxwell as CEO within a year or two. He would not have taken a job that meant being No. 2 for a long spell.

Cahouet's stay proved very short: Mellon Bank Corp. in Pittsburgh invited him to become its CEO. So Cahouet left Fannie in June 1987, about ten months after his arrival. "Mellon was just one of those things that fit," Cahouet said.

Maxwell was stunned—and angry that he hadn't been told of the negotiations between Mellon and Cahouet. Maxwell retaliated by leaking the story of Cahouet's new job to the *Wall Street Journal*, which ran the story on a Monday morning, upstaging the official announcement from Mellon.

Maxwell then talked to his friend Roger Birk, a former chairman and CEO of Merrill Lynch, who already served on Fannie's board. Birk took the job of president, becoming the fifth president to serve under Maxwell.

As RIEDY HAD DISCOVERED, Maxwell had firm aesthetic principles. One day he arrived at work to find that a gaudy neon Fannie Mae sign had been installed in the main lobby of the headquarters. It had been put up without his approval. Colleagues recalled that Maxwell issued an immediate order: "Get that thing down."

At a cocktail party, he noted that Gary Kopff, a vice-president of the company, had his necktie askew. Maxwell instructed Kopff to hold the skinny end of the tie in place by putting it through the loop on the back of the fat end. "If you're going to wear a Hermes tie, wear it properly," Kopff recalled being told by his boss.

Maxwell also wanted Fannie to be thought of as a sophisticated financial corporation, not as an "agency," as it was still often called. He pushed for the use of Fannie Mae as the corporate name rather than the formal Federal National Mortgage Association or FNMA.

FROM THE OUTSIDE, FANNIE was being pressured again to work harder to help the poor become homeowners. One woman who made a deep impression was Gale Cincotta, a Chicago mother of six who was married to the owner of a gas station. Cincotta campaigned on behalf of poor residents of Chicago's West Side. At one point, she nailed a rat to the door of an alderman's house to convince him to do something about rodent infestations.

Cincotta's influence spread far beyond Chicago, partly through her creation of an organization called National People's Action. The group lobbied for the Home Mortgage Disclosure Act of 1975, which requires banks to provide detailed information on their mortgage-lending practices, and for the Community Reinvestment Act of 1977, or CRA, which requires banks to lend and invest in neighborhoods where they collect deposits. Those laws were needed, Cincotta once said, because banks "were sucking capital out of our neighborhoods."

The CRA legislation, along with requirements for Fannie and Freddie to step up their financing for poor people, changed the priorities of mortgage lenders. It was no longer enough to make money for shareholders; it became necessary to show that your institution was helping to improve American society. Whether this shift was beneficial or detrimental to the U.S. economy remains a subject of debate.

Eventually, Cincotta came knocking on Fannie's door and worked with executives there on programs to encourage more mortgage lending to people who had trouble getting credit. Edward Pinto, who was chief credit officer at Fannie in the late 1980s, told me that Cincotta at that time espoused high lending standards to avoid foreclosures and influenced Fannie's policies for serving poor neighborhoods.

In Pittsburgh, Fannie scored political points in the late 1980s by helping finance the conversion of a downtown YMCA building into a 270-room shelter for homeless people. In this project and many others later, Fannie teamed up with the Enterprise Foundation, a nonprofit housing group founded by James Rouse, a Maryland property developer.

Maxwell insisted that the company could support low-income housing without hurting shareholders. "Remember," the *Financial World* quoted him as saying in 1989, "we don't do this as a charity. We make money doing these things. I'm not hired to give away stockholders' money."

MORTGAGE SECURITIES WERE GROWING more complicated, and that entangled Fannie and Freddie in new disputes over the boundaries between their business and those of purely private companies. As part of a 1986 overhaul of federal taxes, Congress created another baffling acronym: Remic (Real Estate Mortgage Investment Conduit). These legal structures allowed mortgage securities to be divided into segments with various maturities and other characteristics, while avoiding double taxation.

Remics were destined to become popular with investors and create profits for the firms that assembled and marketed them. Wall Street firms and some savings and loan institutions didn't want Fannie to dominate this new business. They appealed to HUD to shut Fannie out.

Fannie argued that it didn't need HUD's approval; it wasn't really entering a new business but merely participating in an updated version of the old one. HUD insisted on a review.

J. Michael Dorsey, who was HUD's general counsel at the time, told me later that the department wanted to study how the Remic business would affect Fannie's financial stability and whether Remics should be left to purely private companies. Several big Wall Street firms—including Salomon Brothers, Goldman Sachs and Merrill Lynch—encouraged HUD to resist Fannie's demands. Fannie was furious. "The Wall Street guys double-crossed Fannie" by pressing HUD to limit the company's move into Remics, William Maloni, who was a Fannie lobbyist at the time, told me.

Officials from Salomon told the *Wall Street Journal* that Fannie retaliated by reducing the amount of bond-market business it gave to Salomon. Fannie's regular sales of bonds were a huge source of income for Wall Street firms like Salomon. So they generally avoided offending Fannie. Bruce McMillen, Fannie's chief financial officer, confirmed that his company had cut back on its dealings with Salomon. But he said that wasn't because of the dispute over Remics. Rather, he said, it was "because they do not give us any indication that they value our business very highly."

Fannie applied pressure through Congress. Representative Henry Gonzalez, a Texas Democrat, sent a letter to HUD Secretary Samuel Pierce to protest delays in making a decision on the issue.

Maxwell also went public. In a March 1987 speech at a mortgage bankers' convention in Kansas City, Missouri, he denounced savings and loan companies for standing in Fannie's way on the Remic issue: "Can we not fairly conclude that a handful of giant, deregulated portfolio lenders want a greatly weakened secondary market…in order to raise rates as high as possible and cut back the variety of mortgages available to the home buyer?"

The savings and loans shot back at Fannie and Freddie. "I don't think the country is well served by having them dominate the entire industry," said Dennis Jacobe, research director of the U.S. League of Savings Institutions.

In April 1988, HUD Secretary Pierce loosened some of the restrictions it had put on Fannie's issuance of Remics. He still wouldn't give Fannie the unlimited authority it sought. Fannie battled on.

Dorsey, HUD's general counsel, received a phone call in 1988 from a Fannie executive telling him that a provision was being added to a House bill that would eliminate HUD's authority to decide whether Fannie could enter new businesses. Rather than lose this authority, Dorsey told me, HUD made a quiet deal with people in Congress: HUD would keep its power to review new Fannie programs, but Fannie would get unlimited authority to issue Remics.

"That was the kind of thing that happened all the time," Dorsey said. "If you tried to effectively regulate them, they'd just go to Congress and get their way."

Maloni, the Fannie lobbyist, confirmed that Fannie persuaded Congress to take away HUD's authority unless it let Fannie issue Remics. He said the threat was justified for the reason always cited by the company and its backers: anything that thwarted Fannie's efforts to make the mortgage market more efficient, he said, would "drive up the cost of housing."

WITH REMICS AND OTHER types of mortgage securities trading in an increasingly sophisticated market, some people believed Fannie and Freddie had by now accomplished their original mission: creating an efficient market to ensure that investors' dollars could flow steadily into home mortgages. Among those people was James Murray, one of the senior Fannie executives who had been pushed out by Maxwell. He argued that Fannie and Freddie no longer needed a government charter and should become purely private companies.

People in the Reagan administration—notably David Stockman, the budget director—occasionally called for "privatizing" Fannie and Freddie. Of course, the companies were already in the private sector in the sense that they were owned by shareholders, not the government. But true "privatization" would mean giving up their federal charters, their roles in public housing policy and the special borrowing privileges that allowed them to raise money at low interest rates. That was a course advocated by Federal Reserve Board Vice-Chairman Preston Martin, among others.

David Stockman (left) with President Reagan. Stockman, the budget director, wanted to end government backing for Fannie and Freddie. *Courtesy of the Library of Congress.*

Speaking to the American Educational League in March 1986, Martin called for "reducing the federal presence in housing finance," though only gradually, to avoid disrupting the market. The aim, he said, should be to make Fannie and Freddie private in 1990 or 1991. "Many objectives of federal involvement have by now largely been met for mortgage borrowers," the Fed vice-chairman said, "and in my view the costs to society of continuing such wide-scale involvement exceed the benefits." Among those costs was the danger that taxpayers might have to pay for any catastrophic losses at Fannie or Freddie.

Maxwell himself had suggested early in his time at Fannie that he was willing to consider privatization. This discussion was sometimes referred to as "giving back the keys." Stuart McFarland, a senior Fannie executive under Maxwell in the early 1980s, told me the idea died out, partly because some members of the board opposed it. Among those directors was Henry Cashen, the former Nixon White House aide, who had a small role in ousting Lapin. Talk of privatization "never went anywhere," Cashen told me. "What Fannie Mae was doing at the time was very productive in terms of low-cost housing."

In January 1987, however, the president's annual budget proposal said the Reagan administration was "studying ways of privatizing" Fannie and Freddie. The policy statement deplored "their continued encroachment on the market served by private firms." The President's Commission on Privatization in 1988 also called for ending all federal benefits and backing for Fannie and Freddie, leaving them "fully privatized" after a transition period.

For a time, the Reagan administration also pushed the idea of imposing "user fees" on borrowings by Fannie and Freddie to offset the advantages they had over purely private companies. Fannie squashed that idea. Instead, it persuaded Congress to amend the charters of Fannie and Freddie in a way that banned any such fees as part of the Housing and Community Development Act of 1987.

Maxwell finally commissioned a study on the pros and cons of privatization. He hoped the study would resolve a debate he found tiresome. "I was sick of being asked about it" by Reagan administration officials who saw the company as "this terrible socialistic thing," Maxwell told me. He hoped that "if we made a good faith effort" to consider the merits of privatization, the administration would "get off our back."

To conduct this study, Maxwell hired Wall Street investment bank Shearson Lehman Hutton. Shearson got the job because Maxwell had happened to meet James Arthur Johnson, then a managing director at Shearson, at a dinner party hosted by a mutual friend. Johnson, a Minnesotan, had managed Walter Mondale's unsuccessful run for president in 1984. "We hit it off," Maxwell said later. He found Johnson to be an "extraordinary person" with "an amazing ability to focus."

The question of privatization was complicated. Getting rid of the ties to the federal government would free Fannie from regulatory constraints and political pressures. The company would be able to diversify into other businesses, reducing its reliance on the volatile housing industry. But privatization would mean Fannie would no longer be viewed as having the financial backing of Uncle Sam. So it would have to pay much more to borrow money.

One problem was that congressional approval would be needed for any change in the company's status. Once Congress took up the debate, the terms of the transition would become an unpredictable matter of politics. "To go to Congress would have been very risky because God only knows what they would have dreamed up," Maxwell said. "You can't control that process once it gets going."

Wall Street generally wasn't excited by the idea of Fannie giving up access to cheap money. An August 1987 article in *Financial World* quoted Peter Treadway, the former chief economist of Fannie who by then was an analyst at Smith Barney, as saying, "If you take away Fannie Mae's agency status, it will wind up insolvent or out of the mortgage business because it will be unable to get favorable funding."

The Mortgage Bankers Association of America also was cool to the idea. "Either you believe that housing is a social priority or you don't," said Warren Lasko, an executive vice-president of the mortgage banking trade group.

When it came time to write his report, Johnson recommended against privatization. Maxwell believed Fannie's business model wouldn't work without the low borrowing costs that came with implied government backing. The privatization talk, Maxwell said later, "was totally divorced from reality."

Although some members of the Reagan administration still wanted privatization, there was little backing for the idea in Congress. Fannie's skillful lobbying was paying off. In a 1988 interview with *American Banker*, Roger Birk, then president of Fannie, seemed totally relaxed about preserving the company's status: "Obviously, Fannie Mae's activities in providing a liquid secondary market have a benefit to society in terms of lower mortgage rates," he said. "Our activity doesn't cost the government anything. In fact, we have a huge tax bill. And I can tell you that there is zero appetite in Congress for a change, for privatization—not 9%, not 25%, but zero."

Frank Cahouet, who served briefly as president of Fannie in the mid-1980s, had his own view about why the company's executives never embraced privatization: they were too comfortable. "It's a pretty good life," he told me. "You've got a driver, you get invitations to all the best [social events]." He figured he wore his tuxedo more times in the ten months he worked at Fannie than in the preceding twenty years. "Wall Street comes and tells you how brilliant you are....Wall Street says you can be leveraged [in debt] to an infinite amount. Maybe they're right....You're not there to create a lot of problems....You want to do the right thing, but you're not there to get into a squabble or a fistfight with a lot of Senators."

He recalled attending a Fannie management meeting at the plush Hotel del Coronado in San Diego. "You don't want to rock the boat," Cahouet said, "because it's a comfortable boat."

BUT WHY DID THE Reagan administration, with its zeal for free markets and small government, let Fannie stay in that comfortable boat?

"We had too many other problems, and we didn't have enough political capital to take on Fannie and Freddie," Peter Wallison, who served as general counsel in the Treasury under President Reagan, told me. The administration was dealing with the collapse of hundreds of savings and loan institutions, a debt crisis in Latin America and the ups and downs of the economy. "All of those things were much more important" than Fannie and Freddie, which were then much smaller than they would become in the 1990s and early 2000s, Wallison said. "Fannie and Freddie were way down the list" of priorities.

Even if a change in the status of Fannie and Freddie had been a top priority, "they were going to be tough opponents," he said.

Fannie's lobbying was effective partly because the company had the money to hire plenty of smart people to make its case. The message boiled down to this: we are all about keeping the American housing market healthy. That resonated with politicians. Most voters owned homes or aspired to own them. No politician wanted to be blamed for messing up the housing market.

"They beat us politically," Lawrence Kudlow, who was an associate budget director in the Reagan White House, told me.

The lobbying, Maxwell said, was merely self-defense: "I would have been thrilled to forgo this largely distasteful part of my job if I had had confidence the Congress would not have done something that would both have required us to continue to serve the secondary market and made it impossible for us to have done that job."

Others felt Fannie was developing a habit of lashing back at anyone who dared criticize it. In 1990, after the *Economist* magazine ran articles critical of Fannie and Freddie, Fannie canceled its advertising in the magazine. "The feeling was: Why should we give money to people who are constantly criticizing us?" explained Maloni, the Fannie lobbyist.

Michael Basham ran up against Fannie's agents when he became a deputy assistant secretary at the U.S. Treasury in 1989 under the first President Bush. Basham was responsible for some of the Treasury's dealings with Fannie and Freddie. He soon found himself getting lunch invitations from James Johnson (which he accepted) and invitations to poker nights held by Maloni (which he declined). At a dinner party one night, Basham was seated next to a lawyer who represented Fannie. Basham avoided talking about relations between Fannie and the Treasury. Then, on his way out the door, in a lighthearted reference to the endless

A cartoon published by the *Economist* in 1990 mocked the growing appetites of Fannie and Freddie for debt. Fannie stopped advertising in the magazine. *Drawing by David Simonds.*

debates over government housing policy, he quipped, "Well, I guess I'll see you in the trenches."

The next day, Basham learned that the lawyer had reported this remark to Maxwell as an apparently hostile comment and that Maxwell had complained to Basham's bosses at the Treasury. Basham recalled being "chewed out" for making indiscreet remarks. "These guys were incredibly powerful lobbyists," Basham said. "They had their fingers in everything." When he left the Treasury to join the Wall Street firm Smith Barney, Basham said, he was advised not to talk publicly about Fannie and Freddie to avoid their wrath—and the risk of losing the fees they paid Wall Street for arranging debt sales.

FANNIE AND FREDDIE WERE about to grow much bigger and stronger. By the late 1980s, hundreds of savings and loan institutions were failing, often because of ill-advised lending for real estate and commercial projects. The S&Ls' dominance of mortgage lending was over. More of the market would go to mortgage bankers.

The decline of S&Ls meant a bigger share of all mortgage loans would flow to Fannie or Freddie. Originally, they were set up to be the buyers of mortgages only when other buyers retreated from the market. Now Fannie and Freddie were becoming the dominant buyers of mortgages at all times.

The bigger and more powerful they became, the harder they would be to fight. The Reagan administration and Congress, distracted by other issues, had missed a chance to rein in Fannie and Freddie.

Even so, Fannie and Freddie were not completely off the hook. The S&Ls' collapse forced Congress to look more closely at financial regulation in general, and that scrutiny eventually included supervision of Fannie and Freddie. One lesson of the S&L debacle was that lax regulation of politically powerful financial institutions could lead to disaster. The bailout of federally insured S&Ls eventually would cost taxpayers an estimated $124 billion, according to the FDIC Banking Review.

To clean up the S&L mess, Congress passed the Financial Institutions Reform, Recovery and Enforcement Act, known as FIREA, signed into law in August 1989 by President George H.W. Bush. That law toughened regulation of the surviving S&Ls and created mechanisms to repay insured depositors and deal with other costs of the closure of more than one thousand S&Ls.

All but lost in the brouhaha over the S&L problem were provisions of the legislation that dealt with Fannie and Freddie. One of those was a tweaking of the "statement of purpose" in their charters. The revised language directed them to "provide stability" and "ongoing assistance to the secondary market for home mortgages." Under the 1968 legislation, their purpose was described as providing "supplemental assistance" to the mortgage market. This subtle change served to bolster and make legitimate the idea that Fannie and Freddie were to be major players in the mortgage market at all times, on an "ongoing" basis, rather than just when credit was scarce.

Congress also recognized that, just like the federal insurance of S&L deposits, the implied federal backing of Fannie and Freddie created a potentially huge liability for taxpayers. Rather than trying to eliminate this contingent liability, Congress took the easy route and ordered studies of the risk by the Treasury and General Accounting Office.

So federal bureaucrats once again dredged through the history of government-sponsored companies and rehearsed the risks and benefits of having them. The first Treasury study, released in May 1990 and weighing in at 480 pages, found problems with Fannie's risk controls. For instance, Fannie had not documented some of its critical procedures, including some related to managing mortgage-default risks. The Treasury chided Fannie for "failure to maintain written procedures for complicated computer models." Fannie's computer systems sometimes went awry. When the Treasury asked for financial data, it found that some of the numbers spat out by Fannie's computers were inaccurate and inconsistent.

In a forecast that would prove spectacularly wrong, the Treasury predicted that Fannie's growth would slow in the 1990s, partly because the initial burst of baby-boomer home buying was past.

The Treasury also found that Fannie should hold more capital as a cushion against financial upsets. How much more? The Treasury didn't specify an amount. It noted that setting a minimum requirement "for an entity as unique as Fannie Mae must be somewhat subjective." The Treasury chewed over the risks of recessions, waves of mortgage defaults and wild swings in interest rates. A change in interest rates of 4 or 5 percentage points could wipe out Fannie's net worth if the company was forced to mark its mortgage holdings to their market values, the Treasury wrote.

BUT FANNIE HAD PREEMPTED the Treasury's report with an audacious maneuver—perhaps its most brilliant lobbying coup ever. Before the Treasury report came out, the company hired Volcker, the former Federal Reserve chairman, as a consultant to assess the adequacy of Fannie's capital. In his March 6, 1990 report to the company, Volcker said that if Fannie followed its plans for ensuring it had adequate capital, "the Company would be in a position to maintain its solvency in the face of difficulties in the housing markets and an interest rate environment significantly more adverse than any experienced in the post–World War II period." The risk of a taxpayer bailout "would be remote," he added.

Volcker's blessing was a huge advantage for Fannie. He was a revered financial figure, the man who as Fed chairman had put out the inflationary fires of the late 1970s. If he said Fannie's plan was sound, few would dare disagree.

It was hard to blame Congress for wanting to trust a reassuring, avuncular authority like Volcker. There was, after all, no scientific way to prove how much capital Fannie and Freddie should hold. It was "a matter of judgment," as Volcker put it.

So why not just hold at least as much capital as the typical big bank? Make us hold too much capital, Fannie executives would say, and we will have to charge more for mortgages, and that will hurt the housing market or at the very least prevent lots of poor and even middle-class people from buying their own homes.

Having obtained the Volcker seal of approval, Fannie then announced plans to raise its capital to $6 billion by the end of 1991 from $3.7 billion in early 1990. At a news conference, Maxwell suggested that the increased capital would be more than enough. He argued that Fannie's business wasn't nearly so risky as that of big banks, with their dubious lending to commercial real estate developers and Third World governments. "There are no unpleasant surprises because of the nature of our assets," he said. "We don't have any see-through buildings, any Third World countries or any strip shopping malls. We just have those mortgages."

Long afterward, during an interview in 2011, Volcker told me he "had the impression [Fannie] really didn't come completely clean" with him on the historical default data and had omitted certain data that would have made the record look worse. He no longer remembered how he got that impression, but his 1990 report noted that he had not "independently verified" data provided by Fannie.

When I asked him for a comment, Maxwell said, "We would never have thought of giving Paul Volcker incorrect or incomplete information. We really did want his opinion, and we assured him it would govern our decision, as it did."

In retrospect, Volcker said, he probably would not have blessed Fannie's capital plans "knowing what I know now." Of course, he said, Fannie was then much smaller, and mortgage standards were stricter than they would later become, so the risks to the taxpayers did not loom nearly as large as they would a decade later.

As instructed by Congress, the Treasury issued a second report in April 1991 covering not just Fannie and Freddie but other so-called government-sponsored enterprises, or GSEs, such as the Federal Home Loan Banks and the Student Loan Marketing Association, known as Sallie Mae. Among other things, the report warned:

> *The principal GSEs are few in number; they have highly qualified staffs; they have strong support for their programs from special interest groups; and they have significant resources with which to influence political outcomes. A weak financial regulator would find GSE political power overwhelming and even the most powerful and respected government agencies would find regulating such entities a challenge.*

In its May 1991 report, the General Accounting Office advocated the creation of a tough new regulator for Fannie and Freddie to replace HUD. The GAO recommended creating a Federal Enterprise Regulatory Board with authority to set capital requirements. "Enforcement authorities should track those available to bank and thrift regulators," the GAO said.

Fannie wanted nothing of the sort. In its letter of response, the company wrote that "the full panoply of enforcement authorities GAO suggests would be counterproductive to maintaining Fannie Mae's efficiency and effectiveness. Such enforcement authorities may well encourage a regulator to rely on after-the-fact enforcement, and will not foster regulation based on full understanding of the company and high quality, frequent monitoring designed to detect any problems early." There was no reason to create "a new, free-standing bureaucracy" to regulate Fannie and Freddie because HUD could do the job if given "more effective tools," Fannie's letter said.

Fannie depicted its business as low-risk: "Fannie Mae is limited to one line of business in which we are expert and which has risks that are quantifiable, based on historic experience." The company said its standards for determining how much capital was needed were perfectly adequate.

"There is now a consensus that Fannie Mae does not pose a significant risk to the American taxpayers," said Fannie's letter, signed by Ellen Seidman, vice-president for strategic planning.

Maxwell could prepare to retire as the savior of Fannie Mae. In James Johnson, Maxwell had found a kindred spirit and successor. To prepare for his eventual appointment as CEO, Johnson joined Fannie as vice-chairman in January 1990. When Johnson was officially named the successor in September 1990, Maxwell declared to the press, "The condition of the company has never been stronger. It will remain that way in the future."

THOUGH MAXWELL HAD SAVED the company from financial ruin, he also set it on a perilous political course. When Fannie had a clear choice—to remove itself from politics or fight to keep its congressionally granted privileges—Maxwell and Johnson chose the latter course.

Fannie and Freddie were heading into more than a decade of immensely profitable growth as they became the dominant providers of funding for home mortgages. At the end of 1990, Fannie and Freddie held mortgages and related securities totaling $136.0 billion, or 4.7 percent of all U.S. home mortgage debt outstanding. By the end of 2002, they had increased those holdings to $1.4 trillion, or 20.0 percent of home mortgage debt outstanding. (These figures cover only the mortgages they owned, not the larger amount of mortgage securities held by others on which the two companies guaranteed payments.)

The more powerful Fannie and Freddie grew, the more enemies they would create. The huge salaries they could now afford to pay would incite envy. With increasing alarm, large banks and mortgage-insurance companies would view Fannie and Freddie as unfairly subsidized rivals. Politicians and advocates for housing interests would expect Fannie and Freddie to earn their privileged status by doing more and more to help poor people afford homes. Other politicians, opposing government intervention in the economy, would grow angrier about the rapidly growing power of government-backed companies.

Caught between jealous rivals and insatiable political demands, Fannie and Freddie would expand their already formidable lobbying arsenals to defend the privileges they chose to retain. The bigger they became, the harder they would fall.

Maxwell had also made a fateful choice for the company in his selection of Johnson to lead Fannie into the 1990s. Johnson was clearly a political figure, one of the most powerful Democratic Party insiders in the nation. A company that had tried to be viewed as nonpartisan would come to be seen by resentful Republicans as a tool of the Democrats, pushing their housing-policy goals. Republicans began to see Fannie as a refuge—or "terrorist training ground," as some later put it—for Democratic leaders desiring lucrative jobs between Democratic administrations.

UPON RETIRING IN JANUARY 1991, Maxwell ignited one final controversy: he chose to take his pension in a lump sum of $20 million rather than in smaller payments spread over the rest of his life. Maxwell found it more prudent not to rely on Fannie's future ability to meet that pension obligation on a month-by-month basis. His decision triggered headlines about what then looked like a stupendous sum for any executive and even today looks generous. Added to his final year's compensation, the reported sum came to $27 million.

When newspaper reporters called, Fannie spokesman David Jeffers defended his former boss: "He earned it. He deserved every penny."

Maxwell told the *Washington Post*, "I am the first to say it's a very large amount of money. I never, in my wildest dreams, believed that any time in my life I would have a lot of money. Now that I have it and it's an object of considerable interest, it's a little unsettling."

David Maxwell in a portrait taken long after his retirement from Fannie Mae. *Courtesy of the Maxwell family.*

Another newspaper, *USA Today*, compared Maxwell's big payday to that of a New York Mets baseball pitcher, Dwight Gooden, who had recently signed a three-year contract totaling $15.5 million. Gooden "should consider pitching for Fannie Mae," the newspaper commented. A congressman, Charles Schumer of New York, later said of Maxwell's package, "I like him. I think he did a good job. But that's an obscenity."

Early the next year, Maxwell tried to limit the damage by giving up an additional $5.5 million of compensation that the company owed him. Instead, that money was given to the Fannie Mae Foundation, a charity set up by the company.

In a letter to Johnson, Maxwell defended himself by saying that "my management team and I took a company that was losing $1 million every business day and turned it into a company that was earning $4 million every business day when I retired in 1991." He acknowledged, however, that his pay had become a political issue: "I have concluded it would better shield Fannie Mae from any criticism that could develop into unwise legislative or regulatory provisions if I simply did not accept the money."

In his 2001 management book *Good to Great*, Jim Collins described Maxwell's performance at Fannie as brilliant: "Maxwell focused first on getting the right people on the Fannie Mae management team....Maxwell made it absolutely clear that there would only be seats for A players who were going to put forth an A+ effort, and if you weren't up for it, you had better get off the bus, and get off now."

Oakley Hunter, Maxwell's predecessor, took a dimmer view. Hunter, according to a former colleague, resented critical remarks by Maxwell about how the company was run in the pre-Maxwell days. That resentment may have colored Hunter's assessment of Maxwell. Even so, Hunter's jeremiad is worth considering, partly because it would be echoed by many others in years to come. He spelled it out in a November 7, 1991 letter to Senator Don Riegle, chairman of the Senate Banking Committee. In his letter, Hunter complained that Fannie had grown too political, notably by forming a Political Action Committee to make contributions to congressional candidates. He also wrote that executive compensation at Fannie had "run amok." In Hunter's view, increases in the stock price weren't necessarily due to the brilliance of management. Though Maxwell was "an able and intelligent individual," Hunter wrote, he "did not turn the company around." Rather, it was the steep drop in interest rates that saved Fannie, Hunter argued.

The implied federal guarantee gave Fannie "an immense leg up over competitors because interest costs are the principal expense of doing business." Hunter added, "They are immune from takeovers, and their executives enjoy the best of both worlds, private and public. Their pay is comparable with the top echelons of the private sector, and they have the protection of the safety net and the psychic income of the public sector. They are not entrepreneurs. It is not their wealth at risk."

Hunter accused Fannie of making excess profits, noting that the company's return on equity was 33.8 percent in 1990 and that the lowest rate of the past four years was 24.9 percent. Fannie's returns were double the average for companies included in the S&P 500 stock index.

In the Hunter era, profits were more modest. The goal in those days, he wrote, was "to attract the equity and borrowed capital necessary to finance its operations carried on for the benefit of the public it served, but not to maximize profits at the expense of the public it served."

AND SO MAXWELL COULD not glide quietly into retirement. In the post-Maxwell period, Fannie would thrive for another fifteen years but never quite manage to win the political debate. When Fannie made big profits, it would be accused of enriching its shareholders and executives while neglecting the "mission" of helping poor people buy houses. When, in 2008 and beyond, Fannie reported immense losses, it would be accused of having gambled recklessly, putting taxpayers at risk. The happy medium never arrived.

Chapter 7

A Hell of a Machine

Jim Johnson, a cool and sometimes aloof political operative who became chairman and CEO at the end of January 1991, presided elegantly over a fleeting period in which Fannie was at the apex of its power, able to please shareholders with ever-larger profits while crushing most of its political enemies. He often chatted urbanely with visitors while perched in a wingback chair near a fireplace in his office suite, featuring a silky Oriental rug. Liveried doormen, resembling those in posh hotels, ushered guests to and fro.

Johnson could treat cabinet members, Wall Street CEOs and senators as peers, if not slightly lesser beings. He was not merely chairman of the nation's most profitable financial institution. For part of this period, he was also chairman of the board of trustees at the Brookings Institution, a center of progressive thought, and chairman of the John F. Kennedy Center for the Performing Arts, Washington's highest temple of culture.

When he traveled on business, it was in the style of a presidential candidate. An aide traveled in advance to ensure that arrangements would suit his meticulous preferences and that he would meet all the local politicians worth cultivating as friends of Fannie. If a limousine was to pick him up after an appointment, his staff knew that it had better be exactly where he was told to expect it. Though his perfectionism often exasperated subordinates, many found him admirable.

Johnson's roots were more humble. His paternal grandparents emigrated from Norway to Swift County, Minnesota, in the 1870s. One of his grandmothers lived in a log cabin on the prairie south of Benson, Minnesota. When Johnson was a boy in the late 1940s and early 1950s, his father was becoming a powerful figure in Minnesota. His father, Alfred Ingvald "A.I." Johnson, grew up on a farm near Benson and became an entrepreneur. He and a partner owned the Jack Sprat grocery and dry goods store in Benson. After World War II, he became a real estate broker and home builder and served for two decades in the state legislature, including as speaker of the House. The elder Johnson was a member of Minnesota's Democratic-Farmer-Labor Party, or DFL, created in the 1940s through a merger of the Democratic Party and the Farmer-Labor Party. The DFL cultivated national political leaders including Hubert Humphrey, Eugene McCarthy and Walter Mondale. James Johnson's mother, Adeline, taught Latin, German and social studies at the Benson high school.

The young Johnson earned a bachelor's degree in political science from the University of Minnesota, where he served as student body president. "He was naturally very introverted," a friend said, but he wanted a public role and so "forced himself to be extroverted." Next he acquired a master's degree in public policy from Princeton. As a leader of protests against the Vietnam war, he met Bill Clinton at a meeting of activists on Martha's Vineyard in 1969. Both were heading into the transition from angry young man to pragmatic political pro. Johnson worked on the political campaigns of Eugene McCarthy, Edmund Muskie, George McGovern and Jimmy Carter. During the Carter administration, he was executive assistant to Vice President Mondale. In 1984, he headed Mondale's campaign against Reagan for president. It was not a great success: Mondale prevailed only in his home state of Minnesota and in the District of Columbia.

One charm of American politics is that even the losers win, going on to lucrative and prestigious jobs. Johnson joined the Wall Street investment banking firm of Shearson Lehman Hutton as a managing director. He married Maxine Isaacs, who taught at Harvard's Kennedy School of Government. Around that time, in the mid-1980s, he attended a Washington dinner party hosted by Betty Ann Ottinger, a psychoanalyst, and met David Maxwell.

Maxwell introduced Johnson to his calling. At Fannie, Johnson would find a platform to pursue social causes that had not always proved popular in his days as a political pro. He could lift up the downtrodden. And there was no need to take a vow of poverty: he could earn millions of dollars every year.

A Hell of a Machine

DURING JOHNSON'S REIGN AT Fannie, profits flowed reliably. Net income rose every year in the 1990s, more than tripling from $1.17 billion in 1990 to $3.91 billion in 1999. But it was in the political realm that Johnson showed his greatest mastery.

There was a big battle to be fought. Having done its best to sort out the S&L crisis, Congress in 1991 finally was getting around to the question of how to reduce the risk that Fannie and Freddie would blow up and force another bailout. The House and Senate were working toward legislation to improve oversight of Fannie and Freddie, an effort supported by President George H.W. Bush. There was growing belief that a new regulator must be created. HUD had neither the interest nor the expertise for the job.

Competitors and critics were sniping. News of Maxwell's retirement package had irked powerful people on Capitol Hill. The reports from the Treasury and General Accounting Office reminded everyone of the financial risks.

Representative Jim Leach, a Republican from Iowa and member of the House Banking Committee, argued that Fannie and Freddie were taking over business that should be left to the private sector and creating potentially huge risks for the taxpayer. He advocated higher capital requirements and the repeal of some of the companies' privileges, such as exemptions from state and local taxes. Having seen S&Ls implode and big banks make bad loans to Latin America, Representative Leach considered himself a "hawk" on capital. He did not believe Fannie and Freddie should be allowed to hold much less of it than other financial institutions did.

Fannie was willing to go along with Congress's desire for a new regulator. But Fannie executives feared their critics "wanted to smother us with regulation," as one put it. Fannie's goal was clear: keep the new regulator from having enough power to thwart the company's vision of what was best for itself, its shareholders, the housing market and the nation.

Ellen Seidman, a senior Fannie executive at the time, told me there was internal debate over how strong the regulator should be. Some felt it would be helpful to have a regulator strong enough to be seen as credible; that might allay fears that the company constituted a major risk to the economy and taxpayers. Others feared the regulator would box Fannie into an uncomfortably tight space. The debate came down on the side of not wanting the regulator to be very strong. It wasn't only a desire to avoid irksome regulations, Seidman said: "We all really believed in what we did" at Fannie and didn't want that work squashed by excessive regulation.

The Bush administration sent its proposals for legislation to Congress in May 1991. Initially, Treasury officials favored creating a new regulator within that department, known for its skepticism of Fannie and Freddie. But the administration ended up pleasing Fannie and Freddie by proposing that the new regulator should be an independent arm of HUD, more sympathetic to the housing lobby. The director of this new regulator would be nominated by the president, subject to confirmation by the Senate.

The administration's plan troubled Representative J.J. Pickle, a Texas Democrat who was chairman of the House Ways and Means oversight subcommittee. At a hearing in May 1991, Representative Pickle said he feared the new regulator wouldn't be truly independent if it was under the wing of HUD. "I recognize that there are enormous political pressures being brought to bear on all these issues," said Representative Pickle.

Treasury Undersecretary Robert Glauber, who had testified on an earlier version of the bill in favor of putting the regulator inside the Treasury, now

The Department of Housing and Urban Development, shown here, was chosen over the Treasury as overseer for the agency regulating Fannie and Freddie under legislation passed in 1992. *Courtesy of the Library of Congress.*

assured the committee that the regulator would have enough independence from HUD and could take its case to Congress if that department tried to block any needed action.

Fannie and Freddie were unhappy with another Bush administration plan that would give the regulator power to raise their capital requirements. At a hearing in the House in late May, Johnson said the plan gave the regulator "entirely too much" flexibility to raise capital requirements, something that could push up mortgage payments for homeowners. He said Congress, not the regulator, should set capital standards for Fannie and Freddie because only Congress had the political mandate to balance the needs of housing policy with those of financial safety.

Referring to the rich retirement package for Maxwell, Representative Gonzalez, who was chairman of the House Banking Committee, suggested that Fannie's shareholders could shoulder higher capital requirements without raising the cost of mortgages. Representative Joseph Kennedy, a Democrat from Massachusetts, said Fannie had "gotten too greedy" and was "out of control."

A few days later, in early June, Johnson went to New York to brief investors and analysts. He assured them that Fannie expected Congress to pass legislation that wouldn't hobble the company. Congress, he predicted, would recognize that "government intrusion into the business of a well-capitalized, well-functioning company should be low."

In July, Representative Gonzalez released his own legislative proposal, co-sponsored by Representative Chalmers Wylie, an Ohio Republican, and Representative Marge Roukema, a Republican from New Jersey. Their bill set specific capital levels for Fannie and Freddie, in line with those favored by the companies. This provision would leave the regulator with less flexibility on capital than would be provided by the Bush administration plan—a victory for Fannie and Freddie. But the Gonzalez bill also would require Fannie and Freddie to set aside an amount equaling 20 percent of the previous year's dividends to support rental housing for poor people. Fannie objected to that constraint. "We are not in the subsidy business," a Fannie spokesman said.

At hearings on the legislation in July, the National Association of Realtors said both the Bush administration and the Gonzalez plans would create overly strict capital requirements that might prevent the companies from giving enough support to housing. Rick Adams, a Realtor from San Antonio, said in his written testimony to Congress: "It's fair to say that today's housing industry would be lost without Fannie Mae and Freddie Mac. The liquidity they have brought to the mortgage market has resulted in lower mortgage rates, more consistent sources of financing and a wider choice of financing for the consumer."

At the end of July, the House Banking Committee compromised on the capital standards. The regulator would be left without any immediate ability to push up the requirements set by Congress but would be instructed to devise an additional "risk-based" capital standard. The provision setting a fixed percentage of dividend payments aside for low-income housing was transformed into a mere goal.

Johnson endorsed this watered-down plan, calling it "tough, dynamic and fair." The vote in the banking committee was 49–1 in favor of the compromise. Only Representative Leach voted no.

Representative Joseph Kennedy's amendment to put caps on pay at Fannie and Freddie was defeated. Among those hired by Fannie to lobby against that idea was Stuart Eizenstat, who had been President Carter's chief domestic policy adviser. "I don't think I've ever been lobbied by such a broad cross-section of influential Democrats—strategists, businessmen, everybody from the Washington hierarchy," Representative Kennedy said.

Thomas Stanton, a Washington lawyer whose book *A State of Risk* and behind-the-scenes crusading helped spur Congress to improve regulation of Fannie and Freddie, said the legislation would "perpetuate a system of wafer-thin capital." In a *Washington Post* column, Robert J. Samuelson agreed that the capital requirements were too low. Congress should not be lulled by the currently robust profits at Fannie and Freddie, he wrote. "Just because they're safe and solid today is no reason to shun prudent safeguards. The real risks are not the ones that we can see but the ones that we (and even the best computer models) cannot. This was the bedrock lesson of the S&L crisis."

On September 25, 1991, the legislation was presented for a vote by the full House. Representative Leach had his final chance to deplore the low capital requirements written into the law: "If one kind of institution is allowed excessive leveraging [of debt in relation to capital], the taxpayer can too quickly be put on the line for management stupidity, foul play or bad luck." Representative Leach added that Congress was giving Fannie and Freddie unfair advantages over competitors and legislating "the privatization of profit coupled with the socialization of cost and risk."

Representative Wylie replied that if capital requirements were too high, "money would not be made available for housing." As for the risk of a bailout, he said, "We think we have drafted a proposal here which would suggest that at no time would there be any risk to the taxpayers."

Representative Leach proposed amendments, including one to raise the basic capital requirement. Representative Gonzalez called that proposal "draconian." The higher capital requirement, he warned, would prevent "that goose from laying that golden egg." Representative Bruce Vento of Minnesota rose to say that higher capital requirements would increase interest rates on home loans, hurting those seeking to "fulfill the American Dream." The amendments were defeated.

The House approved the legislation 412–8. Nearly all Republicans and Democrats were on board with Fannie and Freddie. Representative Leach was among the 8 who voted no. He later complained that the legislation was "written largely by lawyers" for Fannie and Freddie. "In fact and indeed," Leach wrote afterward, "Fannie Mae and Freddie Mac are beginning to seem like an arrogant, two-headed monopoly controlling 90% of the market."

Representative Leach didn't hold a grudge. Five years later, when Johnson wrote a book extolling homeownership, he asked Leach to write the foreword. Leach obliged, writing that Johnson's book "lights a lamp of hope." Despite their political differences, Leach considered Johnson a friend.

The legislative battle moved on to the Senate, famous for taking its time. When an early draft of the Senate legislation made the rounds in November, Fannie pounced. Maloni, the Fannie senior vice-president responsible for lobbying, sent a letter denouncing the draft as "an exceptionally broad and intrusive grant of regulatory authority" that would "stifle the private market vitality" of the company. Fannie disliked provisions that would give HUD power to veto new types of financing by Fannie and impose penalties on any failure to meet goals for support to affordable housing.

While Johnson was the polished, suave face of Fannie, Maloni was the pit bull. A native of Pittsburgh, he was as quick to find fault with the coaches of his beloved Steelers football team as he was to blitz any regulatory idea that might constrain Fannie. He didn't believe in an understated approach. Long after his retirement, he told me, "I always told my people, 'I would rather throw one too many bricks than one too few.'"

Given Fannie's smashmouth defense, nothing was going to be easy about this debate. It became clear that the Senate wouldn't act on the legislation before 1992. With little more public debate, the Senate Banking Committee in early April 1992 passed a bill similar to the House legislation. "Their current financial health is good," said Senator Riegle. The aim of the legislation was "to keep it that way."

Only one member of the committee, Senator Phil Gramm, a Texas Republican, dissented. He warned that the goals set for financing of affordable housing could undermine the companies' finances and that the new regulator would impose more rules without strengthening Fannie and Freddie. "I personally don't think we have gone far enough in this bill," he told the committee.

In mid-1992, as the legislation moved toward enactment, Johnson told the *Wall Street Journal* that the bill would "remove any cloud that remains about our governmental mandate…and allow Fannie Mae to get on with housing Americans and making more money for its shareholders." In a later letter to that newspaper, he said a regulator with too much power could stifle Fannie's creativity: "Were we subject to a regulator inclined to micromanage every element of our business, this innovation could be quickly snuffed out. This is why we have sought statutory definition of our new regulator's role."

On July 1, 1992, the Senate approved the bill 77–19. In September, staff members of the Senate and House worked on the technicalities of resolving differences between the two versions of the legislation. Late in the month, Fannie officials objected to minor changes in the legislative language that they said would give the regulator too much leeway on capital requirements under a risk-based formula to be developed by the regulator. Johnson sent a letter to Congress denouncing the new language and withdrawing the company's support for the bill. He said it would allow "excessively wide discretion to set virtually any capital level [the regulator] desires and to enforce it by taking over the operations of Fannie Mae or Freddie Mac."

The Bush administration was furious. Assistant Treasury Secretary John Dugan told the press that Fannie "apparently wants to stay unregulated by bolting from the process at the 11th hour." He added, "The great danger is that members of Congress will cave in to one of the most powerful financial lobbies in Washington."

Fannie, an entity created by the government fifty-four years earlier to perform a financial chore, now was so powerful that the same government was not sure it could enact legislation affecting Fannie without first securing Fannie's consent.

Negotiations ensued involving Fannie, Treasury Secretary Nicholas Brady and congressional leaders. In the end, the language was tweaked. Fannie agreed to support the bill. In early October, the House and Senate gave formal approval to the bill.

A Hell of a Machine

"We should have done better," Representative Pickle lamented on the House floor. "We have, once again, left the public purse exposed to the risks of private greed and corporate misjudgment. But, as little progress as this is, it is something. It is a step forward."

President Bush signed the bill into law on October 28, 1992.

THE 1992 ACT REQUIRED Fannie and Freddie to hold capital equaling 2.50 percent of assets held on their balance sheets and 0.45 percent of those not included on their balance sheets, mainly guarantees on mortgage securities owned by others. That 2.50 percent standard was less than half the capital held by most banks.

The law also instructed the new regulator to devise supplemental risk-based capital standards that could be higher than the statutory standards, depending on the types of assets held. (The regulator didn't manage to issue final regulations for those risk-based standards until September 2001.)

The 1992 act also set into law goals for the percentage of Fannie and Freddie's loan purchases or guarantees that were to finance homes for people with less than the median income or those living in inner cities or other areas deemed to be neglected by mortgage lenders.

The new regulatory agency, clumsily named the Office of Federal Housing Enterprise Oversight, or Ofheo, was a weakling. Unlike bank regulators, it lacked flexibility to adjust capital requirements. Bank regulators were allowed to determine their own budgets. But Ofheo was required to get approval from Congress for its budget each year—an ordeal that gave congressional friends of Fannie and Freddie a chance to pressure the regulator. Almost every year, Congress delayed approving the Ofheo budget, leaving the agency unsure how much it could spend and forcing it to put off hiring plans. "We had almost no funds, and that was by design," Patrick Lawler, who worked as chief economist at Ofheo, said later.

Armando Falcon, a former director of Ofheo, estimated in 2010 that if the agency had been funded like federal bank regulators, it would have had at least sixty examiners supervising Fannie and Freddie. In fact, he said, Ofheo had only about fifteen to twenty.

IT WAS LEFT TO a new president, Bill Clinton, to appoint the first director of Ofheo: Aida Alvarez. Alvarez, who was born in Puerto Rico and was a graduate of Harvard College, worked early in her career as a journalist for the *New York Post* and a New York City television station and then as a spokeswoman for a New York City hospital agency. Later, she spent seven years as an investment banker with Bear Stearns and First Boston. Her job at both banks involved finding local government bodies wishing to raise money through tax-exempt bonds. On a trip to Texas, she met Henry Cisneros, the mayor of San Antonio and one of the rising stars in the Democratic firmament. Soon Alvarez was introducing Cisneros to Hispanic leaders in New York. Through him, she met Bill Clinton.

"One thing led to another," she told me in an interview in 2011. During Clinton's presidential campaign in 1992, Alvarez served as an adviser on Hispanic and women's issues. Once Clinton was elected, she was in line for a federal appointment. That turned out to be the challenging, but not very glamorous, task of setting up an agency to monitor Fannie and Freddie.

Almost immediately, she was fighting for money. Upon arrival in Washington, she learned that the House of Representatives had appropriated $5.7 million for the agency's annual budget. Congressional staffers told her that amount was an estimate by Fannie and Freddie of how much Ofheo would need.

"I thought, 'Whoa, this is not the way it's going to be,'" she recalled. She wanted about twice that amount. When she made her case to Senate staff members, the Republicans resisted. Republicans tended to want tight limits on the size of federal agencies. But Alvarez also believed Fannie and Freddie wanted to keep her agency puny and reliant on consultants rather than staff members.

Stymied in the Senate, she telephoned Leland Brendsel, Freddie Mac's CEO, and Johnson at Fannie. Brendsel, a low-profile executive who was raised on a farm in South Dakota and earned a doctorate in financial economics at Northwestern University, did not return her call. Johnson expressed annoyance that he had been pulled out of a board meeting. Johnson assured her that he had never instructed anyone to block her budget request. She asked him to prod Senator Alfonse D'Amato, a New York Republican who was considered particularly reluctant to let Ofheo have its way on the budget.

Johnson sent a fax to Senator D'Amato, supporting Alvarez's budget plan, and relayed a copy of the fax to her. She forwarded the fax to Freddie's Brendsel, hoping to get a reaction out of him. Finally, Brendsel returned her call—and told her she didn't need all the money she was requesting. She noted that he didn't want her to micromanage his company but that he now seemed to be micromanaging her. She then suggested she might have to tell reporters that Freddie was trying to thwart her at Ofheo. Brendsel produced a supportive letter to Senator D'Amato.

Congress approved a $10.7 million budget, but Senator D'Amato pushed through an amendment limiting the agency to forty-five full-time employees, well below the sixty sought by Alvarez. Senator D'Amato said Ofheo had "failed to provide Congress with an acceptable business plan to justify" its staffing proposal. He wanted "to limit the size of a new federal bureaucracy before it grows out of control."

That struggle set the pattern for Ofheo, which had little support on Capitol Hill, where Fannie and Freddie walked tall. "Every time we would ask for an increase [in funding], it was a battle for every single dollar," Alvarez said.

Almost from the start, some Fannie executives failed to hide their disdain for Ofheo. "We thought they were amateurs," said Maloni, the Fannie lobbyist. Still, Alvarez said she generally got along well with Johnson and Brendsel and "never felt personally disrespected." Even with a much bigger budget, Ofheo would have been subject to political pressure, of course. Even the larger and more prestigious federal bank regulatory agencies failed to crack down early enough on the lax lending policies that eventually led to a housing bust. As Representative Leach later put it, "Having the power to regulate doesn't mean they have the wisdom to regulate."

So Fannie succeeded in keeping its capital requirements low and its regulator weak. As it later turned out, Fannie and Freddie would have been better off with a strong regulator able to enforce conservative standards for capital holdings and credit risks. Such a regime would have been less lucrative but might have ensured the survival of the companies. With a stronger regulator, Fannie and Freddie could more easily have said no to the various parties pressuring them—shareholders, lenders and housing advocates: "No, sorry, the regulator won't let us do that."

THOUGH THE LEGISLATIVE BATTLE had been won, Fannie did not let up in its lobbying. People who could be useful—such as congressional committee staffers or others with political influence—sometimes got job offers. Among those hired by Fannie in the early 1990s was Herb Moses, then a companion of Representative Barney Frank, who was deeply involved in housing issues. A spokesman for Representative Frank told me Moses was "way, way qualified" for the job.

Flattery also could be useful. At a reception for bankers in 1994, Johnson bestowed the Fannie Mae Housing Hero award on Representative Gonzalez, citing his "lifetime of accomplishments in ensuring that millions of families have decent, safe and affordable housing throughout the nation." Johnson called the award "Fannie Mae's version of the Oscar."

Fannie funded a charitable foundation to spread largesse throughout the land and built a network of regional offices to curry favor with governors, mayors and other notables—anyone who might be called upon to bombard Congress with warnings against tampering with Fannie's prerogatives.

Fannie lobbyists kept track of how much housing the company had financed in each congressional district—and made sure each Congressman knew about it. Then there were the little touches: Fannie supplied the softball teams on Capitol Hill with bases, identifying the company as "The USA's Housing Partner."

At the same time, Fannie and Freddie felt growing pressures. A 1992 study by Alicia Munnell and other researchers at the Federal Reserve Bank of Boston, "Mortgage Lending in Boston: Interpreting HMDA Data," provided statistical evidence that lenders were more inclined to deny mortgage loans to black and Hispanic applicants than to whites with similar financial situations. That study fueled demands for change from minority groups whose political support Fannie and Freddie needed.

The study reverberated through the entire mortgage industry. Angelo Mozilo, a co-founder of Countrywide Financial, one of the nation's biggest mortgage lenders, said later that the study jolted his company into rethinking its policies. Many people from minority groups had never had formal bank loans or credit cards and so lacked a payments record. That alone might keep them from qualifying for a mortgage. Countrywide began looking for other ways to assess their willingness and ability to make payments, such as their utility bills.

Countrywide started making more loans to people who didn't fit the usual mold. Those loans "performed much better than expected," Mozilo told the Financial Crisis Inquiry Commission in September 2010. Lending to people of modest means, when done carefully, could be profitable and did not have to be (as it often was) predatory.

Fannie also had to react. In March 1994, the company announced that by the end of the decade it would make $1 trillion available to finance housing for "minorities, low- and moderate-income families, new immigrants, families who live in central cities and distressed areas, and people with special housing needs."

A month later, Johnson traveled to Baltimore to announce that $750 million would be invested there over five years "to finance affordable housing and homeownership opportunities." He held a press conference with Mayor Kurt Schmoke and toured poor neighborhoods. Mayor Schmoke called it "a great shot in the arm for the city." The plan included an offering of loans with down payments of 5 percent. U.S. Senator Paul Sarbanes and Representative Kweisi Mfume contributed laudatory quotes for the press release. It was an exercise that would be repeated across the land. Fannie's press release for an investment in the twenty-nine-home Gables of Wingate development in Charlotte, North Carolina, in 2001 shared credit with U.S. Representative Mel Watt for helping revive a neighborhood.

Johnson crisscrossed the country to open "partnership offices." These branches—eventually totaling more than fifty—were touted as a way to find investment opportunities but also were vital to a strategy of building political support. When the St. Louis office opened in 1995, Johnson shared the stage with Mayor Freeman Bosley, Senator Christopher "Kit" Bond and U.S. Representative Richard Gephardt. When Fannie needed help in lobbying Congress, it could use these local offices to call in political debts across the country. Some Fannie executives called these lobbying drives "fire drills."

Resisting Fannie was a thankless task. Representative Leach said most of his Iowa constituents paid no attention to debates about regulation of Fannie and Freddie; whenever he defied the two companies' wishes, though, he heard from irate Realtors, home builders and advocates for housing projects.

FANNIE'S SUPPORT FOR AFFORDABLE housing meshed with the goals of the Clinton administration. On November 5, 1994, President Clinton called for a national drive to increase the homeownership rate and directed HUD to come up with a "national homeownership strategy."

The U.S. homeownership rate had jumped to 65.6 percent in 1980 from 43.6 percent in 1940. The rate then declined modestly during the 1980s. At the end of 1994, it stood at 64.1 percent, or 1.5 percentage points below the 1980 peak. Rates for blacks and Hispanics were far lower.

HUD's "homeownership strategy" report, dated May 1995, listed the usual arguments in favor of helping more people own homes: homeownership would stabilize neighborhoods, help families generate wealth and "exercise more responsibility over their living environment," create "incentives for improving private property and public spaces" and boost the economy. "Every new home creates 2.1 jobs directly related to construction, and many more jobs through increased demand for household goods and services," the report said.

Many companies were eager to join this HUD crusade. Among the fifty-six organizations that took part were Fannie and Freddie. Others included trade associations representing bankers, title insurers, home builders and real estate brokers—all parties that would gain from any increase in building and selling houses.

The report called for one hundred "action steps" aimed at creating as many as eight million homeowners within six years. These included reviews of regulations that might impede building, more zoning for high-density housing and steps to encourage financing of manufactured housing, or what most Americans still called trailers. The report noted approvingly that Fannie and Freddie had allowed loans with down payments as low as 3 percent.

The goal was to increase the national homeownership rate to as much as 67.5 percent by the end of the year 2000. In fact, the rate increased to exactly 67.5 percent by that date, according to Census Bureau data.

The mid-1990s were heady times for those who fervently believed that making homeownership easier to attain would transform lives and neighborhoods and for those who could profit from making more loans and selling more homes—and especially for the many people who both believed in this dogma and profited from it.

In 1995, Fannie distributed a brochure called "Opening Doors With Fannie Mae's Community Lending Products." It opened with a gush:

> *Most people share a common dream—one that is solidly rooted in the history of our country and deeply etched in our national character. It is a dream of owning a home and of having the stability, security and bonds of community that homeownership provides. At Fannie Mae, we are committed to making that dream come true for every family who can possibly achieve it.*

The brochure listed new flexible mortgages with such features as reduced income requirements and minimum down payments as low as 3 percent, far below the traditional norm of 20 percent or more. One of these programs, the "start-up mortgage," allowed borrowers to make only interest payments for the first year rather than starting to chip away at the principal.

Closing costs are often onerous for first-time buyers with little or no savings. These costs include taxes and fees from lenders and other parties, such as inspectors and providers of flood-zone reports. They are due at the closing of the transaction and typically total at least several thousand dollars.

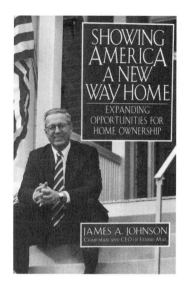

SHOWING
AMERICA
A NEW
WAY HOME

EXPANDING
OPPORTUNITIES FOR
HOME OWNERSHIP

JAMES A. JOHNSON
CHAIRMAN AND CEO OF FANNIE MAE

The cover of James Johnson's
1996 book extolling Fannie's role
in expanding homeownership.

The Fannie program allowed those costs to be covered by gifts (from a family member or charity, for instance), grants (from a housing agency) or unsecured loans (from nonprofits, government agencies or mortgage lenders).

Some critics worried that borrowers would be more likely to default if they put little or no money into the deal. Fannie said it required home-buyer education in many cases in an attempt to ensure that borrowers were ready for ownership.

In 1996, Johnson's book *Showing America a New Way Home* was a battle cry for Fannie executives. "We must pursue powerful policies that will increase the rate of home ownership among minorities to equal that of whites," Johnson wrote. "I believe nothing would do more to advance social justice, heal the wounds of past discrimination, and bank the fires of future tension and division than to ensure truly equal access to home ownership."

As he tried to maintain bipartisan support, Johnson realized the risk that Fannie would be seen as a tool of the Democrats. To bolster support among Republicans, he engaged as a lobbyist Kenneth Duberstein, who had served as White House chief of staff under President Reagan. Duberstein became a member of Fannie's board in 1998.

In 1991, Johnson appointed another Republican as Fannie's chief spokesman, John Buckley, a nephew of the conservative writer William F. Buckley. John Buckley, a novelist and former journalist, had worked in public relations for the Reagan reelection campaign and as a spokesman for U.S. Representative Jack Kemp, among other Republican roles. As a conservative, Buckley had to think hard about Fannie's model, he later told me. "Whether or not you believed it was a legitimate birth, it was a fact," and a major pillar of the housing industry, he concluded. As a moderate Jack Kemp–style Republican, Buckley was not "allergic" to all government intervention in the economy. His Uncle Jim—former U.S. Senator James Buckley—believed Fannie shouldn't exist. Meanwhile, "my uncle Bill saw me as doing the Lord's work in trying to tame a New Deal institution to private sector ends."

As a PR man, Buckley felt "the company had to define itself" before someone else did. His boss, Johnson, wanted to stress "the service we were providing to those most in need." Fannie began buying television ads, first locally in Washington and later on national broadcasts, to explain its mission. "That's when the Mortgage Bankers Association started to freak out," Buckley said. Some mortgage lenders feared Fannie was trying to build up a consumer brand name in the hope of eventually dealing directly with borrowers—a charge denied by Fannie.

Fannie also became a sponsor of the National Basketball Association. The goal, Buckley said, was to reach more minorities who aspired to homeownership. In March 1998, the *Houston Chronicle* reported that members of the Rockets basketball team would "landscape, plant shrubs, lay sod and install a basketball goal for a newly built 'Home Team' house in the Fifth Ward neighborhood" as part of a project funded by a Fannie Mae Foundation grant.

ALL OF THIS ADVERTISING, PR and lobbying did not prevent critics from occasionally trying to take away some of the privileges dear to Fannie and Freddie. In 1995, the Congressional Budget Office, or CBO, a nonpartisan research arm of Congress, proposed charging Fannie and Freddie fees equaling half the estimated benefits they received from their government backing. The fees would have raised about $700 million a year for the government. The CBO acknowledged that part of those fees might be passed on to mortgage borrowers, perhaps pushing mortgage interest rates up as much as a tenth of a percentage point. Fannie denounced the proposed fees as "a tax on homeownership." The Clinton administration considered the fees but eventually backed off.

Then came a barrage of federal reports rehashing the question of whether the government should still provide its implicit backing of Fannie and Freddie, allowing them to piggyback on Uncle Sam's credit rating. The reports—by the Congressional Budget Office, the General Accounting Office, HUD and the Treasury—had been ordered by Congress in 1992 as part of the legislation that created Ofheo.

In May 1996, the CBO's report questioned the companies' privileged status. "Improving access to mortgage finance may have been a social benefit worth paying for in the past," the report said. "It is now available without subsidy from fully private firms." The CBO also found that a large part of the benefits of federal support flowed to executives and shareholders rather than home buyers. "As a means of funneling federal subsidies to homebuyers…[the corporations] are a spongy conduit—soaking up nearly $1 for every $2 delivered," the CBO report said. The CBO acknowledged the difficulty of ending those privileges, given the political might of Fannie and Freddie: "Once one agrees to share a canoe with a bear, it is hard to get him out without obtaining his agreement or getting wet."

Fannie's retort was swift: "This is the work of economic pencil brains who wouldn't recognize something that works for ordinary home buyers if it bit them in the erasers," said David Jeffers, a vice-president in the company's PR department. Shortly after that outburst, Johnson stopped by Jeffers's office and said, "Let's take a walk." Jeffers admitted he had gone too far in using the term "pencil brains."

Though he wanted to maintain a high tone, Johnson was relentless in rebutting any suggestion that the Fannie model was not the best possible answer for America and sometimes seemed contemptuous of those who pushed alternative visions. As he told the Associated Press later that year, "When people try to impose costs on us and try to in some way undermine our ability to fulfill our public mission, we fight back very vigorously."

As for the GAO, its report cautioned that ending federal support for Fannie and Freddie would raise their borrowing costs. For mortgage borrowers, that might mean a rise in interest rates of 0.15 to 0.35 of a percentage point, the GAO said. It also warned that cutting the federal cord to Fannie and Freddie might reduce the availability of mortgage credit to poor people.

The Treasury, also required to produce a report, was in a delicate position. Treasury Secretary Robert Rubin, as a friend of Fannie's Johnson, recused himself from the process. In the end, Treasury underlings took the safest course, earnestly reviewing the pros and cons of privatization and coming to no conclusion. Lawrence Summers, a deputy secretary of the Treasury who would later become Treasury secretary and then president of Harvard University, presented the Treasury's findings to the House banking subcommittee on capital markets on July 24, 1996.

Fannie and Freddie had much smaller capital requirements than fully private financial firms, meaning they had less of a cushion against any losses that might arise from mortgage defaults or unexpected moves in interest rates. The Treasury found that their capital at the end of 1995 worked out to 2.75 percent of assets, compared with an average of 7.80 percent for banks and other savings institutions whose deposits were federally insured.

On the plus side, the Treasury described as "plausible" estimates that Fannie and Freddie's special status meant that mortgage rates for borrowers were around 0.30 of a percentage point lower than they otherwise would be. That worked out to $4 billion of savings annually for American home buyers.

On the other hand, now that mortgage securities were a well-established means of enticing money from a wide array of investors into housing finance, there was little doubt that the market for mortgages "could operate efficiently and effectively" if Fannie and Freddie lost their government backing, Summers said.

So what should Congress do? "Ending or modifying government sponsorship would entail risk, but would have potential benefits," Summers testified. "Its potential effect on mortgage interest rates would represent an important risk, as would any potential negative consequence for the availability of credit for affordable housing. Potential benefits could include increased market competition, more efficient credit allocation, reduced U.S. government borrowing costs, and reduced potential risk to taxpayers." It would be "premature," he added, to reach firm conclusions about whether to end or modify the government sponsorship of Fannie and Freddie.

This waffling exasperated Representative Richard Baker, the Louisiana Republican who was chairman of the subcommittee. "It seems that after more than two years of study we have a report that says, 'Standing still is risky, and doing something is risky,'" Representative Baker told Summers.

The result of all these reports and discussions was that Congress did nothing.

FANNIE GOT A CHANCE to take a victory lap at another hearing of Representative Baker's subcommittee in July 1996. Representing Fannie at that hearing was one of its executive vice-presidents, Robert B. Zoellick. "The plain, observable fact is that Fannie Mae is a critical part of the best housing finance system in the world," Zoellick told Congress. "No other country has created such an effective and efficient linkage between its housing finance and capital markets."

The rest of the world was envious, Zoellick said:

> *Somewhat ironically, at the same time we have been receiving a host of government analyses probing whether Fannie Mae works, we also have been asked to meet with a steady stream of visitors from all over the world— from Latin America, Western Europe, Eastern Europe, Russia, East Asia, South Asia, Africa, Australia—seeking to learn how to replicate the phenomenal success of America's housing finance system.*

A Hell of a Machine

A delusion was developing in Washington—to be repeated over and over in the years ahead, before the fall of Fannie and Freddie—that America's quirky way of financing mortgages was, as many put it, "the envy of the world." In fact, the U.S. system was rarely adopted in other countries, and the U.S. rate of homeownership was below that of many other lands, including Singapore, Spain and Ireland. These facts were seldom mentioned.

Fannie nurtured this delusion, sometimes with specious arguments. Johnson told the National Press Club in 1996 that America's housing-finance system was "the most successful in the world." In much of America, he said, "the typical house costs three times the annual income of the owner." In Tokyo, he said, "it's 12 times." He did not mention the scarcity of land in Japan, where population per square mile was about ten times greater than in the United States. Housing in the United States was cheaper than elsewhere mainly because there was far more land available, not because of Fannie or Freddie.

WHILE FANNIE DEFEATED ITS critics in Washington, it also faced grumbling in the rest of the mortgage industry. Many people in the industry relied heavily on being able to sell their mortgages to Fannie and Freddie and so avoided criticizing them in public. But resentment occasionally surfaced.

Mortgage banks, mostly small, local operations, generally liked the idea of having Fannie and Freddie around to buy mortgages. Without Fannie and Freddie, the mortgage bankers feared, giant commercial banks would dominate mortgage lending and squeeze out the little guys. But the mortgage bankers thought Fannie and Freddie were charging them excessive fees for guaranteeing mortgages against default. Those fees frequently were in the range of 0.20 percent to 0.30 percent of the unpaid loan balance on an annual basis, soaking up a big part of the profit margin on a loan.

Giant banks, too, had mixed feelings about Fannie and Freddie. Even big commercial banks, which had the capacity to hold mortgages on their books, liked having the option of selling loans to Fannie and Freddie. But some people at the big banks also thought Fannie and Freddie charged too much for their services and were trying to take over the entire mortgage business. Wall Street firms feasted on the fees they got from arranging Fannie and Freddie's frequent sales of bonds. But the Wall Street firms competed with Fannie and Freddie in the business of putting together mortgage securities and selling them to investors.

Tom LaMalfa, a partner in a mortgage research firm, took a shot at Fannie and Freddie when he was invited to speak at a convention of the Mortgage Bankers Association in San Francisco in 1996. LaMalfa told the mortgage bankers that Fannie and Freddie were "extracting the lion's share of revenue and net income from mortgage banking." They "are eating your companies' and industry's breakfast and lunch. They are siphoning its revenues and profits. They commoditize the market. They increase the cost of credit. They create mega-liabilities with minuscule capital to support it."

As LaMalfa later recalled, "Many Fannie and Freddie employees walked out, but when my talk ended, I received a standing ovation from maybe two-thirds of the audience." Fannie stopped buying research from his firm shortly afterward, LaMalfa said.

APPRECIATED OR NOT, FANNIE raced on. Its assets more than doubled from $133 billion in 1990 to $351 billion in 1996. They would reach an apex of about $1 trillion in 2003 and 2004.

As part of his growth strategy, Johnson embraced the country's fastest-growing mortgage lender, Countrywide Home Loans, and its tough-talking boss, Angelo Mozilo, the son of a butcher from the Bronx. Countrywide—later a symbol of excess in the great housing bubble—became by far the biggest seller of loans to Fannie, accounting for 25 to 30 percent of its business at times, according to Fannie executives. Mozilo and Johnson became golfing buddies.

By the mid-1990s, Fannie and Freddie owned or guaranteed around half of all home mortgages in the United States. They effectively set the standards determining which borrowers were eligible for loans and on what terms. Lending decisions were becoming less a matter of individual human judgment or the whims of a banker sitting self-importantly behind a desk. The lending decision now was more likely to be based on computer programs containing all the complicated determinants of loan eligibility and terms. Countrywide, big banks and Fannie and Freddie rushed to develop their own technologies for this so-called automated underwriting. Fannie bickered with the big banks over whose technology should be used. In the end, they compromised, making their systems work together.

Along with the rise of automated underwriting came the spread of credit scores. These numbers, such as the well-known FICO score created by Fair, Isaac & Co., rate borrowers largely on the basis of their past performance in paying bills and making loan payments on time, as well as their recent record of seeking credit. Fannie executives believed credit scores could be a better predictor of a borrower's behavior than other considerations, such as income, occupation and savings. The entire mortgage industry began to rely heavily on credit scores—eventually, too heavily, as common sense and other old-fashioned methods of assessing borrowers were neglected in favor of the speedy simplicity of scores.

This automation did not remove all human judgment, of course. People still fed the computers with the rules used to determine eligibility for loans. Loan officers or brokers who got a "no" from the computer could punch in different information—perhaps even false information—until they got a "yes." The lending process became less subjective, and probably more fair, but remained subject to human frailty.

Automation created expectations that people should be able to get a home loan almost as fast as they could get a hamburger at McDonald's. Lenders raced to verify the claims people made about incomes, occupations, savings, taxes and debts. This quest for speed eventually led to more so-called "no-doc" loans as lenders decided that many borrowers—especially those with good credit scores—didn't need to provide all the verifying documents. Lenders began competing on convenience, not just on interest rates and fees. In the end, at the top of the housing bubble, even borrowers with poor credit scores often were excused from the bother of rounding up their pay stubs and tax records before getting a loan.

LIKE MAXWELL, JOHNSON DECIDED to step down while he was winning. In April 1998, he announced that Franklin D. Raines would succeed him at the end of that year as chairman and chief executive officer. Raines, who had spent the previous two years as President Clinton's budget director, already had experience at Fannie Mae as a vice-chairman from 1991 to 1996.

In a farewell interview with the *Washington Post* in December 1998, Johnson was going out with a flourish:

> *There is a revolution going on in homeownership in America. At the beginning of this decade there were 59 million American families who owned their own homes. There are now 69 million American families who own their homes. We think everything gets better with more homeownership. If you look at all the data, you have better schools, less crime, more civic participation, more voting, more stable neighborhoods. Less teenage pregnancy. You can go through a list of everything under the sun that gets*

better as homeownership goes up neighborhood by neighborhood around the country. And we have been working very aggressively on that....

We're reaching out as a whole industry more and more to people who are below the median income where they live, more and more to African Americans, more and more to Hispanics, more and more to new immigrants. And it's working. We have systematically reduced the level of down payment required. We have more and more people getting into homes.

Fannie was at the top of its game—respected and feared on Capitol Hill, on Wall Street and among the thousands of state and local entities that worked to promote low-income housing. Stephen Ashley, a mortgage banker who later became chairman of Fannie, recalled the company's Johnson-era apogee this way: "This was a hell of a machine at work."

JOHNSON'S RETIREMENT, HOWEVER, WAS marred by the Fannie stigma that afflicted other ex-CEOs of the company. In 2006, an embarrassing regulatory report found that Fannie failed to inform shareholders of a consulting contract it gave him after he stepped down. That deal gave Johnson fees of about $390,000 a year, plus two support-staff members, a car and partial payment for a driver, an Ofheo report said. That was in addition to Johnson's pension of $852,000 a year.

In 2005, Johnson offered to reduce the payments temporarily to $300,000 a year and give up the support staff and car, Ofheo said. It quoted a letter from Johnson as stating, "I should do my part to assist Fannie Mae's efforts to reduce expenditures at this difficult time." Two former directors told me Johnson was kept on the payroll partly because of his close ties to Fannie's most important customer, Countrywide's Angelo Mozilo. Johnson occasionally called Fannie executives to pass on information he picked up from his chats with Mozilo and others in the mortgage and housing business.

Johnson became a director of Goldman Sachs and remained a powerful Democratic insider. In June 2008, however, he resigned as an adviser to the Obama presidential campaign after *Wall Street Journal* reports about mortgage loans he received from Countrywide, where Mozilo ran a program providing preferential loans for his pals. A lawyer for Johnson said the loans were made on normal terms.

After a lengthy investigation, however, the House Committee on Oversight and Government Reform in June 2012 released internal Countrywide e-mails indicating that Johnson had received below-market interest rates on three loans, including ones on properties in Washington, D.C., and Palm Desert, California. Countrywide also provided mortgage loans or lines of credit on Johnson's condominium at the Ritz-Carlton in Washington and a home near the Sun Valley ski resort in Idaho, according to the report. Johnson liked the service he got at Countrywide so well that he often referred his friends and allies to a VIP loan desk there. The report quoted Mozilo informing a colleague by e-mail in 2007 that special terms for Johnson were "just a small token of my appreciation for the business that he sends to us and for his loyalty to the Company."

Chapter 8

The Tragedy of Frank Raines

As his successor, Johnson chose someone who personified the American dream: Franklin Delano Raines, named in honor of a late president who still inspired the Left and infuriated the Right.

One of six children of a custodian for the city park service and a mother who cleaned offices for Boeing in Seattle, Raines began working part time in a grocery store at age eight. He proved a gifted student, excelled on his high school debate team and was a quarterback on the football team, despite his slight frame. To build a home for the family, his father dug a foundation by hand and salvaged lumber from a condemned house nearby.

Young Frank won a scholarship to Harvard. Both Democrats and Republicans saw his potential. While an undergraduate at Harvard, he won a summer internship in the Nixon White House, where Egil Krogh, a Nixon aide, found him "super bright." For a time, Raines wasn't sure whether to be a moderate Republican or a Democrat; by his junior year at Harvard, he considered himself a committed Democrat. Later, as a Rhodes scholar, he spent two years studying at Oxford in England, which he later remembered as cold and lonely. He went on to earn a law degree at Harvard.

He briefly practiced law in Seattle and considered running for Congress as a Democrat but shelved that idea when he got an offer in 1977 to work in the White House on the domestic policy staff. He then became an associate director at the Office of Management and Budget. Late in the Carter administration, he decided he wanted to get out of the government but didn't want to practice law. "Friends said, 'You should be an investment banker.' I said, 'What's that?'" he later recalled.

He soon found out and was hired as an investment banker for Lazard Freres, where he helped line up municipal bond business. The job involved traveling several days a week to meet local officials and pitch for their business. He helped raise money for the District of Columbia, Cleveland and the Chicago public schools. In 1985, he was made a general partner. By 1991, he felt bored and burned out.

Raines was not sure what he wanted to do next. Johnson, who knew everyone who mattered in Democratic circles, approached him about the possibility of working at Fannie. Raines knew little about Fannie. One thing he *did* know was powerfully attractive: the headquarters was within a mile of his District of Columbia home. It was just across Wisconsin Avenue from the posh, private Sidwell Friends School his children attended.

In June 1991, Johnson introduced Raines, forty-two years old, as the company's new vice-chairman and Lawrence Small, a former Citicorp officer, as chief operating officer. "Larry Small and Frank Raines will help write the next chapter in the Fannie Mae story," Johnson said.

President Clinton poached Raines in 1996, making him director of the Office of Management and Budget. Johnson lured him back in 1998 with a promise that he would become CEO at the beginning of 1999.

Like Johnson, Raines was a powerful Democratic insider, sometimes mentioned as a potential future Treasury secretary. The Raines ascension stirred Republican resentment and suspicion of Fannie—a dangerous trend for a company that needed bipartisan backing. By now, however, Fannie was so powerful that its executives could afford to give their critics an occasional poke in the eye.

ONE OF RAINES'S FIRST moves as CEO at Fannie Mae was to set a goal of doubling earnings per share, or EPS, from $3.23 in 1998 to $6.46 in 2003. All employees were then given "EPS Challenge" stock options that would give them a bonus in January 2004 if Fannie hit the target. That would mean revving up the company's earnings growth to 14.9 percent a year from the already brisk 11.5 percent over the preceding five years.

Fannie executives took the goal seriously. Sampath Rajappa, a senior vice-president, in 2000 gave a talk to the company's internal auditors, later recounted in an Ofheo report. He reminded them of Raines's goal of doubling annual earnings per share to $6.46:

By now every one of you must have 6.46 branded in your brains. You must be able to say it in your sleep, you must be able to recite it forwards and backwards, you must have a raging fire in your belly that burns away all doubts, you must live, breathe and dream 6.46, you must be obsessed on 6.46....After all, thanks to Frank [Raines], we have a lot of money riding on it....We must do this with a fiery determination, not on some days, not on most days but day in and day out, give it your best, not 50%, not 75%, not 100%, but 150%. Remember, Frank has given us an opportunity to earn not just our salaries, benefits, raises, [employee stock purchases] but substantially over and above if we make 6.46.

Raines had assumed command amid a giddy stock market boom. Many Americans were convinced that the Internet and other technological advances were changing almost everything and leading to a brighter world where the old rules did not apply. Fannie was no longer just a mortgage company; it was a technology and information company. Soon it would have a website called eFannie.com to deal with its customers.

"We gather enormous amounts of information," Raines told the *Washington Post*.

We have the largest stock of information now on mortgage finance of any entity in the world. We now have a data warehouse that's tracked every loan that's come through Fannie Mae over the years from initiation to conclusion and we have now used that information along with research correlations of what is correlated to success in mortgage [lending]. A lot of the rules were based on rules of thumb. We've found that a lot of things that we thought were very important to success weren't.

What about that old idea of a 20 percent down payment? "Well, 20% down is not nearly as well correlated as two things. One is that you've got the ability to pay. You're not trying to overextend yourself. And second, a demonstrated willingness to pay. Willingness to pay being even more important than ability—paying rent, utility bills, credit cards."

Raines was highly intelligent and articulate. But he was less at ease socially than were his predecessors, Maxwell and Johnson. Colleagues described him as shy or introverted. Some said he didn't always explain why he was pursuing a particular policy and tended to figure things out on his own, making others feel left out of decision making.

He was not always sensitive to political risks. One example was his publicly proclaimed goal of doubling earnings per share in five years. For an ordinary company, this might be unexceptional, a stretch goal from a new CEO. For Fannie's critics, however, it was a provocation. It gave them an opening to raise questions about where the priority was—in the public "mission" or the private profits?

Raines saw a need for tough goals to keep the organization from stagnating. He believed rapid earnings growth was consistent with the mission.

In an essay he wrote for the *Washington Times* in December 1999, Raines described Fannie as being "at the center of the housing finance system," a statement that, although true, implied that other parts of the system—banks, brokers, mortgage insurers—were peripheral, mere minions to Fannie.

Jealousy was part of the problem. In 2000, Raines invited a group of mortgage bankers to an elegant party at his hilltop vacation home in Bermuda. As the guests left, one of them heard the executive of a second-tier bank mutter, "Gee, in my next life I want to come back as a government employee." In the minds of some people, Fannie was still akin to a government agency—but one where the top people got fabulously rich.

In the view of Raines, Fannie's role was to lead an industry churning out several trillion dollars of home loans annually. Fannie's position in mortgages, he once said, was like that of Coca-Cola in soft drinks: Fannie made the vital syrup; lenders squirted it into the bottles.

This fizzy analogy didn't sit well with Fannie's biggest business partner, Mozilo of Countrywide. "I perceive a bottler as a subordinate to the person who makes the syrup," Mozilo grumped. "After building a company for thirty-two years, I didn't like being put in a subordinate role." Raines patched things up with the prickly Mozilo, but others in the mortgage business were growing warier of Fannie and Freddie.

In mid-1999, a group of financial companies formed a loose coalition called FM Watch, designed to monitor Fannie and Freddie and lobby against any attempt to expand their power or annex more of the mortgage market. Members of FM Watch included the big banks Chase Manhattan and Wells Fargo.

Raines quickly dubbed FM Watch "the coalition for higher mortgage costs." Appearing at a meeting of the New York Financial Writers Association, he said, "What this coalition really wants is to move Fannie Mae out of the way so they can charge consumers more." Fannie published a brochure called "The Facts About Fannie Mae and the Mortgage Market." It quoted Volcker's reassurances on Fannie's capital and concluded that the

Fannie-Freddie system had "produced the most sophisticated, efficient and equitable housing finance system in the world."

FM Watch arose partly because of a belief that Fannie and Freddie were plotting to push mortgage insurance companies to the margins of the business. Mortgage insurers sell coverage that protects lenders—or other institutions like Fannie and Freddie that buy or guarantee loans—from losses due to defaults. The Fannie and Freddie charters required such coverage when they bought or guaranteed loans that amounted to more than 80 percent of the home's estimated value. This provision created a steady flow of business for mortgage insurers.

In early October 1998, lobbyists for Freddie slipped into a congressional appropriations bill an amendment to revise the company's charter to make it less reliant on mortgage insurance. The amendment would have permitted Freddie to cover the risk in different ways. Freddie wanted to set up accounts into which a small portion of borrowers' monthly payments would flow to cover any eventual loan losses. The amendment passed in the House, but mortgage insurers soon found out about it. They feared Fannie and Freddie would use the new authority to bypass them. Mortgage insurers quickly rallied Congress to kill the amendment; suspicion of Fannie's and Freddie's aims lingered.

In December 1998, Fannie invited representatives of mortgage insurance companies to discuss ways to reduce borrowing costs so more poor people could afford homes. Fannie denied it was trying to squeeze the mortgage insurers. Still, Raines told the mortgage insurers that if they didn't change their ways and become more flexible, they would end up in the Smithsonian museum, next to the buggy-whip makers. One of his colleagues later recalled wincing at the analogy.

A year later, in late 1999, Raines tangled with Larry Summers, who by then had been promoted to Treasury secretary. The two men had a strained relationship; both were candidates to be the smartest person in just about any room and didn't mind who knew it; neither was a natural diplomat. In a speech to a Washington group called Women in Housing Finance, Summers mentioned the risks to the financial system posed by Fannie and Freddie. Fannie officials—including the most powerful Democratic insiders, Thomas Donilon and Jamie Gorelick—barraged the Treasury with protests. Raines paid a visit to Summers and offered to give him "econometric" proofs that Fannie did not benefit from a government subsidy, an idea the Treasury secretary considered absurd. Summers, who had a doctorate in economics from Harvard, where he had also taught the subject, noted that his grasp of econometrics was probably firmer than Raines's. (Economists generally agreed that the implied government backing of Fannie and Freddie provided a large subsidy in that it allowed them to borrow much more cheaply than other financial institutions could.)

Fannie's protests were so vehement that they backfired, strengthening the Treasury's resolve to keep raising the issue.

TO DEFLECT CRITICISM, RAINES frequently extolled Fannie's record of helping more poor people and members of minority groups buy homes. Yet pressure kept mounting to do more. In 1999, Martin Luther King III, chief executive of the Southern Christian Leadership Conference, wrote a newspaper column saying Fannie and Freddie were falling short of what the overall mortgage market was doing to help minorities. The homeownership rate for African Americans was only 46 percent, compared with nearly 73 percent for whites. Raines responded that Fannie was leading the market; the data cited by King was "outdated" and based on analysis that was "not solid."

The Clinton administration also was pushing for more. In July 1999, HUD Secretary Andrew Cuomo announced "historic action" to raise the bar for Fannie and Freddie: they would have to increase the percentage of their mortgage financing that went to low- or moderate-income families to 48 percent in 2000 and 50 percent in 2001 from 42 percent, set in 1995. The new rules, Cuomo declared, would over the next decade "provide affordable housing for about 28.1 million low- and moderate-income families."

In stating such a large and precise figure, Cuomo was making some grand and dubious assumptions about the future. He was sure to please some important constituencies, including nonprofit housing groups, advocates for minorities, urban mayors and banks that had made loans to low-income people to meet Community Reinvestment Act requirements and now wanted to sell those loans to Fannie and Freddie. Cuomo said his order would strengthen the economy and create jobs by spurring home construction.

Thus, the Clinton administration could promise to create twenty-eight million new homeowners without asking Congress to appropriate a single cent. It simply ordered Fannie and Freddie to increase financing of homes for the poor and neglected. It was conveniently off budget.

Raines attended Cuomo's press conference and promised to meet the new goals. HUD said it had the authority to impose penalties of up to $10,000 a day for any failure to "make a good faith effort to achieve" the affordable housing goals. That was not enough money to matter much to such big companies, but missing the goals would anger Congress, whose support was needed to maintain Fannie and Freddie's privileges.

Raines yearned to win the debate over how much risk Fannie and Freddie posed to U.S. taxpayers. He hired Arne Christenson, a former chief of staff for U.S. Representative Newt Gingrich, as senior vice-president for regulatory policy. Christenson launched a series called the "Fannie Mae Papers," paying for studies by scholars including Joseph Stiglitz, a Nobel Prize–winning economist from Columbia University, and Peter Orszag, later U.S. budget chief under President Obama.

A March 2002 paper in this series by Professor Stiglitz and others found that the probability of default by Fannie or Freddie was "extremely small." The economists studied the risk-based capital requirements recently imposed by Ofheo, the regulator. These capital requirements were based on a "stress test," producing estimates of how much capital Fannie and Freddie would need to survive a sharp rise or fall in interest rates, coupled with a long-term surge in mortgage defaults. "The implied credit loss rate [under the stress test] is more than five times as large as the national credit loss rate in any year since 1980," the paper said. The probability of the stress-test conditions actually occurring was less than 1 in 500,000, the authors wrote.

They acknowledged "potential shortcomings" of the risk-based capital standard. The test "may fail to reflect the probability of another Great Depression–like scenario," they wrote. There also was a risk that the mathematical model "omits or mischaracterizes important elements of the real economy." But "none of the potential shortcomings appears to be significant enough to alter the basic conclusion that the risk-based capital standard provides substantial protection against insolvency."

Besides, the economists wrote, if the risks inherent in home mortgages weren't concentrated at Fannie and Freddie, they "would likely be held by large banks and other types of financial institutions," which probably would be considered "too big to fail" and so might need to be bailed out by the government. It was a popular argument at Fannie: all this mortgage risk has to be somewhere; it might as well be with us because we know how to manage it.

Years later, Stiglitz offered a very different comment. In a July 2008 article in the *Financial Times*, he wrote that the core of the problem for Fannie and Freddie was that millions of Americans were granted loans "beyond their ability to pay." Compensation of the companies' managers, he wrote, was "designed to encourage excessive risk-taking."

In 2009, I asked Stiglitz about the apparent shift in his view. He said that when he wrote his paper in 2002, "Fannie and Freddie had not at the juncture begun the reckless subprime lending." Though Fannie and Freddie loosened their standards for years, beginning in the 1990s, their exposure grew markedly in 2005 through 2007 as they embraced much riskier loans. In 2002, Stiglitz said, "no one would have ever thought the regulators would allow them to get away with that." Stiglitz and his fellow authors had underestimated the risks of regulatory and management failures. "We assumed," he said, "that the regulator was doing its job."

When the papers came out, though, they helped Fannie project a reputation for reliable management. In a preface to a collection of these papers, Sheila Bair—who had served as an assistant secretary of the U.S. Treasury and would later be chairman of the Federal Deposit Insurance Corp.—wrote that the studies "paint a picture of a company that is world-class in its corporate governance, risk management and pursuit of its statutory mission."

THERE WERE SOME EARLY warnings that the mortgage industry was going off the rails. One came in a June 2001 report from Josh Rosner, a New York financial analyst who favored scruffy jeans and lumpy sweaters rather than the sharp suits worn by his Wall Street rivals. Rosner said much of the growth in housing in the 1990s came from looser lending standards, including loans with reduced down-payment requirements or no money down; greater efforts to serve low-income borrowers; and easing of loan terms for delinquent borrowers that allowed their loans to be reclassified as current. Such lending practices were likely to keep fueling the housing boom, but the market would be vulnerable to any jump in unemployment, which could lead to falling house prices and a surge in foreclosures. "The virtuous circle of increasing homeownership through greater leverage [borrowing] has the potential to become a vicious cycle of lower home prices due to an accelerating rate of foreclosures caused by lower savings," he wrote.

Richard Baker, the Republican congressman from Louisiana, also was raising tough questions. Baker, who had worked in real estate sales and home building before running for Congress in 1985, seemed an unlikely foe for Fannie and Freddie, which ordinarily had fervent support from Realtors and home builders. But Baker said Fannie and Freddie were being operated too much for the sake of their shareholders and not enough for the benefit of poor people seeking to buy homes. "They were given a government privilege, and they abused it," he told me.

In his early years in Congress, Baker had little power and couldn't pursue his agenda for reining in Fannie and Freddie. "I was hollering wolf, and there wasn't any danger in sight," he recalled. In the mid-1990s, his congressional chief of staff, Duane Duncan, defected to become a lobbyist at Fannie. The big salaries Fannie paid were hard to resist. "I told him he had an obligation to his family and to do what was best for him professionally," Baker said. Did Duncan ever alter his former boss's views on Fannie and Freddie? Baker laughed: "It would be like mixing concrete with a straw. There was something about it [that] wasn't going to work."

Baker became chairman of the capital markets subcommittee of the House Financial Services Committee in 1998. That allowed him to put the heat on Fannie and Freddie by holding hearings and demanding information. In March 2000, Baker called hearings on his own legislation to tighten regulation of Fannie, Freddie and the Federal Home Loan Banks. The bill would have given the regulator more flexibility in setting minimum capital standards. Given the lobbying might of Fannie and Freddie, that legislation was never likely to be approved. But Baker seized the chance to give his agenda a public airing.

Treasury Secretary Summers and his staff agreed that Representative Baker's bill was doomed. But the Treasury was invited to testify before Baker's subcommittee and would have to say something. Whatever their political stripe, Treasury officials were typically hardheaded financial people who loathed the fuzzy implied guarantee of Fannie's and Freddie's debts. The Treasury had its own debt to sell and didn't like competition from Fannie and Freddie. Unlike the housing advocates at HUD, Treasury officials didn't consider housing sacred.

Summers told his colleagues it was a "hand on the Bible moment"—time to speak some home truths, even if Fannie and Freddie would not like them. After weeks of consultations within the Treasury and other parts of the Clinton administration, the Treasury sent Gary Gensler, the undersecretary for domestic finance, to testify on March 22, 2000.

Giving the Treasury's view on Representative Baker's bill, Gensler opened his testimony with bland comments, saying Fannie, Freddie and the home loan banks "have done much for home ownership in this country." Then he quoted some striking numbers. With $1.4 trillion of debt outstanding, they had obligations totaling about the same amount as those issued by all of America's state and local governments combined. Fannie and Freddie had about $32.00

of debt for each dollar of capital, while large banks had about $11.50 and the five largest securities firms $25.00. Fannie and Freddie were very profitable, Gensler said: from 1995 through 1999, their average return on equity was 24 percent, compared with 15 percent for large banks.

Now came the part of his testimony that rattled the markets: Gensler said American banks held too much debt issued by Fannie and Freddie and urged Congress to limit those holdings. There were no limits, he noted, on national banks' holdings of debt from Fannie, Freddie or the home loan banks. By contrast, regulators wouldn't allow banks to put more than 10 percent of their capital

Gary Gensler, a Treasury official whose testimony about the risks of Fannie and Freddie rattled the markets in March 2000. *Courtesy of Commodity Futures Trading Commission.*

into corporate bonds of any other single borrower. If Congress were to cap the amount of Fannie and Freddie debt that banks could hold, many would have to sell that debt, reducing its value; with less demand for their paper, Fannie and Freddie would need to pay higher interest rates.

The Treasury supported Representative Baker's proposal to repeal the $2.25 billion lines of credit Fannie and Freddie had at the Treasury. Those lines weren't being used and were so small as to be almost irrelevant for companies that raised hundreds of billions of dollars in the bond markets each year. But they were a potent symbol of government backing. By even suggesting elimination of the lines, Gensler gave the markets a jolt. Prices of Fannie and Freddie debt promptly fell, signaling they would have to offer higher yields the next time they sold bonds.

Fannie fired back a few days later. Jeffers, the company spokesman who had once derided Fannie's critics as "pencil brains," now said the higher borrowing costs triggered by Gensler's remarks had pushed mortgage rates about a quarter percentage point higher. "It's unfortunate when statements made by the Treasury have such an immediate and pronounced effect on American consumers," Jeffers said. "The rise in mortgage costs caused by

Treasury's remarks means about 206,000 families will be disqualified from [obtaining] home loans."

This riposte, according to two of the people involved, was made on instructions from Raines. It irked Summers. He called Raines and told him the Treasury would return fire unless Fannie retracted its statement within forty-five minutes.

Jeffers backed down. "I regret the comments I made regarding the impact of Treasury's testimony," he told a reporter. "There are, of course, many factors that affect both the pricing of bonds and mortgage rates. Our analysis of the impact of Treasury's statement on consumers was neither accurate nor appropriate."

SHAKEN, FANNIE EXECUTIVES LOOKED for ways to make peace. Treasury officials had complained that Fannie and Freddie were not subject to "market discipline," the normal monitoring by investors. Market discipline works swiftly: if investors start to believe a company's behavior is too risky, the company's stock price drops and its borrowing costs surge until the company mends its ways. That discipline did not apply to Fannie and Freddie because investors could assume that the government would back them up if they got into a jam.

To mollify the Treasury and other critics, Fannie executives offered "voluntary initiatives" aimed at showing they were behaving responsibly. In October 2000, executives of Fannie and Freddie stood on a platform with Representative Baker to announce a series of actions:

- They would begin to sell subordinated bonds along with their senior debt. The interest paid on subordinated debt can be cut off if a company has financial difficulties. The theory was that holders of these subordinated bonds, facing more risk, would be vigilant in monitoring the finances of Fannie and Freddie, providing an early warning if the companies went astray.
- They would hold enough cash to last more than three months without new borrowings.
- They would make regular disclosures of the risks they faced from defaults and sudden changes in interest rates.
- They would obtain ratings from a nationally recognized rating agency on their financial conditions.

Fannie executives had hoped these initiatives would completely appease the Treasury. In a statement, the Treasury said the steps had "the potential to promote market discipline and increase transparency." But a Treasury spokeswoman told reporters there were still "a range of issues" related to Fannie and Freddie that "warrant continuing attention from financial authorities, the Congress and their regulators."

So there would be no peace. Fannie would never be able to buy more than the occasional brief truce on the political front. The second Clinton administration was winding down. The Republicans, generally tougher on government-sponsored enterprises, would soon regain control of the White House under President George W. Bush.

THE SURPRISE WAS THAT Raines got off to a fairly good start with George Bush. Part of Bush's "compassionate conservatism" was a belief that the government should favor homeownership. Fannie was delighted to agree.

Raines was particularly comfortable with President Bush's first Treasury secretary, Paul O'Neill. During a television interview in February 2001, O'Neill rejected the idea that Fannie and Freddie were subsidized. "The market might give them a preferential [interest] rate because of the prospect of government support, but they don't really receive a subsidy," O'Neill said, not mentioning that the preferential interest rate was a type of subsidy. He described Raines as "a close personal friend of mine." Years before, the two had served on the board of a nonprofit, Manpower Demonstration Research Corp.

The White House invited Raines to accompany Bush on a visit to Atlanta in June 2002. During a tour of new housing on Atlanta's south side, President Bush promoted his goal of helping five and a half million black and Hispanic families buy homes before the end of the decade. "There is a homeownership gap in America," Bush said. "The difference between Anglo-American and African-American and Hispanic homeownership is too big. Part of being a secure America is to encourage homeownership, so somebody can say, 'This is my home. Welcome to my home.'" Raines got a ride back to Washington with President Bush on Air Force One.

At a White House conference on homeownership in October 2002, Bush and Fannie seemed perfectly in tune. The president said:

> *You see, we want everybody in America to own their own home. That's what we want. This is an ownership society, is a compassionate society.*

The Tragedy of Frank Raines

More and more people own their homes in America today. Two-thirds of all Americans own their homes. Yet we have a problem here in America because fewer than half of the Hispanics and half the African Americans own the home. That's a homeownership gap. It's a gap that we've got to work together to close for the good of our country, for the sake of a more hopeful future.

President Bush pointed to Raines and Leland Brendsel, Freddie's CEO. The president said:

Fannie Mae recently announced a $50 million program to develop 600 homes for the Cherokee Nation in Oklahoma. Franklin [Raines], I appreciate that commitment. They also announced a $12.7 million investment in the condominium project in Harlem. It's the beginnings of a series of initiatives to help meet the goal of five and a half million families. Franklin told me at the meeting where we kicked this off, he said, "I promise you, we will help," and he has, like many others in this room have done.

THE BUSH ADMINISTRATION WASN'T unanimous in seeing Fannie and Freddie as helpful. White House economic advisers, including Larry Lindsey, Kevin Warsh and Allan Hubbard, were critical of the companies, as was a Treasury official, Wayne Abernathy. At a reception, Raines managed to get a few seconds with President Bush and mentioned that "somehow we've gotten sideways with your guys" on the National Economic Council, a panel of White House advisers. One of those advisers, Keith Hennessy, later told me that he and others in the White House thought of Fannie and Freddie as "multibillion-dollar hedge funds" taking unacceptable risks. Hubbard called them "a ticking time bomb."

The National Economic Council coordinated policy on Fannie and Freddie with the Treasury and HUD. One goal was to persuade investors that they shouldn't rely on any implicit guarantee of Fannie's and Freddie's debts. To keep Fannie and Freddie from gathering intelligence on administration plans, Andrew Card, the chief of staff, barred White House staffers from taking calls from the companies or their legions of lobbyists. To further express its disapproval, the Bush White House declined to make the usual five presidential appointments to the boards of Fannie and Freddie. Where Nixon saw an opportunity for patronage, Bush chose symbolism.

He had powerful allies. Officials at the Federal Reserve had long been quietly hostile to Fannie and Freddie. That hostility was now becoming louder. In 2002, two economists from the Federal Reserve Bank of Atlanta, W. Scott Frame and Larry D. Wall, published a report summing up the risks: "A subsidy in the form of an implicit guarantee creates the appearance of something for nothing: a lower-cost funding for the housing GSEs [government-sponsored enterprises] at no cost to taxpayers. However, as with co-signing a loan, a seemingly costless guarantee can turn out to be very costly."

FANNIE AND FREDDIE MADE another attempt to appease their critics in July 2002 by agreeing to register their common stock with the Securities and Exchange Commission and comply with SEC disclosure requirements. They had resisted this idea for years, but U.S. Representative Christopher Shays was pushing for action. Fannie executives chose to act voluntarily rather than risk legislation. "Once the legislation started, we weren't sure where it would end," Arne Christenson, then a senior vice-president at Fannie, later told me.

By making these voluntary moves, Raines felt Fannie had fully responded to the demands of its critics. Yet the critics were not appeased. "Fannie Mae was never forgiven for the circumstances of its birth," he said later. "It didn't matter what we did."

By instinct, Raines wanted to punch back. He told *American Banker* in early 2001:

> *Under attack, I advance. I don't withdraw....There is a school of thought that if you harass Fannie Mae, maybe they'll pull their punches, maybe they'll slow down, maybe they'll not be as good a company. But anybody who knows me knows that would be a very large tactical error. Anyone who thinks that trying to intimidate us would be productive [would] be making a mistake.*

Raines and his colleagues made a strategic mistake in failing to establish smooth relations with their regulator, Ofheo. That agency's director was Armando Falcon Jr., a soft-spoken lawyer from San Antonio who had worked as a Democrat staff member on the House Banking Committee before being appointed to the top job at Ofheo by the Clinton administration in 1999. Fannie officials found it hard to hide their disdain for Falcon, even as critics of Fannie and Freddie in the White House shrewdly befriended him.

Raines tried at one point to improve relations with Falcon by meeting him for lunch, but they were uncomfortable together. Raines later grumbled that "talking to Armando was almost like talking to a rock." Falcon said he tried to establish a rapport with Raines but "it was difficult to break through the veneer and have a real conversation." One problem, Falcon said, was that Fannie executives "viewed me as someone who needed to bend to their will."

Some former Fannie executives later acknowledged that the failure to get along with Falcon was an error: "There's an old saying in the army that you salute the uniform," whether or not you think the person inside that uniform is capable, Christenson said.

Armando Falcon, as a regulator, found accounting problems at Fannie in 2004. *Photo by Masahiro Kobayashi.*

Falcon at times felt political pressure to go easy on Fannie and Freddie. In February 2003, Ofheo was getting ready to release a report from its research staff discussing the financial risks to the economy arising from Fannie's and Freddie's rapidly growing debts. Fannie and Freddie did not want Ofheo to issue the report. As Falcon recalled later, he got a call from Raines a few days before the scheduled release. "He urged me not to release it, and when I reaffirmed my plans, he threatened to bring down me and the agency," Falcon testified to the Financial Crisis Inquiry Commission in 2010. Falcon added that a Treasury official called him to say Fannie lobbyists were calling other agencies to seek help in suppressing the report.

On February 4, 2003, while he was in New York waiting to give a speech on the findings of the report, Falcon got a phone call from the White House personnel office: the president was about to nominate a new director of Ofheo to replace Falcon. Clearly, the White House had authority to nominate a new director, and it was not surprising that a Republican president would replace a Democratic appointee like Falcon. Still, the timing seemed fishy. As Falcon put it, "The next day's news emphasized coverage of the personnel change [at Ofheo] and gave very scant coverage to the findings of the systemic-risk report. This was, of course, exactly the result intended by those who engineered the timing of the announcement of my replacement."

The White House nominee was Mark Brickell, a former managing director of J.P. Morgan. Brickell later ran into opposition in Congress amid suggestions that he might be too sympathetic to Fannie and Freddie. The Bush administration ended up leaving Falcon in place for two more years. That was not good news for Raines.

THOUGH FANNIE'S LOBBYING POWER was immense, its foes were implacable, and they were watching for any chance to take down Fannie and Freddie. Freddie gave them the perfect opportunity.

In December 2002, Raines received anonymous letters containing allegations of accounting and financial-reporting misdeeds at Freddie. Why these allegations concerning Freddie were sent to the CEO of Fannie is a mystery. An aide to Raines faxed the letters to his counterpart at Freddie, Brendsel.

Among the charges was that Freddie, in preparing its 1999 financial statements, had used projections that overestimated income by hundreds of millions of dollars. Freddie's board hired the law firm of Baker Botts to investigate. The law firm in January 2003 told Freddie's directors that the allegations in the anonymous letters "were false in most material respects." While looking into those allegations, however, Baker Botts found other accounting problems.

Some of the problems arose from what was then a new set of accounting rules known as Financial Accounting Standard (FAS) 133, which governs how companies book gains or losses on derivative contracts, such as interest-rate swaps and other complex financial agreements used to hedge against fluctuations in interest rates. FAS 133 would require Fannie and Freddie to reflect in their earnings the often wildly fluctuating values of those derivatives. As a result, the companies worried, investors might get the idea that earnings were unreliable—up sharply one quarter, way down the next. That would shatter the image of companies able to produce steadily rising earnings each quarter—an image that had earned Freddie the nickname of "Steady Freddie."

Fannie also liked to be known as steady. In the annual report for 2000, Raines boasted, "Our 14 years of steady earnings growth demonstrates that Fannie Mae defies the conventional wisdom that financial company earnings are always sensitive to changes in the economy or interest rates."

Thanks to new accounting rules, steady growth was becoming harder to achieve. Accounting rules in general were becoming more complicated as the financial world grew more complex. Those rules required companies to value some holdings at the current market price (often a rough estimate) and others at historical cost, or what the company originally paid. This created a mishmash of past and present values on balance sheets.

FAS 133 was anathema to Fannie's chief financial officer, Timothy Howard, who sent letters to accounting authorities suggesting ways to fix what he saw as the standard's failure to present a true picture of financial condition. But FAS 133 wasn't going away. Both companies tried, in different ways, to keep it from spoiling their numbers. Freddie was the first one caught.

The Baker Botts lawyers found that Freddie in 2000 and 2001 entered into complicated transactions and set policies to delay the recognition of income to smooth out earnings. It wasn't a case of wholesale deceit, according to Baker Botts: "In general, these transactions and policies result in unintentional misapplications of GAAP [generally accepted accounting principles], and were supported by Arthur Andersen," then Freddie's auditor. "There were, however, disclosure shortcomings with respect to these transactions and policies." In some cases, "the misapplication of GAAP resulted from a results-oriented, reverse-engineered and opportunistic approach to achieving an accounting objective." In other words, Steady Freddie had played a bit fast and loose with the rules.

As part of the damage control, Freddie's board in June 2003 ousted Brendsel as chairman and CEO. It also pushed out David Glenn, the president.

If Freddie had bent the accounting rules, what was up at Fannie? The share prices of both companies fell. On July 30, 2003, Raines held a press conference to proclaim that *his* corporate books were clean. "At Fannie Mae, we took no steps to try to mediate the impact of FAS 133. In fact, we did just the opposite," Raines said. "We made sure that [for] every type of derivative transaction we engaged in, we had prior approval, not only from Fannie Mae's internal accountants, but also [from] our external auditors prior to undertaking the transaction."

He called Freddie's accounting fiasco "a management failure" and suggested that nothing of the sort could happen at Fannie: "There is a difference in management. Management does matter. And a management that cares about internal controls does matter," Raines said.

The stock market was punishing Fannie for Freddie's sins, Raines groused: "I think we've suffered unfairly. We did not do these things. We should not be subject to the same penalty that they are being subjected to."

The suffering was just beginning. Falcon, the director of Ofheo, wasn't sure Fannie's accounts were pristine, and he was inclined to play hardball. By 2003, Falcon was fed up with the contempt shown to him by Fannie executives. He was also embarrassed. The Freddie affair made Ofheo look inept. It was Freddie and its legal advisers who found the accounting problems. The regulator had failed to spot them. During a July 2003 hearing, Senator Richard Shelby, chairman of the Senate Banking Committee, scolded Falcon: "You're the regulator, but you've been in the dark. That's troubling."

Ofheo started acting tougher. By late 2003, the regulator was gathering information on Fannie's accounting policies in a "special review." Early in 2004, Ofheo hired the accounting firm of Deloitte & Touche to help with that review.

Fannie tried to discredit Ofheo. A memo from Maloni, the Fannie lobbyist, to Donilon, executive vice-president for law and policy, dated October 31, 2003, suggested a political attack on Steve Blumenthal, the deputy director of Ofheo. "Have a Democrat nail Blumenthal, suggesting that he is setting up the Company in the coming accounting audit," Maloni wrote in an e-mail.

Instead, a Republican stepped up to the plate. Senator Christopher S. "Kit" Bond of Missouri demanded an investigation of Ofheo by the HUD Office of the Inspector General, a policing arm of the department that oversaw Ofheo. Among other things, Senator Bond complained about Ofheo's press release on March 31, 2004, a day before the Senate Banking Committee was to work on a bill to improve regulation of Fannie and Freddie. That Ofheo release said the accounting review by Ofheo "may result in a restatement of prior period results." Senator Bond wrote, "The timing of the news release appears to be a cynical attempt to unfairly influence the political process." Senator Bond also wanted information regarding the release to a *Wall Street Journal* reporter of a letter from Ofheo to Raines regarding accounting matters.

The demand for an investigation wasn't purely Senator Bond's idea; Ofheo later found in Fannie's computer system a draft of the letter later sent by the senator. Duane Duncan, the Fannie lobbyist, admitted to Ofheo under oath that the call for an investigation was initiated by Fannie.

In the summer of 2004, HUD's inspector general interviewed Falcon and others at Ofheo about the issues raised by Senator Bond's letter. Falcon, who considered the inquiry an effort to intimidate him, was a reluctant witness. The report says he ended one interview after ninety minutes, citing fatigue, and canceled two other appointments, saying he was busy.

Ofheo bureaucrats were deeply divided. The regulator's chief accountant, Wanda DeLeo, told the HUD investigators that she believed Falcon and his deputy, Blumenthal, had overstated the initial findings of the accounting review. DeLeo also said the release of the letter "was driven by motives of publicity." In her diary, the HUD report says, DeLeo wrote that her concerns had been brushed aside by her bosses: "I was told that the issue was to have this letter out before Frank Raines testified [before a congressional committee] so he would have to answer questions on this issue. They appear to have completely lost sight of the mission of Ofheo. The sole purpose appears to be publicity."

She added that "action by Ofheo that would be more appropriately handled in an examination framework are [sic] being played out in the press for all the wrong reasons." The normal process, she said, "would have been to have gone back to Fannie, let them see our results and have a chance to respond to whether it was correct, incorrect, or what was going on."

Falcon countered tersely that the letter was released "solely on the basis of safety and soundness."

A former chief examiner of Ofheo, Scott Calhoun, told the investigators that Falcon had pushed a more confrontational approach after the humiliation of having failed to uncover Freddie's accounting problems. Ofheo had been "asleep at the switch," as Blumenthal put it. Now it was showing a more aggressive spirit. Calhoun said the new approach meant "no more worrying about having a working relationship...because you're the cop on the beat. You whack them in the head with a nightstick."

Blumenthal defended the tougher approach. He told the investigators Ofheo had been too eager to be collegial: "Well, that's over now. And now we have a situation where it's a tough regulator. It's looking for problems, and it identifies, it's addressing them."

The HUD inspector general shared the information with U.S. federal prosecutors, who "declined criminal prosecution on this matter," the report says.

SHORTLY AFTER FREDDIE'S ACCOUNTING troubles surfaced in June 2003, Bush administration officials and Representative Baker began talking about the possibility of legislation to clamp tighter controls on the companies. By late June, Baker had proposed legislation to move regulation of Fannie and Freddie from Ofheo to a more powerful body, the U.S. Treasury. In late July, three Republican senators—Elizabeth Dole, John Sununu and Chuck Hagel—offered similar legislation.

The Bush administration joined the calls for a stronger regulator, with more power to set minimum capital, among other things. Two Republican congressional leaders, Representative Michael Oxley and Senator Shelby, promised to move swiftly to prepare legislation.

Not so fast, said the National Association of Home Builders. Jerry Howard, the pugnacious executive vice-president of the builders' trade group, told reporters the legislative plans would "severely damage" the government's commitment to housing.

Representative Barney Frank, the ranking Democrat on the House Financial Services Committee, also urged caution. "I do not think we are facing any kind of crisis," he said.

One issue was whether the new regulator would have stronger powers to approve or disapprove any "new product" proposed by Fannie and Freddie. Some financial companies were wary of what they called "mission creep," a tendency of Fannie and Freddie to spread into new areas of the mortgage business.

Fannie warned that its ability to innovate would be stifled if a new regulator began reviewing every new wrinkle in its programs and procedures. Home builders and advocates for low-income housing fretted that tight regulation would choke off the flow of money from Fannie and Freddie.

Fannie's allies in Congress leaped to the company's defense. At a House hearing, Representative Maxine Waters, a California Democrat, said Congress should "do no harm" to Fannie and Freddie, which she saw as vital sources of mortgage financing for the poor: "We should be enhancing regulation, not making fundamental change." She added, "We do not have a crisis at Freddie Mac. And in particular at Fannie Mae, under the outstanding leadership of Franklin Raines, everything in the 1992 act has worked just fine."

Trying to find a compromise, the House Financial Services Committee drafted legislation that would create a new regulator for Fannie and Freddie inside the Treasury but limit that regulator's authority over new products. The Bush administration said the regulator would be too weak under the

House committee's plan. Wayne Abernathy, an assistant Treasury secretary, argued that weak legislation could give investors a false sense of confidence in the way the companies were regulated. Abernathy and other officials made clear that they preferred no legislation to weak legislation. It soon became apparent that no bill would pass in 2003.

The momentum generated by Freddie's accounting scandal had dissipated. Despite sporadic hearings and maneuvers to find a compromise, it would take five more years—and the worst economic crisis since the 1930s—before Congress acted. By then it would be too late.

AMID THIS DEBATE, FANNIE was vulnerable to the charge that it pampered executives with overly generous pay and benefits. In October 2003, Representative Baker asked Ofheo, the regulator, to provide information on the compensation of the top twenty executives at Fannie and Freddie. Ofheo sent that information to the House Financial Services Committee.

Fannie reacted by sending an e-mail to the committee's staff members to warn that any leak of that pay information (to the press, for instance) would violate the Trade Secrets Act and could lead to "criminal proceedings." The e-mail noted that Kenneth Starr, a Washington lawyer best known for investigating President Clinton's sexual entanglement with an intern, was serving as Fannie's outside counsel.

A year later, Representative Baker displayed the compensation details at a House subcommittee hearing. Dow Jones Newswires used the information to report that twenty-one Fannie executives had received more than $1 million in compensation for 2002.

IN 2004, AS CONGRESS renewed discussion of how to regulate Fannie and Freddie, Fed chairman Alan Greenspan strode into the debate. Greenspan was still seen as an economic miracle worker, and his views commanded almost reverent attention.

Fannie and Freddie posed "very serious risks" to the U.S. financial system, Greenspan told the Senate Banking Committee in February 2004. Congress should restrict their growth "sooner rather than later." The Fed chairman deplored the huge concentration of risk at these two companies. At the end of 2003, Fannie's debt stood at $961.7 billion, up nearly fourfold from a decade before. Freddie's debt, at $744.8 billion, had multiplied by fifteen in the past ten years. The total borrowings of Fannie, Freddie and the twelve

Federal Home Loan Banks had reached about $2.4 trillion—approaching the Treasury's debt of $3.7 trillion. Fannie and Freddie had grown so huge that any stumble by them could upset the global economy.

Greenspan also argued that Fannie and Freddie were doing little to lower mortgage costs for Americans. A Federal Reserve economist, Wayne Passmore, had recently estimated that their purchases of mortgages reduced interest rates for home buyers by as little as 0.07 of a percentage point. (Other estimates at the time ranged from around 0.25 to 0.50 of a percentage point.)

The Fed chairman advised Congress to give a new regulator the power to raise minimum capital requirements for Fannie and Freddie and to limit the amount of debt they could issue.

A day after Greenspan's testimony, the Senate Banking Committee heard from Raines and Freddie's new CEO, Richard Syron, in an elegant wood-paneled hearing room stuffed with journalists and lobbyists. Syron's testimony was folksy and rambling.

Raines, a polished debater since high school, arrived with an assistant carrying thirty-six charts, which she hoisted onto an easel one by one to illustrate his meticulously prepared arguments. He made sure to give credit to his hosts: "Congress has helped create the best housing finance system in the world, a system other countries envy and want to emulate." While Fannie supported creation of a new regulatory agency, Congress should make sure that regulator wouldn't be able to "alter national housing policy by restricting the flow of capital into housing."

At one point, Raines delivered a lengthy technical explanation of capital requirements for financial institutions. Senator Shelby of Alabama, the committee's chairman, finally lost patience, cut off Raines's seminar and said the idea was to create a stronger regulatory agency that would decide such things as capital requirements. "A world-class regulator would hopefully know all this, would they not?" Senator Shelby asked Raines.

But Raines also got some praise. Senator Christopher Dodd, a silver-haired Democrat from Connecticut, told the committee that Fannie and Freddie were "one of the great success stories of all time" and "one of the great engines of economic success in the last 30 or 40 years." Any changes Congress might make, Senator Dodd said, should not be done "with a sledgehammer when a scalpel may be the appropriate tool."

FANNIE'S FOES IN THE Bush administration kept bashing. The Treasury let it be known that it was considering how it might exercise its powers to restrict borrowing by Fannie and Freddie. HUD was drawing up regulations to increase affordable-housing requirements again. The administration was parking tanks on the lawns of Fannie and Freddie. The White House could make life harder for them even if Congress dithered.

In an April speech to the Mortgage Bankers Association, Representative Frank said the Bush administration was exaggerating the risks of failure at Fannie and Freddie in a way that would block legislation. One sticking point, he said, was that the administration was putting too much stress on giving the regulator authority to put Fannie or Freddie into receivership under certain dire circumstances. "I think it is an artificial issue created by the administration," he said. "People tend to pay their mortgages. I don't think we are in any remote danger here. This focus on receivership, I think, is intended to create fears that aren't there."

Fannie tried to stir different fears: it created a television ad, aired in the Washington, D.C. area, showing a couple talking over the kitchen table.

"Uh oh," said the man.

"What?" asked the woman.

"It looks like Congress is talking about new regulations on Fannie Mae."

"Will that keep us from getting that lower mortgage rate?" the woman wondered.

"Some economists say rates may go up."

"But that could mean we won't be able to afford the new house!"

Off camera, a somber voice intoned, "There's a lot at stake as Congress considers changes in home finance. Taking the wrong path will close the door of homeownership to millions of Americans."

IN MAY, OFHEO FOUND that Fannie had used the wrong accounting method to value about $8 billion of securities backed by manufactured-housing loans and aircraft leases. Fannie was forced to agree to use an accounting method favored by Ofheo, even though the company said its old method was legitimate. Falcon was showing he could have his way, despite Ofheo's limited powers. "Either you rise to the challenge or you don't," Falcon told me.

By August 2004, Ofheo was no longer just asking Fannie for information about its accounting procedures. It was sending subpoenas, legally enforceable demands for information. Raines and his chief financial officer, Tim Howard, who had looked unbeatable a year before, were starting to look vulnerable.

In a two-hundred-page report released on September 22, Ofheo said its findings raised "concerns regarding the validity of previously reported financial results, the adequacy of regulatory capital, the quality of management supervision and the overall safety and soundness" of the company. Fannie's desire to show a smooth, continuous rise in earnings was "a central organizing principle" in devising accounting policies, the report said.

Amid all the technicalities, one example cited by Ofheo stood out: the regulator said Fannie "inappropriately deferred" $200 million of estimated expenses in 1998 and recorded them in later periods. The effect of that decision, Ofheo said, was to allow the company to report earnings of $3.23 a share for 1998, exactly the minimum level needed to trigger the largest possible bonuses for executives under the compensation plan.

Fannie had developed "a corporate culture that emphasized stable earnings at the expense of accurate financial disclosures," Ofheo alleged. It added that Fannie's chief financial officer, Howard, was given "inordinate" responsibilities.

Ofheo's bold accusations instantly changed the game. Raines was no longer fully in charge at Fannie. Instead, eight outside directors (ones who were not executives of the company) took the lead in deciding how to respond to the charges.

Leading that committee was Ann McLaughlin Korologos, then sixty-two years old. She had been recruited to Fannie's board by James Johnson a decade before—largely, she believed, because her Republican pedigree provided political balance. The holder of a degree in English literature from Marymount College, she had experience in corporate public relations, as communications director of President Nixon's 1972 reelection campaign and as secretary of labor under President Reagan. She married Tom Korologos, a veteran lobbyist, after divorcing John McLaughlin, a onetime Jesuit priest who worked for Nixon and became a TV political commentator. She headed the commission that investigated the downing of Pan American Flight 103 over Scotland in 1988. She was on the boards of Microsoft and American Airlines. She collected art from the American West.

Now she was suddenly at the helm of one of the world's biggest financial firms. Falcon was no longer dealing with Raines; he was dealing with Korologos. She resisted pressure for an immediate ouster of Raines; she thought the board needed to investigate before making such a drastic move. Still, she quickly established a pragmatic new consensus on the board, in defiance of Raines: a government-sponsored company, reliant on money from investors who expected government backing, could not be at war with the government. "You don't poke your finger in the eye of the regulator," as she later put it.

The directors accepted Ofheo's terms. They agreed the company would change accounting policies, as directed by Ofheo, and temporarily hold at least 30 percent more capital than the usual minimum. Fannie would seek written approval from Ofheo before increasing its dividend or repurchasing shares. The company would review its compensation policies "to avoid any inappropriate incentives." It would appoint a chief risk officer, whose duties would be set in consultation with Ofheo.

RAINES WAS FURIOUS—AND fought back. He and Howard appeared before a House subcommittee on October 6 to defend the company's accounting. Raines denied that the $200 million of expenses had been delayed as part of a scheme to boost executive bonuses. Ofheo had shown no proof, he said.

"The company is in fine shape," Raines said, in calm and confident tones, and Ofheo should have discussed its findings with Fannie's management before going to the company's board. "I don't know of any [other] financial regulator that would have done it this way," Raines said. Other agencies, he said, would have resolved the issues quietly, "without one headline."

In the end, Raines said, it would be up to the Securities and Exchange Commission—not Ofheo—to decide whether Fannie had violated accounting rules.

In his testimony, Falcon said Ofheo normally allowed for give-and-take between its staff and a company before completing a report. In this case, he said, the matters were so serious that they required urgent action. Ofheo's findings "cannot be dismissed as mere differences of interpretation in accounting rules," Falcon said. "Fannie Mae understood the rules and simply chose not to follow them."

Fannie's congressional allies snarled. "We are rushing to judgment today," stated Representative William Lacy Clay, a Democrat from Missouri. "Ofheo has released a preliminary report which has not been proven, but leaked to the press." Representative Clay saw a sinister motivation: "This hearing is about the political lynching of Franklin Raines."

RAINES WAS CONFIDENT THAT the SEC would bless Fannie's books. After all, the company's auditors, KPMG, had approved the company's method of interpreting the FAS 133 accounting rule.

Yet Raines also was worried about Fannie's image and especially its reputation for arrogance. In remarks prepared for an officers' meeting in November 2004, he wrote, "We need to be candid about the fact that we are not perfect. We may have believed our own PR a little too much. We allowed ourselves to be arrogant. We thought we had a lot to teach and little to learn from others."

Fannie's chief operating officer, Daniel Mudd, wrote a memo to Raines the same month: "The old political reality was that we always won, we took no prisoners, and we faced little organized political opposition....We used to, by virtue of our peculiarity, be able to write, or have written, rules that worked for us. We now operate in a world where we will have to be 'normal.'"

THE SHOWDOWN BETWEEN RAINES and Falcon came on December 15, 2004. Raines was summoned to the SEC headquarters in Washington for a meeting on a cold, rainy evening. He arrived with three members of Fannie's board. They ducked into a back door to elude journalists. Nearly thirty people crowded a conference room at SEC headquarters, including Falcon and auditors from KPMG. Neither Falcon nor Raines knew what the SEC had decided.

Donald Nicolaisen, the SEC's chief accountant, announced that Fannie had misapplied the FAS 133 rules. The company had used "hedge accounting"—a way of avoiding the need to mark derivative contracts to their current market value—without meeting the stringent requirements set down by FAS 133.

Stunned, Raines began raising objections. The SEC accounting chief cut off Raines. "Many companies can and do comply with the rules," Nicolaisen said, according to people who were at the meeting. "Sir, hedge accounting is a privilege, not a right," he said. Hedge accounting "is applied only under strict circumstances, and you did not comply."

Raines asked how far off Fannie had been. Nicolaisen held up a sheet of paper. If the paper represented the four corners of the rule, he told Raines, "you were not even on the page."

THE SEC'S RULING SHATTERED the credibility of Raines and Howard. Fannie's board went into emergency mode. Korologos talked individually with each of the other directors about how to proceed. On December 21, six days after the SEC showdown, the board convened at a Four Seasons hotel

Franklin Raines in a portrait taken around 2006. *Courtesy of the Raines family.*

in Washington, avoiding the Fannie headquarters, where journalists might be lurking. Korologos told Raines he would have to leave. Raines made a plea for more time; he wanted his departure to be a retirement, part of an orderly succession. He wanted to avoid a rushed exit, implying guilt.

"No," Korologos said. "It's today."

As usual, Raines kept most of his thoughts to himself. He made his way around the table, shook hands with each director and left.

The directors appointed Mudd as interim CEO. They dismissed KPMG as Fannie's auditor.

So Raines's public life ended in disgrace. Though he had not been given a trial, he was already convicted in the court of loosely informed public opinion. He would become a stock villain on right-wing talk shows, where he was blamed for running Fannie into the ground.

Raines did not run Fannie into the ground. The company's worst decisions about which loans to buy or guarantee came after he was gone. Raines later said he believed he wouldn't have made the same mistakes his successor made. We will never know.

Raines was sometimes arrogant and often undiplomatic. He failed to win the debate over how Fannie should be regulated, though not for lack of effort and debating skill. He collected vast amounts of compensation, totaling $90 million for 1998 through 2003. (Much of that compensation was in stock, whose value later collapsed.) He failed to understand that Wall Street–style pay wasn't politically acceptable at an institution chartered and given special privileges by Congress to help people of modest means afford housing.

Under both Johnson and Raines, Korologos told me later, the top management suffered from arrogance, self-righteousness and an unwillingness to listen to critics: "The culture was rotten at the top."

FANNIE'S BOARD HIRED A former U.S. senator, Warren Rudman, and a team of lawyers from the firm of Paul Weiss to investigate what went wrong. After working for more than a year, Rudman's team in February 2006 released a 2,652-page report concluding that executives had misled the directors about accounting manipulations designed to produce the illusion of steady earnings growth. Scores of other companies also were forced to restate earnings because of confusion over the FAS 133 rule. But the Rudman report found a wide array of other accounting violations.

Some Fannie employees in accounting, financial-reporting and auditing jobs "were either unqualified for their positions, didn't understand their roles or failed to carry out their roles properly," the report said. The computer systems used for accounting were "grossly inadequate."

Rudman's report pointed to Howard, the former chief financial officer, and a former senior accounting executive, Leanne Spencer, as being "primarily responsible" for improper accounting practices. "They put undue emphasis on avoiding earnings volatility and meeting [earnings per share] targets and growth expectations," the report said.

Among many other accounting lapses, the report focused on management decisions that increased reported profit for 1998's fourth quarter and helped inflate bonuses—the issue first raised by Ofheo in

Some of the voluminous reports produced by investigators looking into accounting problems at Fannie and Freddie. *Photo by James R. Hagerty.*

2004. Based on interest-rate movements, the report found, Fannie should have recognized expenses (related to the fluctuating values of loans and mortgage securities) totaling $439 million in that quarter. Instead, the report said, Howard and Spencer chose to delay recognition of $199 million of those expenses and persuaded Raines that their decision was correct, even though the company's auditing firm, KPMG, disagreed. If Fannie had recognized all of the expenses during that quarter, it would have missed its earnings target; bonuses would have been much smaller. "Howard and Spencer then made incomplete and misleading disclosures to the board" about these decisions, the report said.

There were many other ways to make earnings look smoother. When it repaid debt securities early, Fannie calibrated the size of the repurchases to achieve earnings targets "to the penny" rather than doing an analysis to determine what amount of buybacks would be in the company's best long-term interests, the report said.

An internal memo dated November 30, 1998, showed a desire to withhold sensitive accounting information from auditors and even colleagues. The memo from Spencer and Janet Pennewell, another Fannie executive in charge of financial reporting, was to Lawrence Small, who was president and chief operating officer. Small was preparing remarks for a meeting with other officers of the company. Spencer and Pennewell advised him to avoid a specific reference to a plan to delay recognition of financial benefits from an accounting rule change involving certain tax credits.

The memo urged Small to tweak the draft of his planned remarks:

> *Nothing you state is incorrect. However, we would like to soften it a little. Technically, if you "know" about a [sic] accounting change you are supposed to book it. We haven't informed KPMG that we intend to implement this next year and our preference would be to not talk to them about it prior to year-end 1998 so they don't say "book it" at year-end. We've limited discussion of this to the inner circle, so we wouldn't want to broadcast it to the officer group at this point.*

SOMETIMES EXECUTIVES WERE UNEASY about the accounting. The report quoted an e-mail from Louis Hoyes, an executive vice-president, questioning an insurance transaction in January 2002 covering high-risk loans. The Rudman team found that Fannie accounted for this transaction improperly and that the main goal was to shift income from 2002 into later years to help smooth earnings. In his e-mail, Hoyes asked, "Should we be exposing Fannie Mae to this type of political risk to 'move' $40 million of income? I believe not."

As for Raines, "we did not find that he knew that the company's accounting policies departed from [generally accepted accounting principles] in significant ways," the report said. But Raines "contributed to a culture that improperly stressed stable earnings growth." As the CEO, "he was ultimately responsible for the failures that occurred on his watch."

In a letter submitted to the Rudman team, Kevin Downey, a lawyer representing Raines, said the former CEO "took prudent steps to ensure" accurate accounting. A lawyer for Howard said he had "consistently acted in accordance with the highest standards of integrity and the best interests of shareholders." Howard, on the advice of his lawyer, had declined to meet with the Rudman team during the investigation. Spencer's attorney said she had "worked tirelessly to maintain accurate accounting records."

THE REPORT ALSO TURNED up an example of Fannie's efforts to buy political support. In 2001, Fannie paid $800,000 for a 10 percent stake in Gulf Bank of Florida, a small and troubled bank in the Miami area that was short on capital and had pressed Fannie for help. The report quotes Fannie executives as estimating that the price of the stake was $150,000 above market value. Gulf Bank wasn't even in the mortgage business, though it had ambitions in that area. Fannie officials went ahead with the purchase even though they knew regulators had accused Gulf Bank of failing to file currency-transaction reports.

Fannie officials saw value in a cozy relationship with the chairman of Gulf Bank, Salvador Bonilla-Mathe. An internal memo noted that Bonilla-Mathe had "strong ties" with Florida Senator Bob Graham, other members of Congress and Florida Governor Jeb Bush, the president's brother. Those ties "will be invaluable in our needs for support at the Hill in DC," this memo said.

In 2003, Fannie wrote off its entire investment in Gulf Bank, which eventually was closed down. The U.S. Treasury's Financial Crimes Enforcement Network in July 2005 fined the former majority owners of Gulf Bank $700,000 for failing to file "suspicious-activity" reports on money transfers, including some by a convicted money launderer. The enforcement agency found that Gulf Bank had failed to make timely reports on 2,434 currency transactions, showing a "systemic breakdown" in compliance with laws aimed at catching money launderers.

The Tragedy of Frank Raines

Fannie tried to move on from the accounting ordeal. In May 2006, the company agreed to pay fines totaling $400 million to settle charges of improper accounting. In its settlement with Ofheo and the SEC, the company neither admitted nor denied wrongdoing.

ONE WARNING FLAG AT Fannie that few outsiders had noticed was the enormous concentration of power in one man: Howard. Fannie's chief financial officer was supremely self-confident. He was a ferocious tennis player and a trustee of the Washington Opera. He had been at the company since 1982. He understood its inner workings better than anyone else, including the final two CEOs he worked under, Johnson and Raines.

After starting out as an economist under Maxwell, he had risen to be vice-chairman and chief financial officer under Raines. Most chief financial officers are in charge only of the finances. Howard also was responsible for Fannie's main business—borrowing money and investing it in mortgage loans and securities. He supervised accounting, forecasting and investor relations. Raines gave him another duty: chief risk officer. Howard was simultaneously responsible for taking risks, reporting on those risks to the board and the public and ensuring that the company wasn't taking too many risks. The checks and balances in place at better-managed companies were missing.

Howard on at least one occasion tried to control the flow of information from Fannie's internal auditors to the board's audit committee, according to the regulator's report. In March 2004, he sent an e-mail to Spencer noting that he had made it "blisteringly clear" to Sampath Rajappa, the head of internal auditing, that he was not allowed to reply to questions from the board without first consulting Spencer or Howard. (Howard later told me he had not been trying to censor Rajappa. The phrase "blisteringly clear" was an inside joke, Howard said. He also said his goal was to ensure that Rajappa gathered the correct information before responding to questions from the board: "Sam at times had a tendency to respond to questions based only on what he knew at the moment, rather than what he could learn if he went to the authoritative source.")

The Rudman report also found that Howard "filtered the accounting and financial information the board received."

Ofheo officials, interviewing Howard in August 2004, asked whether he would ever inform the board's audit committee of accounting policies his staff deemed "aggressive." "No," Howard replied, "because, again, I don't view the label 'aggressive accounting' as being a bad thing. It is descriptive of the relative positioning compared to the GAAP [generally accepted accounting principles] line. That's why I want to find out more about the specific incidents. And if it's uncomfortably close to the line, we will change it. It's not 'take it to the board.' It's 'don't do it.'"

BY HIS OWN ADMISSION, Howard could be introverted and impatient with those he considered fools. He knew his persona intimidated colleagues. For a time, he worked with the company's consulting psychologist on ways to make himself more approachable. He began holding informal meetings now and then to chat with staff members.

Despite his efforts to be friendlier, other executives were afraid to challenge him. A close colleague told me she considered him "upstanding" and smart and didn't believe he was motivated by greed or would deliberately subvert accounting rules. "Yet he didn't play well with others," she said. "He tried to make his stuff so complicated that no one could have an opinion."

THE JUSTICE DEPARTMENT CHOSE not to pursue criminal action against Raines, Howard or other executives involved in the accounting. The U.S. Attorney's Office for the District of Columbia in October 2004 told Fannie that it was investigating the company's past accounting practices. But that investigation never led to any charges.

There was a baffling barrage of numbers. In December 2006, Fannie announced a restatement that lowered retained earnings as of June 30, 2004, by $6.3 billion. The restatement also *increased* stockholders' equity by $4.1 billion as of that date, reflecting increases in the value of mortgage securities held by Fannie that were reclassified as being "available for sale" as part of the process of correcting accounting violations. The increases in the estimated value of those securities more than offset the reduction in retained earnings. There was no simple number to sum up the damage.

Fannie's earnings per share for 2003 were restated as $7.85, compared with the earlier reported $7.91. That 2003 result proved a high-water mark. Earnings per share fell to $4.94 in 2004. By 2008, Fannie was reporting catastrophic losses.

THEN CAME ANOTHER LEGAL settlement. Ofheo in April 2008 settled an administrative-law proceeding against Raines, Howard and Spencer.

The Tragedy of Frank Raines

Originally, Ofheo sought to impose fines of as much as $100 million and claw back compensation totaling $115 million. Instead, the three executives agreed to pay fines totaling about $3 million, which were to be covered by Fannie's own insurance policies.

Raines agreed to donate proceeds from the sale of $1.8 million of his Fannie stock to programs boosting homeownership or helping people avoid foreclosure. He gave up stock options that were once valued at $15.6 million but eventually became worthless as Fannie's stock price collapsed. He gave up about $5.3 million of other benefits relating to his pension and foregone bonuses. The settlement, Raines said in a prepared statement, "is not an acknowledgment of wrongdoing on my part, because I did not break any laws or rules while leading Fannie Mae."

Howard agreed to donate the proceeds from a sale of $200,000 of Fannie stock to a charity and also gave up stock options and benefits valued at about $240,000. Howard and Spencer continued to deny wrongdoing. Howard's lawyer, Steven Salky, called the settlement a "capitulation" by Ofheo and said Howard was "justifiably proud" of his record at Fannie.

By this time, Howard considered himself retired and was spending his winters at a new home in Puerto Aventuras on Mexico's Caribbean coast. Litigation clouded his idyll.

Tim Howard, former chief financial officer of Fannie, as a retiree in 2012. *Photo by Debra Howard.*

A suit filed by Fannie shareholders in 2004—alleging that Fannie, KPMG, Raines, Howard and Spencer had defrauded them by producing false results—rumbled on in the federal courts. The lead plaintiff was the Ohio Public Employees Retirement System and the State Teachers Retirement System. That put Ohio's attorney general in charge of pursuing the claims.

As of January 2011, Ohio Attorney General Mike DeWine said Fannie had spent $132 million on legal fees related to the case. DeWine accused Fannie of "over-lawyering." During a deposition of Raines in April 2010, DeWine said, thirteen lawyers were on hand to represent the defendants. "They just sat there and billed the taxpayers for their hours," DeWine told Congress.

The shareholder litigation gave Raines and Howard a chance to defend themselves in court. A July 14, 2005 filing by their lawyers said, "When individuals develop an accounting policy or make an accounting decision that later is found to violate GAAP, it does not automatically follow that they knowingly violated GAAP and intentionally deceived investors....This is especially so here, given the complexity of the accounting determinations at issue and the fact that they were approved in advance by KPMG."

OTHER SENIOR FANNIE EXECUTIVES from the Johnson-Raines era were never accused of wrongdoing and went on with glittering careers. Thomas Donilon, head of law and policy (including lobbying) under Raines, became a national security adviser to President Obama. Robert Zoellick, an executive at Fannie in charge of legal and regulatory matters from 1993 to 1997, later served as the top U.S. trade negotiator and deputy secretary of state. In 2007, he became president of the World Bank. Jamie Gorelick, a deputy attorney general under President Clinton, was vice-chairman at Fannie from 1997 to 2003 and then became a partner at the law firm WilmerHale.

FANNIE ESTIMATED THAT THE costs arising from the accounting violations—including fines and outside lawyers and accountants hired by the company to sort through the books—totaled more than $1.3 billion in 2005 and 2006. At one point, Fannie was paying about 2,800 outside accountants, lawyers and other consultants to work on a restatement of earnings and other accounting matters. Fannie's headquarters was so crammed with consultants that some had to work in the cafeteria.

In the end, the legal, regulatory and accounting costs stemming from the scandal would exceed $2 billion. That would have been enough to build more than 8,400 houses at the median price for new homes in April 2012.

The biggest cost of the scandal, however, was the distraction of Fannie's management and regulators at a time when they should have been focused on a much bigger problem: the buildup of risks in the housing and mortgage markets. Regulators had rightly insisted on strict accounting policies at Fannie but should have been even more worried about the loosening of credit standards as U.S. home prices soared to levels that defied common sense.

Chapter 9

Fannie's Fall

In December 2004, Fannie promoted Daniel Mudd to succeed Raines as CEO on an interim basis. Mudd was six feet, four inches, a decorated ex-marine and a marathon runner. Unlike his predecessors, he was registered as a Republican. In contrast with Raines, who was combative and often seemed uncomfortable around people, Mudd came across as relaxed and dryly humorous. He disarmed critics by gently mocking himself.

As the son of Roger Mudd, a nationally admired television journalist, Mudd came from a family accustomed to knowing the best and the brightest in the nation's capital. He was an all-around jock in high school, playing football, baseball, soccer and tennis. At the University of Virginia, he was on the rowing team and earned a bachelor's degree in American history. After graduating and narrowly failing to qualify for the U.S. Olympic rowing squad, he wanted a big adventure. He considered the Peace Corps. The U.S. Marine Corps also tempted him. His mother discouraged that idea. His father advised him to talk to other people, including ex-marines. He made the rounds and then made the plunge.

In October 1983, the marines sent him to Beirut, where a bomb had just blown up a marine base. Shortly after his arrival, he heard some shouting and ran over to help colleagues dig out the body of a dead marine. The mangled body turned out to be someone he knew. Experiences like that, he later said, gave him perspective on the smaller annoyances of life.

After serving three years of active duty in the marines and rising to the rank of first lieutenant, he earned a master's degree in public administration

Dan Mudd during his 1983 deployment as a marine in Beirut. *Courtesy of the Mudd family.*

at Harvard. Later, he worked as a management consultant for Xerox and briefly as a venture capitalist in Germany. In 1991, Mudd got a job at GE Capital, the financial arm of General Electric.

He rose quickly through postings in Europe and Asia. When the Thai baht and other Asian currencies crashed in 1998, the financial panic tested him. He later recalled a tense phone call in which GE's chief executive, Jack Welch, told him to "ring fence the problem" in terms of damage to GE and then scout for opportunities. GE and others found bargains on such things as real estate and credit-card receivables. Then a recruiter persuaded Mudd to join Fannie. In February 2000, he became the mortgage company's chief operating officer, a job that brought him home to Washington.

Until his sudden elevation to CEO, Mudd worked on unglamorous day-to-day operations inside Fannie and was eclipsed by Raines and Howard, the public faces of the company. From his first day as CEO, Mudd tried to present a different kind of public face—more humble, more willing to listen to criticism.

Unlike Raines and Johnson, Mudd did not get the title of chairman. That job went to Stephen Ashley, a courtly mortgage banker who lived on a farm near Rochester, New York, and whose pastimes included fox hunting. Ashley, already a director of Fannie, had been in the mortgage business for four decades and served as president of the Mortgage Bankers Association in 1994. Ashley proclaimed that Fannie had to stop being "arrogant," the "A-word," as he put it.

On his first morning as CEO, Mudd paid a contrite visit to the regulator, Falcon. Rather than settling into the regal office suite used by past Fannie CEOs, he made a point of moving into a cramped space meant for a more junior executive. He spent much of his time in his first months as CEO apologizing for the mistakes and arrogance of his predecessors.

In a speech to home builders in January 2005, Mudd said, "We have a lot of work to do to put our house in order and to restore confidence in Fannie Mae. It's like the old Peanuts cartoon where Charlie Brown is lying awake at night asking, 'Where have I gone wrong?' And a voice answers, 'This is going to take more than one night.'"

Fannie's board liked Mudd's ability to set priorities and mend relations with the regulator. In June 2005, he was reaffirmed as CEO, no longer on an interim basis.

CONGRESS HAD RESUMED ITS long-stalled efforts to pass legislation to improve regulation of Fannie and Freddie. By now, one of the most powerful voices for change was that of Fed chairman Alan Greenspan. He made his case for shrinking Fannie and Freddie at a hearing of the Senate Banking Committee on April 6, 2005. Typically, Greenspan spoke as if he were dictating an abstruse economic research paper rather than trying to make his thoughts clear to the typical voter or senator. On that day, he made himself quite clear.

The problem, he said, was that investors had "concluded that the government will not allow [Fannie and Freddie] to default," even though the prospectuses for their debt securities explicitly stated that the borrowings were *not* backed by the government. The perceived government backing allowed Fannie and Freddie to borrow at low interest rates that were not available to even the top-rated banks and other financial institutions and to "borrow essentially without limit."

For decades, Fannie and Freddie didn't take full advantage of that cheap money; they kept their borrowings fairly modest. But in the past decade or so, in pursuit of rapid growth in their profits, they had gorged on cheap borrowed money and used the proceeds to buy vast amounts of mortgages. Their combined holdings of mortgages had soared to nearly $1.6 trillion, or more than 20 percent of all home mortgages outstanding, in 2003 from $136 billion, or 5 percent, in 1990.

They reaped immense profits because their borrowing costs were far below the interest rates they earned on the mortgages. The two companies' annual returns on the equity of their shareholders often topped 25 percent, compared with the 15 percent or so earned by their large financial rivals.

So they were very big and very profitable; what was wrong with that? The danger was that their size created "systemic risk," as Greenspan put it. They were so large that, if they ran into financial difficulty, their problems could imperil the entire financial system.

How might they get into financial trouble? Greenspan focused on the risks arising from fluctuations in interest rates. There was always the danger that a sudden move in interest rates could slash the value of their mortgage holdings and leave them with borrowing costs above the yields on their mortgages, creating the kind of losses Fannie had suffered in the early 1980s, only this time far larger because the companies had bloated so much. This risk persisted despite the companies' elaborate hedging of their interest-rate risks through derivatives, or financial contracts with other parties that served as a kind of insurance against adverse moves in interest rates. In fact, the very complexity of those derivatives created the risk of error.

Greenspan favored stronger, "world-class" regulation of Fannie and Freddie. But tougher regulation alone could make things worse if it reassured investors that all was well and reinforced the market's view of the companies as "extensions of government and their debt as government debt." To avoid that risk, Greenspan wanted Congress to require Fannie and Freddie gradually, over several years, to reduce the size of their mortgage holdings to an amount that he suggested could be less than one-sixth of the size they were then. The result would be much lower profits but also less "systemic risk."

Fannie and Freddie could continue to create mortgage securities for sale to other investors and to guarantee payments on those securities—a business Greenspan depicted as benign. Mortgage securitization, he said, "does not create substantial systemic risks." The problem was interest-rate risk, he affirmed, not credit risk. Credit risk—the danger of losses arising from defaults by homeowners—was not "an issue of substance" at Fannie and

Freddie, Greenspan said. Under questioning, he reaffirmed that "the risk is not credit risk."

Three years later, it turned out that Greenspan was wrong: the risk *was* credit risk, mounds of dubious loans bought or guaranteed by Fannie and Freddie. Fannie's history had shown that the risk was in fluctuating interest rates of the sort that caused the huge losses in the 1980s. But history proved a poor guide in this case. Of course, Greenspan could not have known in 2005 that Fannie and Freddie would soon start buying and guaranteeing riskier loans in large quantities.

When I asked Greenspan about this issue in 2012, he replied by e-mail, "I didn't consider Fannie and Freddie significant credit risks because I believed their dealings were overwhelmingly in prime mortgages whose default rates had historically been quite low. I was clearly mistaken in that view."

The guarantees Fannie and Freddie provided on mortgage securities meant they had to reimburse investors for any losses from default and foreclosure. The mortgage securitization that Greenspan saw as benign proved to be a deadly tumor—not because mortgage securities are inherently dangerous but because too many of the securities guaranteed by Fannie and Freddie were laden with high-risk mortgages.

So the greatest peril came not from the amount of mortgages and mortgage securities Fannie and Freddie *owned* but from the much larger sum of the ones they owned *plus* the ones they guaranteed through securitization. That was the credit risk, the risk of millions of home loans going unpaid. Greenspan and other regulators had their eyes on the wrong ball.

Greenspan would be proven correct in another sense: the failure of the companies would indeed cause tremors across the global financial markets.

No one under the chandeliers of the wood-paneled Senate hearing room on that day could have known how many millions of Americans were

Jim Bunning, who as a U.S. senator was skeptical of Fannie and Freddie, shown in a 1959 baseball card.

going to lose their homes to foreclosure in the next few years. Even so, Jim Bunning, the former star major-league baseball pitcher who now represented Kentucky in the U.S. Senate, said during the hearing that Congress must finally pass legislation to ensure "the safety and soundness" of Fannie and Freddie without doing any harm to the housing market. "The status quo is not acceptable," he said.

Senator Schumer, the New York Democrat, defended the two mortgage companies. "I think Fannie and Freddie over the years have done an incredibly good job and are an intrinsic part of making America the best-housed people in the world," he said at the hearing. "We have a great housing market here. Fannie and Freddie are intrinsically wrapped up in that market, and you've got to be careful before you do too much dramatic change." He conceded that there had been accounting problems and that regulatory changes were in order.

"But I think something else is in the air here," he said. "I think there are a whole lot of people who want to take advantage of the auditing problems that Fannie and Freddie have [had] to take the whole thing down....When the sink is broken, you don't tear down the house."

BUT CONGRESS COULDN'T DECIDE how to fix that sink. The Senate Banking Committee, chaired by Senator Shelby, in July 2005 narrowly approved a bill that would have created a stronger regulator, with powers to increase capital requirements and limit the size of their mortgage holdings. All eleven Republicans on the committee voted for the bill; all nine Democrats voted against. Senator Harry Reid, a Nevada Democrat, warned that the bill "could cripple the ability of Fannie Mae and Freddie Mac to carry out their mission of expanding homeownership."

In late October 2005, the House was finally wrapping up legislation to create a new regulator with stronger controls over capital requirements at Fannie and Freddie. The House legislation fell far short of what the Bush administration and the Fed wanted. The White House said the regulator envisioned by the House bill would be "considerably weaker" than the regulators monitoring other large financial companies.

The Bush administration also criticized the House bill for failing to give the regulator power to limit the amount of mortgages and mortgage securities that Fannie and Freddie could hold. They already were far too big, the White House argued, and had to be reined in. But Fannie and Freddie were lobbying fiercely against limits on their size. This issue created a showdown between backers of maintaining the status quo, with a few tweaks, and those who wanted to cut Fannie and Freddie down to size.

Republicans held a small majority in the House, so the White House might have been expected to get its way in this ideological struggle. Legislators had to make their choice when Representative Ed Royce, a California Republican who was one of the loudest critics of Fannie and Freddie, offered an amendment to let the regulator force Fannie and Freddie to reduce their mortgage holdings if they were found to create "systemic risks" to the financial system. Fannie and Freddie hated that idea. Advocates for affordable-housing programs hated it too.

The Royce amendment came up for a vote late in the afternoon of October 26, 2005. Royce lost, 346–73. More than two-thirds of the 223 Republicans voting supported the Fannie-Freddie line; so did all but 3 of the 195 Democrats. Congress went on to approve the overall legislation on a 331–90 vote. Fannie and Freddie had proved—decisively—that they could still get their way in Congress.

The Senate, where there was a wider gulf between Democratic and Republican ideas, couldn't agree on any new regulatory formula for Fannie and Freddie in 2005, and so the issue festered.

MUDD, WHOSE JOB INCLUDED the role of punching bag for Fannie's toughest critics, was still taking his lumps. In June 2006, the Senate Banking Committee convened to discuss Ofheo's final report on Fannie's accounting scandal. At the end of a long day in the committee room, Senator Chuck Hagel, a Republican from Nebraska, took his turn:

HAGEL: Mr. Mudd, in light of all this—I mean, first, are you thinking seriously about giving any of this money to charity that you received through all the fraudulent misrepresentations [of Fannie's earnings]? And I'm astounded that you would even stay with this institution. Have you thought about resigning?

MUDD: Senator, I've thought about an awful lot of things. I didn't like the old Fannie Mae any more than I understand, from your emotions and words about this, that you like the old Fannie Mae.

And I thought about leaving the old Fannie Mae a lot of times, and I didn't because I'm not a quitter and I stayed around. And if the standard is, now, if you quit, you get off scot-free, and if you stay around and you try to fix it, you're a bad guy, Senator, I can't do anything about that standard.

HAGEL: What's your compensation?

MUDD: I think, last year, the number was around $8 million, including salary, bonus and long term.

HAGEL: How about this year?

MUDD: I don't know what the targets are. I can—obviously, I'd be happy to send them to you, Senator.

HAGEL: Well, $8 million's not a bad number. I can see why you would also want to stay around for that incentive.

AFTER THE HEARING, AS Mudd loped toward an elevator, a reporter asked him whether he felt beat up. "I'm going to go have a beer," Mudd said.

MANY PEOPLE WERE GETTING rich, or believed they were. In the first years of the new century, Americans found plenty of reasons to think house prices would keep rising. The collapse of technology stocks in early 2000 made Americans warier of the stock market and eager to put their money into something tangible, like real estate. Then, to fight recession, the Federal Reserve slashed interest rates to unusually low levels, making mortgage credit cheap. At the same time, the children of baby boomers were starting to buy their first houses; their parents were beginning to purchase second homes or speculate on rental units. Employment began rising again, creating more demand.

As speculators and ordinary buyers bid up home prices—particularly in Florida, Arizona, Nevada and California—rising prices reinforced a general belief that housing was a sure bet and that anyone who wanted to benefit had better hurry.

The drop in interest rates also led to an immense wave of refinancing of home loans in 2003, enriching mortgage lenders as they raked in fees. By 2004, however, most people who could refinance had already done so. There were fears that home purchases would slow as prices leaped too high for many buyers to afford.

The mortgage industry wanted the party to continue. So lenders served up an even more potent stimulant: "affordability" mortgages, or loans that made it possible to spend far more on a house than would have been considered prudent in the past. These loans kept payments low for an initial period, delaying the pain of full payments. The theory was that by the time higher payments kicked in, the borrower would have more income and the value of the home would be much higher, giving the lender more collateral.

For "subprime" borrowers, those with low credit scores, lenders typically offered a kind of loan known in the trade as a 2/28. The interest rate on such loans was fixed at a relatively low rate for the first two years and then floated at a set margin over an interest-rate index for the next twenty-eight years. In many cases, the "reset" of the interest rate after two years pushed monthly payments up 30 percent or more. The amount of subprime loans outstanding nearly tripled to $1.24 trillion at the peak in 2006 from $479 billion in 2001, according to Inside Mortgage Finance.

Subprime lenders often boasted they were making homeownership possible for more people. In fact, they often were persuading elderly or poor people who already owned homes to refinance and extract cash from their properties in ways that later led to the loss of those homes to foreclosure.

For borrowers with better credit scores, many lenders pushed "interest-only" loans, which allowed the home buyer to pay only the interest in the initial years of the loan and start paying off the principal later, resulting in much higher payments down the road.

Lenders also pushed "option ARMs," a type of adjustable-rate mortgage. These loans gave the borrower several payment choices each month, including paying only the interest or even paying less than the monthly interest normally due. If borrowers chose the latter option—and many did—the unpaid interest was tacked onto the loan, and the balance due increased. The loan might seem very "affordable" from month to month, but the amount owed was growing. Eventually, after the loan balance reached a certain level, the borrower was required to pay the full interest and principal due each month. That might lead to "payment shock."

Lenders were typically basing lending decisions on whether borrowers could afford the initial low payments, not on whether they would be able to afford the higher ones that would come later. In 2004, I asked Vijay Lala, an executive vice-president at Countrywide, why his company was basing its ability-to-pay judgments on the low initial payments rather than determining whether the borrower would be able to handle much bigger payments later. That, he told me, was because "we don't know what the circumstances are going to be five years down the road." Countrywide, Fannie's biggest supplier of loans, was rolling the dice.

Though home prices were still rising rapidly, the surging popularity of these "affordability" mortgages raised questions about how many borrowers eventually would get into trouble. The industry had never made so many of these riskier types of loans to such a broad swath of borrowers. When pressed, Doug Duncan, then chief economist of the Mortgage Borrowers Association, acknowledged, "We're flying blind."

Because these loans held down the initial payments, borrowers could bid higher for their dream houses, and buying a home often required winning a bidding war. That added more fuel to the house-price boom at a time when home prices already were rising much faster than incomes. The median U.S. home price rose 33 percent in the four years ending on June 30, 2004; per capita personal income increased only 10 percent.

Even as prices soared to riskier heights, lenders continued to relax requirements for documentation. Patrick Flanagan, president of New Century Financial's mortgage-lending arm, told me that "many customers don't want to take the time to dig out tax returns and bank statements and call their accountant." Countrywide dubbed its "low-doc" program Fast & Easy; many of those loans were sold to Fannie.

The percentage of subprime borrowers who didn't fully document their income and assets increased from about 17 percent in early 2000 to 44 percent in 2006, according to First American CoreLogic, a research firm. These "low-doc" and "no-doc" mortgages opened the way for fraudulent loan applications and became widely known as "liar loans."

Skimpy down payments also were becoming the norm. Many borrowers paid little or nothing down by taking out two loans to buy a house, financing 100 percent of the purchase, an arrangement known as "piggyback" lending.

When I asked Fannie executives about these increasingly lax loan standards in 2004, they assured me they weren't buying many of the riskier sorts of mortgages. Jef Kinney, a vice-president at Fannie, told me the company was wary of the increased risks. Whenever the mortgage industry comes to the end of a refinancing boom, he said, mortgage lenders and brokers look for ways to maintain volume. "Typically," Kinney said, "this is when they start to push the envelope."

Countrywide was on a rampage. The lender's CEO, Mozilo, set a goal of doubling his company's share of U.S. mortgage originations to 30 percent by 2008. When I interviewed him in 2004, Mozilo dismissed the idea of a housing bubble that might eventually burst. "We don't see that at all," he said.

Wasn't there a danger that Countrywide's drive to double its market share would lead to growth at the expense of profitability? "I'm fairly confident that we're not going to do anything stupid," Mozilo said. "We have a history of not doing anything stupid."

THE CONSENSUS VIEW OF prospects for the housing market remained calm. A paper published by the Federal Reserve Bank of New York in December 2004 examined bubble warnings and concluded that there was "little basis for such concerns." The authors found that "the marked upturn in home prices is largely attributable to strong market fundamentals: Home prices have essentially moved in line with increases in family income and declines in nominal mortgage interest rates."

While many of the supposed experts played down the risks, Americans grew giddier. Many kept drawing down their home equity by refinancing their homes and taking out cash to spend—sometimes on more real estate. In May 2005, I interviewed Ryan Epstein of North Beach, Maryland. A year earlier, he and his wife had whittled down the mortgage on their four-bedroom colonial to $130,000. Then Epstein had a chat with a mortgage broker.

The broker helped the Epsteins refinance their home, valued at about $300,000, to take advantage of lower interest rates. He also encouraged the couple to take out extra cash, a popular option called a cash-out refinancing. The Epsteins used that cash, $25,000, as the down payment on a rental property. That purchase swiftly led to others. By May 2005, Epstein calculated, he had about $1.4 million of equity in nine dwellings— and $2 million in mortgage debt.

"It's a wonderful market out there," Epstein said. He considered real estate a far better bet than stocks. "If you buy stocks," he said, "the next day they can tumble in the toilet." (When I reached him in 2012, Epstein said he sold his rental properties in time to avoid being burned in the crash.)

WHAT WERE LENDERS THINKING? Many relied on flawed risk models and allowed themselves to be lulled by a strong economy into a false sense of security, according to a 2010 study by Clifford Rossi, a former banker who became a finance professor at the University of Maryland. A long stretch of solid economic growth and rapidly rising house prices pushed defaults down to unusually low levels and created a "mirage" of adequate risk management, Rossi wrote. Because defaults were so low, lenders grew more willing to accept risk.

Lenders also found they could make bigger profit margins on riskier loans than on standard fixed-rate ones. Managers in loan-production departments, whose pay depended on rising volumes, were able to shout down any concerns raised by risk managers. The swaggering loan producers had hard data on the current profitability of mortgages and low default rates; nervous risk managers could offer only a fuzzy range of possible future outcomes.

Further muddying the picture was the increasing use of loans that allowed borrowers to simply state—rather than verify—their incomes. That meant the information about borrowers' financial health, plugged into risk models, was unreliable. Credit scores also became less reliable as people learned to game the system. Fraud aggravated the data problems; many home buyers who declared themselves to be owner-occupants were really investors with little attachment to the property.

The complexity of many statistical risk models offered "analytical elegance" and created an illusion of security, Rossi wrote. Computer models trumped common sense.

BRIAN, A POLICE OFFICER who asked me not to use his last name, was among the deluded. In 2005, he and his wife, a real estate agent, bought a four-bedroom house in Scottsdale, Arizona, with enough acreage for their dogs and horses. The price was $650,000. Because the real estate market was still booming, Brian's wife was doing well as an agent. Their combined annual income was around $170,000. Their credit scores were excellent. Because they made a 20 percent down payment, they figured they were being conservative. Surely, they thought, the value of the house would keep growing, especially as they were improving it.

Later, they took out a second mortgage, or home-equity loan, to help pay for their eldest daughter's college costs, home improvements and a wedding. Their mortgage debt eventually mounted to $670,000. While the debt grew, the value of the house was falling as the foreclosure wave engulfed their neighborhood. Home sales were so slow that Brian's wife no longer could earn much as a Realtor. Then the marriage ended in divorce, further depleting the couple's finances.

In late 2011, Brian estimated that the market value of the house was about one-third of the debt he still owed. He had stopped making payments on the loans and was waiting to be evicted through foreclosure. Brian had given away the horses and warned his younger daughter that he wouldn't be able to help pay for her college expenses.

The housing bust left uncompleted homes in the once-booming town of Maricopa, Arizona. *Photo by Steve Velaski.*

WHEN BRIAN BOUGHT THE house in 2005, it wasn't clear that a disaster was looming, though there were reasons to be nervous. In a May 2005 speech, Fed chairman Greenspan suggested that house-price inflation in some parts of the country was starting to look excessive. "At a minimum, there's a little froth in the market," Greenspan said in response to a question at a lunch hosted by the Economic Club of New York. "We don't perceive that there is a national bubble, but it's hard not to see that there are a lot of local bubbles."

That same month, Thomas Lawler, a senior vice-president responsible for risk policy at Fannie, gave a presentation entitled "The Home Price Outlook: Are We Experiencing a Housing Bubble?" One of his slides showed that house prices had begun rising faster than personal income in the late 1990s and were pulling away at an increasing rate by 2003. Riskier loans such as option ARMs had gone "from niche to mainstream." Lots of people were speculating by buying houses to flip. The number of new homes for sale was soaring.

"No one can say that a bubble exists until after the fact," Lawler wrote on his final slide. But "conditions in many parts of the country (though certainly not most of the country) mirror past conditions that preceded regional housing busts. The probability of such an event occurring has risen sharply in certain parts of the country."

Lawler's presentation happened to be made in the same month that *Playboy* magazine's playmate of the month, Jamie Westenhiser, informed readers that she was giving up modeling and "getting into investment-type real estate." In later years, after leaving Fannie, Lawler said the embrace of the housing market by a Playboy bunny was a sure sign that it was peaking. A financial publication, *EuroWeek*, wrote that Westenhiser was "moving from one set of inflated assets to another."

As THE HOUSING MARKET wobbled, Mudd hoped Fannie had turned a corner. After all the trauma of the accounting scandal, he wanted to reward his staff. In December 2006, Fannie held its annual holiday staff party at a Hilton hotel in downtown Washington. The entertainment was by Earth, Wind & Fire, a band whose hit songs included "That's the Way of the World" and "Fantasy."

Though Mudd had promised to reduce Fannie's emphasis on lobbying, the company continued to spend heavily to influence politicians. The Center for Responsive Politics (whose data are available at www.opensecrets. org) reported that Fannie spent about $10 million on lobbying in both 2005 and 2006. By comparison, Citigroup spent $7 million in 2006, while Bank of America spent $2 million and Wells Fargo $1.8 million. (Fannie was known for hiring outside lobbyists in large numbers, partly so that the company's foes couldn't engage them. In 2005, twenty-three lobbying firms were listed as working for Fannie.)

On a combined basis, Fannie and Freddie spent $164 million on lobbying from 1999 to 2008, according to the Financial Crisis Inquiry Commission's report.

FANNIE AND FREDDIE HAD reasons to feel threatened amid growing pressure from two directions: they were losing business as lenders found they could sell more of their loans to other packagers of mortgage securities, including Wall Street firms and big lenders like Countrywide, rather than Fannie or Freddie. Meanwhile, HUD was again jacking up their requirements for helping the poor.

In November 2004, HUD announced higher minimum levels for the percentage of loans bought or guaranteed by the companies that financed borrowers whose incomes were at or below the median for their area. Under the new rules, that percentage would rise in stages to 56 percent in 2008 from 50 percent in 2004. Fannie and Freddie also would need to increase financing of homes for people in "underserved" locations, such as impoverished rural and inner-city areas, and for people with very low incomes, defined as 60 percent or less of the median in their areas.

Even before the bar was raised, Fannie and Freddie were struggling to reach the HUD requirements, known as "goals." Hitting the goals became a cynical game. A May 12, 2005 memo from the majority staff of the House Financial Services Committee, reporting on an investigation by the committee, found that the companies had engaged in "double counting" of loans. A loan could be sold to Freddie or Fannie one year, sold back to the lender the next and then sold again to Fannie or Freddie in a later year, counting toward the goals anew even though no new homeowner had been created.

To meet goals, Fannie and Freddie sometimes bought pools of loans that included ones for commercial properties, including retail properties occupied by Walmart and Old Navy, as well as loans for vacation homes. "The purchase of a second home would indicate that the individuals...were not in need of affordable-housing assistance," the staff memo noted.

The companies "paid tens and sometimes hundreds of millions of dollars in fees as inducements to financial institutions to engage in these transactions" and "engaged in transactions that would not normally be considered to be economically viable in order to meet the goals."

Toward the end of each year, banks knew Fannie and Freddie were desperate to find "goal-rich" mortgages and would pay premiums for them. Fannie and Freddie could be induced to bid against each other.

A bigger problem was that HUD's rules didn't differentiate between loans that were likely to be repaid and those likely to end in foreclosure. Fannie and Freddie both became huge buyers of securities created by Wall Street and others that were backed by subprime loans, notably the 2/28 loans described previously. Those loans would end up defaulting in vast numbers and so could hardly be considered a means of increasing homeownership. Yet they counted toward the goals, and the nearly $200 billion Fannie and Freddie invested in those securities encouraged more misguided subprime lending.

These subprime securities were also a risky investment, even though the ones Fannie bought were rated AAA by Moody's and Standard & Poor's. In a March 2005 memo to Mudd, Adolfo Marzol, then Fannie's chief credit officer, pointed to "concern that the rating agencies may not be properly assessing the risk in these securities." One worry was that a large share of the loans backing the securities financed properties in California and other places where home prices had soared to crazy levels. "Many of the loans…would be susceptible to loss if home price growth rates were to slow or decline," Marzol warned. Another concern was that the borrowers did not fully understand the risks they were taking and might not be ready for "abrupt changes in family cash flows brought on by changes in the mortgage payment," he wrote.

FANNIE AND FREDDIE HAD been dominant in the business of buying mortgages from lenders and pooling those loans into securities sold to investors. By 2004 and 2005, however, Wall Street firms and big mortgage lenders with their own securitization departments were doing more of that business. Rather than focusing mainly on making loans that could be sold to Fannie and Freddie, mortgage lenders found it was more profitable to make the types of loans Wall Street was eager to buy, mostly subprime or "Alt-A," a category between prime and subprime that often included low-doc features and loans for investors buying homes.

Wall Street firms hired thousands of people to buy loans, create securities, trade those securities and write research notes that reassured investors that the securities were sound. Demand for mortgage securities was so great that Wall Street firms had trouble buying mortgages fast enough. Rather than simply buying the loans from others, some Wall Street firms, including

Lehman Brothers and Bear Stearns, built up their own mortgage-lending operations to originate loans through mortgage brokers. They also met demand by creating "synthetic" mortgages, financial contracts designed to mimic the behavior of real mortgages.

With spectacularly bad timing, Merrill Lynch bought a subprime lender, First Franklin Financial, for $1.3 billion in December 2006, just as defaults on subprime loans were starting to pile up.

Wall Street could sell so many mortgage securities partly because it had found a way to make them appealing to a much larger group of potential buyers. Before the housing boom, mortgage securities had been a complicated type of investment bought mainly by investors with specialized knowledge. It took lots of time and expertise to decide which securities to buy and how to value them. Then Wall Street began promoting an easier way to buy into the mortgage market, through financial entities called collateralized debt obligations, or CDOs.

Wall Street firms rushed to create CDOs, which essentially were investment funds. The CDOs then raised money by selling notes and shares to investors. The proceeds were used to buy a variety of mortgage securities, often including the riskiest ones. The CDOs were attractive to insurers, pension funds and other investors that lacked the time or expertise to choose individual mortgage securities. They could buy into a single CDO to gain exposure to a variety of mortgage securities, just as a stock market investor can buy a mutual fund rather than picking individual stocks. CDOs were particularly popular with Asian and European institutional investors looking for a higher yield than they could get on U.S. Treasury bonds.

Wall Street seemed to be taking over the mortgage business. In 2005, mortgage securities created by Fannie accounted for 16 percent of the overall market, down from 30 percent in 2003, according to *Inside Mortgage Finance*. Fannie executives started to worry that they were becoming "irrelevant," as Mudd put it.

AS THEIR SHARE OF the mortgage market dwindled, Mudd and his top aides sweated over how to stay in the game. Wall Street's growing power in mortgages "dramatically impacted our ability to influence what was going on in the market," Robert Levin, a senior Fannie executive, recalled later. One big question for Fannie executives was whether Wall Street's new dominance of the mortgage world was temporary or permanent. Were subprime and

Alt-A loans the new norm? If so, some Fannie executives thought, the company would have to embrace them. If not, perhaps Fannie could simply wait for sanity to return to the market.

Was Fannie going to take more risks or just say no? Internal documents—turned over by Fannie in late 2008 to the House Committee on Oversight and Government Reform—show how the company answered that question. Fannie was "at a strategic crossroads," according to materials prepared for senior vice-presidents of the company attending a retreat in June 2005. There were two "stark choices."

One possibility was to "stay the course," sticking to the company's traditional business of concentrating on the less-risky types of mortgages, mainly those with fixed rates for thirty years, documentation of income and substantial down payments. That path would allow Fannie to "maintain our strong credit discipline" and "preserve capital." Meanwhile, Fannie could "intensify our public voice on concerns" about growing risks in the housing and mortgage markets. Fannie's market share would likely continue to decline; earnings might fall.

The other choice was to "meet the market where the market is," or accept the riskier loans that were now the fastest-growing part of the business. There would be "increased exposure to unknown risks." Revenue would likely be higher, and Fannie could at least slow the decline in its market share.

Fannie executives saw obstacles blocking the "meet-the-market" approach: the company lacked the computer systems and expertise needed to assess risks on some of the riskier types of loans. So Fannie would stay the course for a while but also make "underground" efforts to build its capabilities for buying or guaranteeing the riskier alternative loans. Unless it learned how to play Wall Street's game, the meeting materials said, Fannie might become merely "a niche player."

Fannie wouldn't plunge in immediately. Mudd was a methodical manager. He liked to establish formal, written policies and procedures. He spoke of "building out" policies, computer systems and capabilities in an orderly way. But Fannie was already on a slippery ramp.

Countrywide was increasingly bypassing Fannie. Countrywide created its own mortgage securities and sold them on Wall Street. The share of Countrywide's loans that were acquired by Fannie had dropped from more than 80 percent in 2002 to about 20 percent in early 2005. Countrywide's CEO, Mozilo, had shown he could do without Fannie, but he didn't want Fannie to wither away. He liked having choices. If Wall Street ever stopped buying his loans, he wanted Fannie to be there with a big checkbook. In meetings with Mudd and others at Fannie, Mozilo prodded them to buy more Alt-A loans, lest they become irrelevant.

Tom Lund was at the center of this debate. He had been at Fannie for ten years and in 2003 was named head of the department responsible for buying or guaranteeing loans on single-family homes—the heart of Fannie's business. He regarded himself as conservative on risks and favored staying the course rather than taking on higher-risk loans, according to his later discussions with the Financial Crisis Inquiry Commission. Kenneth Bacon, an executive vice-president of Fannie responsible for financing of apartment buildings, agreed that Lund was conservative and sought to remain "in the normal credit box."

Yet Lund was finding it harder to resist the Alt-A lending boom. Wall Street investment banks seemed to be making lots of money on these loans. So far, there had been no alarming surge in defaults. Rising home prices meant people who fell behind on loan payments could sell their homes or refinance into a loan with easier terms. Where was the crisis?

Lund said others saw him as "the boy who cried wolf." He started to wonder whether he was wrong. Maybe Wall Street knew what it was doing?

"People felt, 'These Wall Street people are doing it [eagerly buying new types of mortgages], and they're pretty smart,'" recalled Pamela Johnson, a lawyer who worked in credit policy at Fannie. Johnson told me she sided with Lund and others who were skeptical about Alt-A and other riskier loans and tried to resist the company's drift toward them. Washington Mutual, then one of the biggest and most aggressive mortgage lenders, with a big emphasis on option ARM loans, shifted its business to Freddie after Fannie balked at buying certain high-risk loans on terms WaMu could accept, Johnson said. Some people inside the company, those who wanted a stronger push to regain market share, cited the loss of WaMu business as a sign that their more risk-averse colleagues were "out of touch with the market," she said.

Eventually, the chase for market share prevailed over the calls for caution. "The goal became: figure out how to take in some of these [risky loan] products responsibly," said Johnson, who considered the loosening of standards a mistake.

Bacon, in a meeting with the financial crisis commission, described the acceptance of greater risks as a drift rather than the result of any single decision:

> *It's very hard for any one person to sit as the market moves and say "I'm smarter than everyone in this market." Everyone was getting into the market,*

and I just can't give you a breaking point. Over time, we started doing things we used not to do....We had customers saying clearly, "If you don't buy [this product], *I'm going to Wall Street." And investors wanted to see market share and returns.*

In early 2006, Fannie's senior management adopted a goal of regaining market share, Lund told the financial crisis commission. The goal was to buy or guarantee at least 25 percent of all new single-family home mortgages by the end of 2006, up from 20 percent in 2005, according to court documents later filed by the SEC. The only way to do that, Lund saw, was to become more aggressive in buying Alt-A loans, which typically had lower requirements to verify or "document" information about the borrower's finances. Buying these riskier low-doc loans also would help Fannie meet affordable-housing targets in some cases, he said, but that was not the primary reason for embracing Alt-A loans.

The door was open a crack. It opened wider and wider over the next year as Fannie executives became more comfortable with Alt-A loans. At an April 2006 meeting on credit risks, the SEC later disclosed, Mudd told his colleagues, "The market is moving to low documentation, and we need to actively pursue the keys to this market." At least 27.8 percent of loans acquired by Fannie in 2006 were of the low-doc sort, up from about 18.0 percent in 2004, according to data released by the SEC in December 2011.

Mudd later tried to explain the company's "strategic rethinking" to investigators from the financial crisis commission: "If you're not relevant, you're unprofitable, and you're not serving the mission."

In early July 2006, Fannie's senior executives—including Mudd, Levin and Michael Williams, the company's chief operating officer—held an off-site meeting at the Hyatt Regency Chesapeake Bay golf resort, spa and marina on the banks of the Choptank River in Cambridge, Maryland. Bad weather washed out plans for golf. Trapped inside the resort, the executives discussed strategy. According to a memo distributed after the event, the Fannie bosses affirmed a "strategy to say 'yes' to our customers by increasing purchases of subprime and Alt-A loans." The company would "improve market relevance."

The Fannie executives promised to buy the riskier loans in a careful, deliberate way. The company's new chief risk officer, Enrico Dallavecchia, was to "develop an approach to both enable growth and ensure the necessary controls are in place." The plan was gradually to increase purchases of Alt-A and snub the riskiest types.

Dallavecchia, whose job was to raise alarm bells about undue risks, had joined Fannie earlier in 2006 after working as a risk officer at J.P. Morgan Chase and as a researcher at the University of Venice in Italy. His honeymoon at Fannie was brief. On a Saturday in October 2006, he sent an e-mail to Mudd complaining that subprime business was "ramping up much faster than what would be consistent with the $5bn limit for year end we agreed upon less than two months ago." He added, "There is a pattern emerging of inadequate regard for the control process."

Mudd replied tersely a day later: "This is a serious matter and if the facts are supportive, we [you and I] will come down hard."

By July 2007, the market was getting worse, and Mudd was trying to cut costs. Dallavecchia was furious about a proposed cut of 16 percent in the budget of the risk department for 2008. In response, Williams sent Dallavecchia an e-mail: "Given the importance of the CRO [chief risk officer] function, we would expect you to push back and tell us where you need to be."

Dallavecchia was not appeased. "Giving me a number to ask for pushback is treating me like a child or a second class citizen," he e-mailed back. That wasn't all. "The company has one of the weakest control processes I ever witness [sic] in my career," Dallavecchia wrote. "This company really doesn't get it....We are already back to the old days of scraping on controls and people."

Dallavecchia then forwarded the e-mail exchange to Mudd, along with additional remarks, at 10:15 p.m. on a Monday: "It was inappropriate what was said today to the Board [of directors] as if I had all the necessary means and budget to act on the strategic plan. I do not even think that what I was given for 2008 is adequate for the current risk, considering how far we already are from adequate market practices."

He also was unhappy with some of his colleagues: "I am more than anything very upset because I thought I had joined a team and I realize I am in the usual place where people smile and act nicely but they keep running the company as they always did." Though he was supposed to be building up the risk-control capabilities, "I get a 16pct budget cut. Do I look so stupid?"

Just before seven o'clock the next morning, Mudd e-mailed back: "My experience is that email is not a very good venue for conversation, venting, or negotiating. If you feel you have been dealt with in bad faith, address it man to man....Resources are tight. Everyone has cuts....Please come to see me today face to face."

ONCE FANNIE STARTED TO say yes to Alt-A, it became harder to say no. Countrywide and other lenders began to sell more and more Alt-A loans to Fannie. An e-mail from Michael Quinn, a Fannie executive, to Mudd and others on April 17, 2008, showed that Fannie by then owned or guaranteed $312 billion of Alt-A loans, accounting for about 12 percent of its total single-family mortgage holdings and guarantees. A disproportionate part of that Alt-A exposure was for loans on homes in California and Florida bought by speculators. Though Alt-A was 12 percent of the company's overall mortgage holdings and guarantees, it accounted for 42 percent of default-related losses in the first quarter of 2008.

Fannie had jumped into Alt-A at the worst possible moment. The housing market was starting to crumble, destroying the value of the homes that were the collateral for those loans. As Fannie charged in, Wall Street was retreating from high-risk mortgages.

HOME SALES STARTED FALLING in the second half of 2005, and by mid-2006, home prices were declining in many parts of the country. Defaults were starting to trend up.

In August 2006, I drove to Herndon, Virginia, to watch the auction of a five-bedroom home then owned by Joan Guth. She had been trying to sell her house since September 2005 and initially priced it at $1.1 million. Guth planned to use the proceeds to buy a retirement home in Florida. But her home in Herndon attracted few serious lookers. In March 2006, she cut her asking price to $899,900. Still no takers. Finally, on the advice of her broker, she called in an auction firm. She and her family decided they would accept the highest bid, though they specified it would have to be at least $675,000.

While riding her bike, Kristin Eddy, an occupational therapist who lived in a town house nearby, had noticed Guth's grand dark-green turreted home with its wraparound verandahs. "I've had my eye on that house for a long time—as a dream," Eddy told me. When it first went on the market, it was way beyond her price range. Then she noticed a sign announcing the auction.

On the morning of August 5, the auctioneer, Stephen Karbelk, set up loudspeakers on Guth's side lawn and played an Elton John ballad containing the line "I'd buy a big house where we both could live." Guth handed bottles of chilled water to the several dozen bidders and curious neighbors who showed up. "I have a whole stomach full of butterflies," she said.

Eddy figured her chances of winning were near zero. Yet when the auction began, it became clear that there were only two serious bidders. Although the auctioneer strained to generate excitement, the bidding petered out within minutes. Eddy was the high bidder—at $475,000.

Looking stricken, Guth and one of her sons huddled with their broker for a few minutes. Then they told the auctioneer they wouldn't accept the bid. The auction was over.

Guth said she would move and leave the house empty until she could sell it at a reasonable price. Late that afternoon, Eddy offered to raise her offer to $525,000. The Guths wavered for two days before agreeing to accept $530,000—about half the original asking price.

Guth was among the first wave of many millions of American homeowners to discover that their homes were worth far less than they imagined. Still, people in the real estate industry maintained a brave front. David Lereah, then chief economist of the National Association of Realtors, told me in September 2006 that he expected a "soft landing" for housing "but a longer soft landing than we thought." Lower prices would draw investors and other buyers back into the market, he said.

Two months later, in November 2006, at a Realtors convention, Lereah proclaimed, "The bad news is just about behind us….There are signs of recovery." (Lereah had a spotty record of prognostication. In his 2005 book, *Are You Missing the Real Estate Boom*, he declared, "There has never been a better time" to buy real estate.)

If there were any signs of recovery, they soon vanished. Small subprime lenders began going bankrupt in late 2006. In early 2007, the larger subprime lenders began to totter. Belatedly, lenders began tightening their standards. Some stopped allowing subprime borrowers to buy homes with no down payment. Many subprime lenders were stuck with loans they couldn't sell. They also were forced to buy back earlier loans that had failed to meet quality standards specified in the loan-sales agreements. After buying back a bad loan, a lender has to mark it down to market value. These developments consumed the capital of lenders that had scant reserves.

In March 2007, New Century Financial, one of the largest subprime lenders, ran out of funds and was forced to stop making loans. Nearly all lenders specializing in subprime would disappear before the year was out. Operators of a website called Implode-o-Meter tried to keep track of all the dead or dying lenders.

At a mortgage bankers' meeting in New York in May 2007, Lund, Fannie's executive in charge of acquiring single-family mortgages, offered reassuring words to reporters: "I feel pretty optimistic about the way the market is headed." The crazier lending practices were ending as weak subprime lenders went bust. "The market, in our view, is returning to the sensible center," Lund said.

The center could not hold. In June, news emerged of heavy losses at two hedge funds run by Bear Stearns, a New York–based investment bank that was an aggressive trader of mortgage securities. The funds had made bullish bets on the mortgage market and now faced big losses. As investors pulled their money out of the funds, Bear Stearns was forced to prop up the funds with loans.

In early July, the two big U.S. debt-rating companies, S&P and Moody's, rattled the financial markets by downgrading hundreds of bonds backed by subprime mortgages as more and more borrowers fell behind or defaulted. The rating agencies' message boiled down to this: these mortgages are much riskier than we originally thought. It wasn't only subprime mortgages that were doing badly. Defaults also were rising swiftly on prime and Alt-A mortgages.

S&P held a conference call to give investors and others a chance to ask questions about the downgrades. "Why now?" asked Steve Eisman, managing director at a hedge fund. "Delinquencies have been a disaster for many months. It couldn't be that you just woke up to it."

"We did it as fast as we could, given the information we had," replied Tom Warrack, a managing director at S&P.

Fannie executives still believed the collapse of the weaker subprime lenders would lead to more sensible lending standards. Meanwhile, investors were growing less eager to buy mortgage securities without any government backing. That meant more business was flowing to Fannie and Freddie rather than Wall Street packagers of mortgage securities.

After a two-day meeting in June 2007 in a college classroom near the Fannie headquarters, the company's senior executives produced a five-year strategic plan calling for the company to take more risks. "We will take and manage more mortgage credit risk," the document said, affirming a practice that was already in effect. That would be accomplished by moving "deeper in the credit spectrum," or buying riskier sorts of loans. Fannie expected to buy or guarantee about $114 billion of Alt-A loans in 2007, for instance, up from $40 billion in 2004.

To finance such loans "safely," the document said, Fannie would need ways "to slice off and distribute credit risk into the market," finding others to take on or insure against risks that Fannie didn't choose to retain. Even though Fannie had already begun buying more high-risk loans, the company wasn't quite ready to assess the risks, the document admitted: "We need to buy and build long-term expertise of what can go badly in more credit-sensitive sectors." Fannie executives rated the company's expertise in credit-risk management as medium to low. Outside of familiar prime loans, Fannie was "under-skilled."

Of course, there was already a safe way to finance homes, based on such proven practices as requiring large down payments, verifying borrowers' incomes and scouring loans for fraud. But Fannie would attempt a more complicated strategy of taking more risk on loans and transferring some of that risk to other parties. Fannie called this alchemy a "risk transformation facility."

Fannie had been too cautious, the document concluded: "We're still remarkably risk-averse." Though Wall Street and some mortgage lenders had stumbled, Fannie could do better and "help lenders extend mortgage credit to more families, the right way, at lower cost."

Fannie also could make more money than ever, the executives told themselves. Even though the housing market was already slumping, the strategic plan projected earnings growing steadily from $4.5 billion in 2007 to $7.3 billion in 2011.

"We have reestablished a sound enterprise that serves a strong and growing market," the plan said. All was not well, though: "While we have put the customer on top, we struggle to provide the service, products and solutions they need when they need them. We are not as competitive as we need to be. Our systems are too complex and lack flexibility." Credit losses were growing. Meeting the HUD goals for financing homes for low- and moderate-income people was "a continual stretch."

Fannie executives thought the housing slump would be shallow and brief: "The negative trends of the past several years will work themselves out over the next year or so."

The idea of "privatization"—giving up the federal backing implied by Fannie's charter and becoming a normal company—had been studied again by the company's board and top executives, with hired help from executives at Citigroup and consultants at McKinsey & Co. Once again, Fannie rejected privatization. The consultants estimated that the charter was worth $30 billion and Fannie could earn far more with it than without it.

"Our business model…is a good one, so good that others want to 'take us out,'" the document said. Despite the "complexities (or even contradictions) of running a for-profit business with a public mission," there was value in having that policy role: "Our mission gives our work meaning and motivation."

COUNTRYWIDE, THE BIGGEST U.S. mortgage lender at the time, making or providing funding for roughly one in every six home mortgages, also expected to be one of the survivors of the housing and mortgage crisis. Wall Street analysts predicted that Countrywide would emerge stronger; weaker rivals were dying, leaving more of the market to Countrywide's vast loan-sales machine, stoked by stock options and commissions.

Countrywide's pugnacious CEO, Mozilo, got his start in the business at age fourteen as a messenger for a New York mortgage company. In 1969, when Mozilo was about thirty, he and a colleague set up their own mortgage company. Once his company was established as a nationwide financial powerhouse, Mozilo regularly reminded Wall Street analysts that he had been in the mortgage business for more than fifty years and knew all about the ups and downs. Because Countrywide was the biggest seller of loans to Fannie, Mudd and his colleagues needed to hope that Mozilo really did know what he was doing.

By mid-July 2007, even Countrywide was having trouble. A spike in mortgage defaults had reduced earnings. Like other lenders, Countrywide depended on short-term commercial paper borrowings to provide funds for new home loans, bridging the gap between the time Countrywide provided cash to the borrower and its sale of the loan to Fannie or some other investor. Now investors were fleeing the commercial paper market, depriving Countrywide of one of its main sources of funding.

Mozilo, then sixty-eight years old, had done well out of the housing and mortgage boom of the previous few years. In 2007, his base salary, bonus and equity-incentive pay amounted to $42 million. He reaped another $72 million by exercising stock options. With his deep golfer's tan and penchant for sharp suits, he had become the face of the mortgage industry on business TV programs.

Mozilo often referred to his rivals with contempt. In a conference call with investment analysts in 2007, he said the big Wall Street firms competing with Countrywide "didn't know anything about the mortgage business." He once dismissed efforts by rivals to gain tax advantages—by turning themselves into real-estate investment trusts—as akin to "putting lipstick on a pig." When I asked him about a proposal for shareholders to be allowed a nonbinding vote on executive compensation, he said shareholders had "no clue" how much Countrywide needed to pay to attract talent.

But some of the swagger was gone. In a July 24, 2007 conference call with analysts, Mozilo said that getting out of all the riskier types of loans before the housing market tanked "would have been an insight that only, I think, a superior spirit could have had at that time." Countrywide had not wanted to give up market share to other lenders willing to make those risky loans.

"Knowing what we know now," Mozilo said, "we would have done a lot of things differently....The fact is we didn't know."

In early August, Countrywide warned that "unprecedented disruptions" in credit markets would have an "unknown" effect on its business. Mozilo needed a savior. On August 22, Countrywide announced it had raised $2 billion by selling an equity stake to Bank of America.

WHILE COUNTRYWIDE STRUGGLED, FANNIE executives still hoped to be the saviors of the mortgage and housing markets. "This crisis came along and reminded people of one of the reasons we're around," Mudd told me in September 2007 as he had a lunch of soup and ginger ale in Fannie's employee cafeteria. (He was eating light as part of his training for a rowing race.) Fannie could keep providing money for home mortgages when other investors fled the market—the original reason for creating Fannie in 1938. Fannie had avoided the worst excesses in mortgage lending and now could "help sustain" the market, he said. Despite all the political pressures and market scares, he said, "it's fun to see this machine work and solve the problem it was built to do."

A few miles away, at Freddie's headquarters in the Washington suburb of McLean, Virginia, executives also were touting their role as rescuers. A note on Freddie's website, entitled "Shelter in a Storm," declared, "Even when other lenders stop lending, we continue to provide a steady source of home funding."

Fannie and Freddie were regaining their market dominance. Amid fears over falling house prices and surging defaults, Wall Street firms had grown much less willing and able to buy mortgages. So Countrywide and other lenders had to sell more of their loans to Fannie and Freddie. Among U.S. mortgage securities sold to investors in October 2007, 72 percent were guaranteed by Fannie or Freddie, up from 41 percent in 2005.

Other federal entities also were taking a bigger role in keeping money flowing into mortgages. Lenders were making more loans that met the standards of the Federal Housing Administration, so those loans could be insured by the FHA and put into government-guaranteed mortgage securities. After almost disappearing during the housing boom, FHA lending was hugely popular again. Investors now distrusted mortgage securities packaged by Wall Street but were still eager to buy government-backed securities.

Meanwhile, because Countrywide and other mortgage lenders could no longer raise money by selling commercial paper, they were turning to the Federal Home Loan Banks for short-term loans. By the end of September, Countrywide's borrowings from the Federal Home Loan Bank of Atlanta totaled $51 billion, up 77 percent from three months earlier.

Uncle Sam and his progeny—Fannie, Freddie, the FHA and the home loan banks—were rapidly taking over the mortgage business.

It soon became clear that the government-backed rescuers of the market might need some help themselves. In November 2007, Fannie reported a loss for the third quarter of $1.40 billion, and Freddie recorded a $2.03 billion loss. Those losses resulted largely from the need to make provisions for the expected cost of defaults as more homeowners drifted toward foreclosure. The companies were taking losses both on the mortgages they owned and on those held by other investors in the form of securities guaranteed by Fannie and Freddie.

Fannie and Freddie would need more capital, both to cover losses and to help prop up the housing market, as the Treasury and Congress wanted them to do. In mid-November, Fannie raised $500 million by selling preferred stock. Freddie then raised $6 billion by selling preferred shares in late November. In early December, Fannie sold more preferred to raise $7 billion. To preserve more capital, Fannie cut its quarterly dividend to thirty-five cents a share from fifty cents.

Selling preferred shares meant that a big chunk of future profits would go to the preferred holders rather than the owners of common shares. At an investor conference in December, Freddie's CEO, Syron, apologized to the common shareholders: "We wanted to dilute common shareholders like we wanted to shoot ourselves in the head with a gun."

Fannie and Freddie also raised the fees they charged to guarantee loans, forcing lenders in turn to charge higher mortgage interest rates and turn away more loan applicants who had low credit scores or couldn't afford substantial down payments. Lenders and some politicians, meanwhile, were pushing Fannie and Freddie to take more risks, in the hope that freer credit would bring buyers back to the housing market. "It's very important at this time for Fannie and Freddie to step up to the plate," Countrywide's Mozilo said at a mortgage conference in Washington in early December.

While Fannie and Freddie were stepping up to the plate, Mozilo was striking out. Countrywide's stock price was falling again as investors wondered whether it could survive, even with the $2 billion capital infusion it had received from Bank of America. Countrywide was stuck with billions of dollars of high-risk loans it couldn't sell to Fannie or anyone else.

Mozilo finally gave up and agreed in early January 2008 to sell the company for about $4 billion to Bank of America. (That was down from Countrywide's market value of $24 billion a year earlier, but it proved no bargain for Bank of America. The *Wall Street Journal* reported in July 2012 that the acquisition ended up costing Bank of America an additional $40 billion in real-estate losses, legal expenses and settlements with state and federal regulators.)

Countrywide was finished as an independent entity. The loans it had sold to Fannie would continue to fester for years.

By EARLY 2008, a general sense of impending disaster was spreading.

Congress and the Bush administration were prodding Fannie and Freddie to support the housing market by allowing more people to buy homes. One obstacle was that regulations limited the maximum size of loans they could buy or guarantee. The limit varied from one county to another, depending on the median housing cost for the area, but even in the highest-cost areas, such as California and New York City, the maximum loan size was $417,000—known as the "conforming loan limit." Mortgages above that level were called "jumbo loans."

The conforming loan limit was supposed to prevent Fannie and Freddie from financing homes for wealthy people. During the housing boom, however, prices rose so high in parts of the country that even a modest ranch home—the sort normally bought by middle-class people—could cost $500,000 or more.

For years, interest rates on jumbo loans had been only about a quarter to a half percentage point above those on so-called conforming loans, the ones backed by Fannie or Freddie. In 2007 and 2008, however, as private investors became wary of buying any loans that weren't backed by a government-related entity, rates on jumbos soared to a percentage point or more above the conforming rate. That made it harder to find buyers for homes costing more than $417,000, depressing the housing market further in California and other high-cost areas. Politicians from those areas demanded help.

In late January, the Bush administration and congressional leaders agreed to raise the conforming loan limit to $729,750 in the highest-cost areas. Aside from loans that could be backed by Fannie, Freddie or the FHA, the market had virtually dried up. People who couldn't qualify for those loans generally had to pay cash or give up on buying a home.

James Lockhart, the director of Ofheo, the regulator, had good news and bad news for Congress when he testified before the Senate Banking Committee on February 7, 2008: Fannie and Freddie had "become the dominant funding mechanism for the entire mortgage system in these troubling times. They are fulfilling their missions....In doing so, they have been reducing risks in the market, but concentrating mortgage risks on themselves."

Many in Washington thought Fannie and Freddie could do more, despite their precarious financial positions. Senator Schumer of New York wrote to Lockhart on February 25 to say that the companies should be encouraged to provide more funding for mortgages, particularly as a way to refinance borrowers who were "stuck in unaffordable loans."

In late February, Fannie reported a loss of $2.1 billion for 2007, and Freddie posted a loss of $3.1 billion. It was the first annual loss ever for Freddie and the first in twenty-two years for Fannie. Both companies were being forced to write down the value of their mortgage holdings and make provisions for losses on defaulting mortgages. Both were vastly underestimating those losses.

Despite the losses, Lockhart announced that he would remove the limits on the size of the companies' mortgage holdings that had been imposed by Ofheo as part of the penalty for their accounting-rule violations. He said Ofheo also would discuss an easing of another penalty applied after the accounting scandals: a requirement that they hold 30 percent more capital than the minimum specified by the 1992 legislation. This was known as a capital surcharge.

Fannie and Freddie were going to have more scope to expand. But could they justify taking on even more risk?

Michael A.J. Farrell, chief executive of Annaly Capital Management, a fund management firm in New York, said it was time for Fannie and

Freddie to serve their country, not their shareholders. He wrote an e-mail to Robert Steel, the Treasury's undersecretary for domestic finance, on March 6, 2008. Farrell was worried about the "dearth of buyers" for mortgage securities and the risk of "massive" sales of those securities by desperate investors who were being forced to repay creditors. He wanted some big buyers to come in and mop up the surplus mortgages that everyone was trying to unload. Fannie and Freddie seemed to be the biggest mops around. Farrell acknowledged that the shareholders of Fannie and Freddie might not like the idea but said, "From where I sit, the big picture is that right now whatever is best for the economy and the financial security of America trumps the ROI [return on investment] for Fannie and Freddie shareholders."

Others were starting to question whether Fannie and Freddie could survive. In its March 10 issue, the financial weekly *Barron's* ran a cover story entitled "Is Fannie Mae Toast?" by Jonathan R. Laing. The article suggested that the two companies "may soon be in need of a bailout." *Barron's* cited their growing losses on riskier types of mortgages and questioned the credibility of Fannie's balance sheet. For example, the balance sheet included $13 billion of deferred tax assets, or tax benefits that could be used in the future only if Fannie had earnings sufficient to create a large tax liability—something that was becoming less likely in the near future. If those assets were excluded, Fannie would fall short of its capital requirements.

The *Barron's* article also questioned Fannie's estimates for its liability to make good on guarantees of defaulted mortgages and the value it was putting on securities backed by subprime and Alt-A loans. "Fannie was clearly looking for love—and market share—in some of the wrong places," Laing wrote.

Most investors and Wall Street analysts weren't yet ready to believe that Fannie and Freddie would collapse. But there were growing fears that they would have to sell large amounts of shares to raise capital to cover their losses, diluting the value of previously issued shares. On the first trading day after the *Barron's* article, Fannie's stock dropped 13 percent on the New York Stock Exchange to $19.81. Freddie shares fell 12 percent to $17.39.

The Treasury and Ofheo both wanted Fannie and Freddie to raise more capital soon. Freddie's board was resisting. At a conference for investors on March 12, 2008, at the Hudson Theatre in Manhattan's Times Square, Freddie's CEO, Syron, promised to take care of his shareholders as well as the "mission" of supporting the housing market. "We expect to thrive to the benefit of our shareholders, and also for the benefit of the country," he said.

Ken Posner, then an analyst at Morgan Stanley, reminded him of his "fiduciary duty" to existing shareholders. "You would not raise capital unless you thought it would benefit existing shareholders," Posner said. "I just want to make sure I have got that right."

Syron replied, "You got it right."

Then, in an apparent allusion to pressure on him from regulators and lawmakers, he added, "This company will bow to no one…on our responsibility to shareholders." In the next few days, Syron got angry calls from Capitol Hill over that remark, which seemed at odds with the idea that Freddie had a public mission and a duty to the country as a whole, not just to its shareholders. He later conceded that he should have said Freddie would be "second to none" in meeting its fiduciary duties to shareholders.

THE SPOTLIGHT SHIFTED FROM Fannie and Freddie for a few days in March 2008 as it became clear that Bear Stearns, one of the Wall Street investment banks that had been most aggressive in creating and trading mortgage securities, was near collapse.

Like other investment banks, Bear depended on the willingness of its creditors to keep extending short-term loans to finance its trading positions. Now creditors were so worried about losses at Bear that they were forcing the bank either to put up more collateral or repay debts immediately. The Treasury and Federal Reserve were trying to find a way to prevent a bankruptcy at Bear and the risk that creditors would soon yank their money out of other big Wall Street firms. After a weekend of emergency talks, Treasury Secretary Henry Paulson and his colleagues arranged for J.P. Morgan Chase to acquire Bear, with financial help from the Federal Reserve to protect J.P. Morgan from the unfathomable risks in Bear's mortgage holdings.

As he recounted in his memoir, *On the Brink*, Paulson hoped that "some positive news from Fannie and Freddie" might help calm financial markets that had been rattled by the Bear fiasco. Paulson thought Fannie and Freddie were needed to avoid a complete drying up of funds for mortgage lending and further severe damage to the housing market and economy. "They more than anyone else were the engine we needed to get through the problem," he later told investigators for the Financial Crisis Inquiry Commission. Paulson prodded Steel, the Treasury undersecretary, to speed up efforts to reach a deal with Fannie, Freddie and Ofheo that would remove some of the companies' financial restrictions if they agreed to raise more capital.

Mudd, who had cultivated a good rapport with Steel, was eager to play along. In an e-mail to Steel in early March, Mudd sketched out the possibilities for a compromise and added: "It would be great for the markets, the government and the companies to link arms and get it done. I'll call. Best, Dan."

Mudd wanted to escape the regulator's "unrestricted" control over Fannie's capital, imposed at the time of the accounting scandal. The regulator, Lockhart, wanted assurances that Fannie and Freddie would raise enough capital. It would be "perverse," he wrote in a March 17 e-mail to Steel, for Fannie and Freddie to take even more credit risk "without any new capital."

Two days later, the Treasury, Ofheo, Fannie and Freddie announced their plan to calm the markets: Fannie and Freddie promised to raise "significant capital" and buy more mortgage securities in an attempt to drive down mortgage interest rates and spur the housing market. As a reward, their regulatory capital requirements would be loosened. Since the accounting scandals, Ofheo had demanded that Fannie and Freddie hold 30 percent more capital than their usual minimum levels. As part of the deal, Ofheo reduced that capital surcharge to 20 percent.

It was an odd compromise. The regulator was reducing the capital requirement while making the companies promise to raise more capital. But the companies wanted more flexibility for the future on capital. And the authorities wanted Fannie and Freddie to buy more mortgages immediately.

Fannie and Freddie relished the idea that the Bush administration was casting them in the role of saviors of the mortgage market. "Do a little examination and ask yourself, 'What do you think the housing market in the U.S. would look like without [Fannie and Freddie] now?'" Syron said at a press briefing.

The two companies also saw the chance to buy mortgage securities from others at bargain prices. "It's kind of a shopper's paradise right now," Mudd said.

Lockhart tried to knock down the idea that Fannie and Freddie were dangerously short of capital: "Let me be clear," he said in a press release, "both companies have prudent cushions above the Ofheo-directed capital requirements....We believe they can play an even more positive role in providing the stability and liquidity the markets need right now."

Not everyone was happy to see Fannie and Freddie taking on more risk. "I think it's a huge gamble on the back of the U.S. Treasury," said Senator Mel Martinez, a Republican from Florida.

In many parts of the country, home prices were dropping at frightening rates as foreclosures added to a glut of properties on the market. In some areas, including Las Vegas and San Diego, foreclosures accounted for more than 40 percent of all home sales in early 2008. Inside the city limits of Detroit, the average price for homes sold in the first two months of 2008 was $22,000, down 54 percent from a year earlier.

Some homes were almost worthless. At an auction of foreclosed homes in Pittsburgh in April 2006, a modest but structurally sound house, on which Citigroup had made a $33,600 subprime loan in 2001, was sold to an investor for $700—less than many people paid for a suit of clothing. Fannie owned 33,729 foreclosed homes at the end of 2007, up 34 percent from a year earlier. By the end of 2008, that total had nearly doubled to 63,538.

AFTER MOST OF THE damage had already been done, Fannie and Freddie in late 2007 and early 2008 were busily trying to tighten their standards. Fannie imposed a minimum credit score for borrowers. Both companies adjusted the prices they paid for various types of loans in a way that raised interest rates for borrowers. The National Association of Realtors denounced those loan-pricing adjustments as "a tax on homeownership," borrowing a phrase Fannie lobbyists had formerly used when politicians threatened to impose fees on Fannie.

Fannie's friends were angry. Unless Fannie and Freddie did more to support the housing market and prevent foreclosures, said Senator Schumer, "they're going to lose some of their supporters."

IN MAY 2008, AFTER reporting a loss of $2.19 billion for the first quarter and warning of more big losses ahead, Fannie began preparations to raise more capital. It ended up raising $7.40 billion through sales of new shares, fulfilling its March agreement with the Treasury and Ofheo. While Fannie was arranging those share sales, though, Lockhart gave a speech at a conference in Chicago, where he described Fannie and Freddie as "a point of vulnerability for the financial system" because their capital was meager in relation to their mortgage holdings and obligations.

WHILE FANNIE RAISED CAPITAL, Freddie dithered, and worries about the housing market grew. House prices had fallen so far by mid-2008 that about twelve million households, nearly one in six, owed more on their mortgage loans than their houses were worth, Moody's estimated. In other words, they were "under water."

People began wondering why they should bother even to try paying off those debts. In many circles, it was no longer considered unusual or unethical to be behind on payments or even to walk away from them. Neighborhoods recently considered desirable were becoming derelict as homes emptied and weeds sprouted. What could Americans depend on if they couldn't depend on real estate?

Congress wanted to find ways to help struggling borrowers refinance into loans they could afford. The problem was finding a way for the federal government to help without seeming to provide a federal bailout for irresponsible people who had borrowed too much. Yet again, Fannie and Freddie were going to come in handy in camouflaging the federal government's subsidies for housing.

In late May 2008, Republican Senator Shelby and his Democratic counterpart, Senator Dodd, came up with a compromise plan that would allow the Federal Housing Administration to insure $300 billion in refinanced loans for struggling homeowners. To quell fears that taxpayers would end up paying for defaults on these loans, the senators adopted a provision that would use fees paid by Fannie and Freddie to cover at least part of the cost for any losses on these FHA-insured loans. At the same time, the legislation would finally create a new, stronger regulator to keep Fannie and Freddie in line. On May 20, the Senate Banking Committee approved this plan with a 19–2 vote. Work began on reconciling the differences in the Senate plan with legislation earlier approved by the House.

BEFORE CONGRESS COULD FINISH this task, investors began wondering whether Fannie and Freddie could survive the summer. By late June, another large mortgage lender, IndyMac Bancorp, was on the brink of collapse. Then, on July 7, the share prices of Fannie and Freddie dropped more than 15 percent. By now, Fannie shares were down 76 percent from a year earlier, and Freddie shares had fallen 80 percent. One of the triggers for the July 7 drop was a report from analysts at Lehman Brothers discussing the possibility that changes in accounting rules could force Fannie and Freddie to raise tens of billions of dollars in new capital. More generally, investors were scared, and some were no longer entirely convinced that

Fannie and Freddie could avert a government rescue that would involve wiping out the value of private shareholders' equity.

The stocks recovered a bit the next day as Lockhart said accounting rules wouldn't determine capital requirements and made reassuring remarks about the capital Fannie already had raised and Freddie planned to round up. Soon, however, Fannie and Freddie shares were plunging anew.

"Regulators, government officials and others can say they have enough capital," said James Ellman, a hedge fund manager, "but Mr. Market doesn't believe it. The market is telling us that neither Fannie nor Freddie has enough capital to cover the projected losses." William Poole, a former president of the Federal Reserve Bank of St. Louis, further rattled the market by declaring in an interview with the Bloomberg news service that Fannie and Freddie were "insolvent."

The keepers of Freddie's corporate website had not caught up with this change in fortunes; the site still included this description of the company: "Freddie Mac operates in a single, safe business: residential mortgages backed by the equity of millions of American homes across the nation."

OFFICIALS IN THE BUSH administration were starting to make contingency plans to shore up Fannie and Freddie. Bear Stearns had not been allowed to fail. Surely Fannie and Freddie, far bigger and more central to the functioning of the U.S. economy, could not be allowed to fail—especially not when they were the main hope of keeping more than a trickle of money flowing into mortgages and preventing a complete collapse of house prices.

Treasury Secretary Paulson told President Bush he would need to ask Congress for power to put capital into Fannie and Freddie. "Although [Bush] disliked everything the GSEs [Fannie and Freddie] represented, he understood that we needed them to provide housing finance or we weren't going to get through the crisis," Paulson wrote in his memoir. "The first order of business, he said, was 'save their ass.'"

Over the weekend of July 12 and 13, the Treasury, the Federal Reserve and other regulators rushed to do just that. As they patched together a rescue plan, Paulson and his staff consulted with congressional leaders and the top executives of Fannie and Freddie. Buddy Piszel, chief financial officer of Freddie, was awakened by a call at 1:30 a.m. on Sunday from the company's chief legal officer, wanting to discuss the latest details.

At 6:00 p.m. on Sunday, just in time to calm nerves before the opening of financial markets in Asia on Monday morning, Paulson stood before television cameras on the steps of the Treasury, a granite Greek Revival palace, and announced a plan to ask Congress to give the Treasury temporary authority to provide loans or equity capital to Fannie and Freddie if needed to allow them to "continue to serve their mission." The Fed's Board of Governors, after a highly unusual Sunday afternoon meeting, voted unanimously to give the Federal Reserve Bank of New York authority to lend money to the companies if necessary.

Neither the Treasury nor the Fed specified how much money they might provide to Fannie and Freddie. Congressional leaders promised to act quickly to give the Treasury the authority it sought to bolster the companies' finances. "This could be on the president's desk next week," Representative Barney Frank said.

"Fannie Mae and Freddie Mac play a central role in our housing finance system and must continue to do so in their current form as shareholder-owned companies," Paulson said. The somewhat muddled message was that the government was backing up Fannie and Freddie but they were not being nationalized.

The Bush administration for years had tried to discourage the idea that the federal government stood behind the debt owed by Fannie and Freddie. Now, to avoid panic in the markets, it was trying to reinforce the implied government guarantee so they could continue to buy mortgages. The buyers of bonds and notes issued by Fannie and Freddie included banks and central banks around the world—institutions that the U.S. Treasury also relied on for its debt sales. As the world's biggest debtor, the United States could not afford to lose creditors' faith in its ability and willingness to repay even the debts of quasi-government entities like Fannie and Freddie.

But making sure they could pay their debts did not mean bailing out the shareholders of Fannie and Freddie. Their stock prices continued to fall the day after the weekend rescue package, though the rate of decline slowed.

Several days later, Paulson defended the plan before the Senate Banking Committee. Some senators questioned the wisdom of propping up Fannie and Freddie. "Some of us don't like the idea of an unlimited sum of federal dollars backstopping" Fannie and Freddie, said Senator Bunning.

Paulson argued that it was better to avoid saying exactly how much money the government might make available to support Fannie and Freddie. It was more "confidence-inspiring" to leave that ultimate level of possible support unspecified, he said.

"If you've got a squirt gun in your pocket," the Treasury secretary explained, "you may have to take it out. If you've got a bazooka, and people know you've got it, you may not have to take it out."

Senator Shelby was worried that the Treasury was going to "go easy on the GSEs and just prop them up, regardless of their problems," Paulson later wrote. He recalled assuring Senator Shelby, "You don't know me, Senator. If I find a problem, I'm going to deal with it. I'm a tough guy."

The executives of Fannie and Freddie had been given a reprieve. With reinforced government backing, they could continue to operate. But they had lost control of their destinies. In the event that emergency federal funding was provided, Representative Frank said, the CEO of Fannie or Freddie would have to consult the government on everything, even "before it can pay its water bill for the toilet." When I asked Freddie's CEO, Syron, about that comment, he said he hoped to avoid seeking government funds: "I'm kind of partial to indoor plumbing."

FINALLY, AFTER FIVE YEARS of delays and desultory debate, Congress in late July passed housing legislation that included the creation of a more powerful regulator for Fannie and Freddie. As is often the case in Congress, it took a crisis to force the compromises necessary to finish legislation. The Housing and Economic Recovery Act of 2008, signed into law by President Bush on July 30, authorized the Treasury to provide funding for Fannie and Freddie, giving Paulson the "bazooka" he sought. It also created a new regulator, the Federal Housing Finance Agency, to replace Ofheo. This new agency had more powers to set minimum capital requirements for Fannie and Freddie. Lockhart, who had headed Ofheo, now was the top official at the new regulatory agency, known as the FHFA.

The law also clarified the regulator's powers to take over the management of the companies through either a conservatorship or a receivership, leaving a large amount of discretion to the regulator to determine whether that was necessary.

FANNIE AND FREDDIE SCRAMBLED to deal with both their own problems and the shattered finances of millions of homeowners whose mortgage loans the companies owned or guaranteed. In late July, they increased the fees paid to loan servicers as incentives to arrange modifications of loan terms or take other steps to avert foreclosures. (Loan servicers are companies, often owned by banks, that collect payments and handle defaults and foreclosures, among other administrative tasks.) Fannie and Freddie gave servicers more time to work out agreements to lower payments for struggling borrowers.

In what looked like desperation, Fannie in some cases was financing new loans to delinquent borrowers so they could catch up on their mortgage bills. Under this HomeSaver Advances program, people were essentially borrowing from Peter to repay Paul. Before the program was abandoned in 2010, Fannie had financed 115,357 HomeSaver Advances. These loans were not backed by any collateral.

In some cases, these foreclosure-prevention efforts were giving a chance to borrowers who might still be able to save their homes. In many cases, though, Fannie and Freddie were merely delaying the inevitable. Most of the troubled borrowers were facing more than a temporary cash-flow squeeze. Incomes had fallen. Jobs had been lost. Divorces and disease had changed circumstances. House values had plummeted. Loans that once seemed plausible now looked like fantasy.

About 70 percent of the borrowers who got help through the HomeSaver Advance program quickly defaulted again, according to the FHFA's report on Fannie for 2008. As of the end of 2008, Fannie reported that it had $461 million of these unsecured HomeSaver loans on its books. Fannie declined to say how many were ever repaid.

In early August 2008, Freddie reported a loss of $821.0 million for the second quarter and said the "fair value" of its net assets was a negative $5.6 billion as of June 30. In other words, the estimated market value of its assets was below estimated liabilities. Some would consider Freddie broke. But Freddie officials argued that the negative number merely reflected the temporarily distressed state of the mortgage market.

Freddie also said it aimed to raise at least $5.5 billion through sales of new common and preferred shares—but would wait for market conditions to improve. "There's no need for us to rush," said Piszel, Freddie's chief financial officer.

A few days later, Fannie reported a far bigger second-quarter loss: $2.3 billion. Like Freddie, Fannie said it expected further losses. Fannie also said it might need to raise more capital. Falling home prices were increasing losses on each mortgage default. "The housing market has returned to Earth fast and hard," Mudd said.

In one sign of the times, Credit Suisse in June 2008 sold a 1,230-square-foot home in Corona, California, that the bank had acquired through foreclosure. The sale price was $198,000, down from $450,000 when the same house was sold just eighteen months earlier.

The market value of foreclosed homes dwindled day by day. As long as it owned a foreclosed property, Fannie had to pay for such expenses as taxes, insurance and lawn care. Frequently, thieves broke into vacant foreclosed homes to rip out copper wiring and other items that could be sold. Mold oozed across walls; backyard pools turned to swamps. Damage and vandalism further reduced the value of homes, often by tens of thousands of dollars.

Both Fannie and Freddie wanted to raise more capital. But potential buyers of new stock feared those shares would be worthless if the Treasury had to rescue the companies. Throughout August, Mudd and his colleagues were pleading for assurances that the Treasury would provide capital if needed but would do so in a way that would protect the value of existing shares and other securities.

"The market kind of needs to know what the program is," Mudd told me later. He thought he had a good dialogue going with senior people in the Treasury—that there was mutual understanding of the situation. But he could not get any clear answers.

What Mudd did not know—what almost nobody knew—was that the Treasury and the Fed were preparing for an imminent government takeover of Fannie and Freddie.

FANNIE AND FREDDIE STILL had more capital than the minimum set by the regulatory standards dating to 1992, according to their own accounting. But accounting rules allow for fallible human judgment, and the regulatory standard was flawed. Treasury Secretary Paulson wanted to know the true state of their affairs.

Nearly all the Wall Street investment analysts who followed Fannie and Freddie had failed to predict that they would be in such a perilous condition. Even so, Paulson decided the Treasury staff needed to hire expertise from Wall Street to dig more deeply into their books. He hired a venerable Wall Street investment bank, Morgan Stanley.

In late July, Morgan Stanley provided a team of about forty people, headed by Ruth Porat and Robert Scully, to determine whether the companies were solvent and what could be done to shore them up. Some of the Morgan Stanley people were based in Mumbai, India, where they could run computer analyses of Fannie and Freddie data while their colleagues in America slept. The bankers demanded large amounts of data from Fannie and Freddie—and in some cases were surprised by the companies' apparent difficulty in finding that data.

Many of the Morgan Stanley bankers set up temporary headquarters in a Treasury conference room across the hall from Paulson's office. Paulson—fueled with Diet Coke, jittery, bursting with ideas and questions—frequently popped in to talk with the Wall Street crew.

The number crunching, analysis and spinning of scenarios went on late into the evenings and through the weekends. Porat had to make excuses to her family. She assured them she was doing vital work for the nation. "Mommy is saving America," her youngest son commented.

The Morgan Stanley team didn't discover clear-cut accounting improprieties but did find that the companies' assumptions about future losses were far too optimistic. One big problem was that potential future tax credits—items carried on the balance sheet as assets—would need to be written off because the companies wouldn't have profits in the near future. Fannie and Freddie also had been too optimistic about how much they could recover from mortgage insurers, companies that sold insurance against losses on defaults. "I think there was a kind of a hope-and-a-prayer management style," a member of the investigating team said later.

At the start of the process, the expectation was that Fannie and Freddie could still raise large amounts of money from private investors, perhaps including so-called sovereign wealth funds, investment pools run by foreign governments on behalf of their citizens. Within about two weeks, however, the Morgan Stanley bankers believed that the losses at Fannie and Freddie would be so immense that money available from private investors wouldn't be enough. "We concluded that the capital hole was so big that we couldn't plug it with private money," Scully told me later.

Private investors who over the past year had put money into Fannie and Freddie already had lost huge sums as their stock prices sank near zero. Morgan Stanley bankers sounded out large investors by telephone on their interest in buying new shares in Fannie or Freddie. The smart money was no longer interested.

Without a capital injection from the government, the Morgan Stanley team concluded, Freddie would be insolvent in the fourth quarter of 2008 and Fannie in the first quarter of 2009.

PAULSON FELT PRESSURE TO find a solution soon. The housing market would collapse without money for mortgage lending. Officials of foreign governments and central banks were calling their counterparts at the Fed and the Treasury to demand clarity. Did Uncle Sam stand behind those debts or not? The ambiguity of an implied guarantee was no longer good enough. Most of the big foreign investors had already stopped buying bonds and notes issued by Fannie and Freddie. Without greater assurances of government backing, they would soon be selling the debt they still owned at whatever price the market would offer. That could set off a crash that would destroy confidence in financial markets around the world.

Amid all this anxiety, Paulson went on vacation. In early August, he and his family flew to China to see the sights, learn tai chi and watch part of the Summer Olympics, where the American swimmer Michael Phelps was making history by winning eight gold medals. At the Great Wall, Paulson gashed his bald head on a low ceiling while walking through a guard tower. He found time for phone calls with his staff in Washington and for meetings with Chinese officials, who wanted to know what was up with Fannie and Freddie. Paulson assured them, as he later wrote, "that everything would be all right."

When he returned to Washington on August 15, Paulson felt it was time to fulfill that promise to the Chinese. He was unwilling to give in to the pleas from Fannie and Freddie for assurances to private investors that it would be safe to put more equity into the companies. That would cement the notion that the shareholders of Fannie and Freddie were protected by the government. Paulson was willing to take action to protect holders of Fannie and Freddie debt, including China's central bank. But he was not going to save the shareholders. Owners of a company are supposed to lose their investment when the company fails.

All this meant there would be no new capital from private investors; now it was only a question of how the Treasury would provide capital. It would not be politic to tell American voters that the government was providing billions of dollars so that the executives of Fannie and Freddie could carry on with business as usual. The money would have to be made available as part of a new order of business.

That left two options under the recently approved federal housing legislation. One was receivership, the legal process of selling off a company's assets to repay debts and going out of business. The other was conservatorship, a legal process that would allow the regulator to seize control of the company from its board of directors and run it as a going concern.

Receivership was more appealing to those with a strong ideological aversion to quasi-government entities like Fannie and Freddie. Receivership would eliminate the companies, and it would be hard for Congress to bring them back after such an ignominious ending. Paulson initially thought receivership was the answer. But his advisers warned that receivership would frighten the markets. Creditors would demand immediate guarantees that they would be repaid. Companies that had entered into interest-rate swaps and other complex hedging agreements with Fannie and Freddie would need to know whether those obligations would be honored and, if so, exactly how. "We felt it would scare the hell out of the market," Lockhart said later.

Under receivership, the main providers of funding for home mortgages would be going out of business at a time when private money for mortgages had dried up. The country might have to struggle through a period of months or even years with only small amounts of private money available to finance house purchases. The housing market would be dependent on cash buyers. The Bush administration would have to explain how it was going to make sure mortgage lending would continue without Fannie and Freddie. There was no obvious alternative to them that could be conjured right away.

These fears quickly steered the internal discussion among the Treasury, Fed and White House toward conservatorship. Conservatorship would allow Fannie and Freddie to keep operating, under government control, while politicians pondered what kind of mortgage-finance system eventually would replace them. It was a way of leaving that headache for the next administration.

On August 19, Paulson informed Fed chairman Ben Bernanke of the conservatorship plan. Bernanke endorsed it. Paulson initially hoped to put the companies into conservatorship by September 1. But there wouldn't be time to get everything ready in August. Lawyers brought in from the New York firm of Wachtell, Lipton, Rosen & Katz would have to prepare stacks of documents. Lockhart's regulatory agency, now called the FHFA, would have to make the legal case that conservatorship was necessary.

There was another delicate problem: for all his powers as Treasury secretary and even with his "bazooka," Paulson lacked the legal authority to put Fannie and Freddie under government control. Only the FHFA had that authority. Paulson had to persuade Lockhart that conservatorship was the best solution—and had to happen very soon.

Like Paulson, Lockhart wanted a vacation. In mid-August, he flew to Nantucket Island, off Massachusetts, where his family went every summer. Once there, he found he was spending most of his time on the phone with

Treasury officials and others involved in the crisis. After a day, he gave up on the vacation and flew back to Washington. There was an awkward moment when he bumped into the Mudd family in an airport.

Paulson felt that the FHFA was moving too slowly toward embracing conservatorship. But Lockhart was in an uncomfortable spot because the FHFA and its predecessor agency, Ofheo, had regularly stated that Fannie and Freddie met their capital requirements. Only five months earlier, in March, Lockhart and Paulson had agreed that the minimum capital requirement for Fannie and Freddie should be reduced slightly to allow the companies to support the housing market by buying more mortgages. Now they were saying Fannie and Freddie did not have enough capital. It would require a bit of explaining.

Lockhart said later that the FHFA needed time to develop a justification for such a drastic solution: "We needed to make sure we had a strong case," one that could stand up in court. He wanted to avoid the risk of a messy court battle with Fannie or Freddie should one or both be inclined to resist. Lockhart expected that Freddie would capitulate without much fuss. He was less sure about Fannie, which "had always been more aggressive, more pushing back." Although Mudd had started his term as CEO by making a priority of improving relations with the regulator, he later chafed under Lockhart's direction. Mudd "felt we were trying to micromanage him more than we should," Lockhart said.

In late August, FHFA officials began compiling long lists of the sins and omissions of Fannie and Freddie. A thirty-page "confidential memorandum" to Lockhart from Christopher Dickerson, a senior FHFA official, made the case for putting Fannie into conservatorship. A similar document was prepared for Freddie.

The main justification for conservatorship was a simple judgment, and one that proved correct: the capital held by Fannie and Freddie—though technically meeting the minimum standard set by regulations—would not be enough to cover losses from mortgage defaults.

The FHFA could make only a very rough estimate of the damage. The memo from Dickerson projected that losses at Fannie in 2008 would be somewhere between $18 billion and $50 billion. Fannie's "ability to pay its obligations as they come due is subject to question," the memo said with splendid understatement.

The memo, essentially an indictment of Fannie's management, was clumsily drafted but damning. Among the accusations:

- Fannie had been "imprudent" and "unwise" in its heavy purchases of Alt-A loans in 2006 and 2007, taking on much more risk without having computer models capable of measuring that risk. Fannie itself disclosed in a quarterly SEC filing that "certain higher risk loan types, such as Alt-A loans, interest-only loans, loans to borrowers with low credit scores and loans with high loan-to-value ('LTV') ratios, many of which were originated in 2006 and 2007, represented approximately 29% of our single-family conventional mortgage credit book of business as of June 30, 2008." But the true percentage of high-risk loans was probably higher because there was no standard definition of subprime or Alt-A in the industry. Fannie's practice was to classify as prime all loans that the original lender called prime, even if those loans were riskier than what many people would consider prime. This practice appears to have masked the degree to which Fannie had lowered its standards.
- Some of the models used to assess potential losses relied on historical experience from the 1990s, when mortgage-lending standards were more conservative and house prices had not yet soared to unsustainable levels. The models "assumed a much healthier economic environment than exists currently."
- "Early warning reports that showed poor performance of new mortgage products, such as Alt-A mortgages, were ignored."
- Fannie's reporting on its Alt-A holdings was "inadequate and incomplete." In 2006, Fannie changed its internal definition of Alt-A loans and reclassified $10 billion of Alt-A loans as "prime."
- Fannie was inconsistent in its demands for lenders to buy back loans that fell short of quality standards. Some lenders had to take back bad loans faster than others. Countrywide, by far the biggest seller of loans to Fannie, was given more time, and a huge backlog of faulty Countrywide loans built up in Fannie's portfolio. "Countrywide's repurchases were allowed to backlog for years," the memo stated.
- The restatement of earnings had consumed "enormous resources, limiting the Enterprise's ability to make progress in other much-needed areas."
- Oversight of the company by the board and management was "inadequate," leading to a "myriad of unsafe or unsound practices."

While the FHFA staff was drafting this indictment, the Treasury's Ken Wilson was sounding out candidates to take over the CEO jobs at Fannie and Freddie. One of Wilson's calls was to Herbert Allison, who had retired a few months earlier as head of TIAA-CREF, the teachers' pension fund manager. Allison had promised his wife he would not go back to full-time work. When his cellphone rang, he was having lunch with her on a verandah at Caneel Bay on the Caribbean island of St. John. Wilson explained that the government would need to appoint new chief executives at Fannie and Freddie. He wondered if Allison would be interested. Half an hour later, Treasury Secretary Paulson called to urge Allison to accept.

Allison knew little about Fannie, other than that it was in serious financial trouble. "I didn't have any time to deliberate, so I made a decision on the phone," he told me. "I felt that saying no was not an option."

MUDD, STILL UNAWARE HE was about to be fired, had not given up hope of persuading the Treasury to provide reassurances about the future that might allow Fannie to raise more capital and fight on. He suggested to Treasury officials that they might announce exactly how they would put money into the company when needed—for instance, up to $2 billion or so in a combination of common stock, preferred stock, mortgage-backed securities and debt. Treasury officials listened politely but were noncommittal.

Some members of Fannie's board were growing restive. They wanted to keep Mudd in place, at least for the time being, but replace some of his subordinates to see if performance might improve. Mudd resisted. Stephen Ashley, the board chairman, visited him at home one evening to press the case for a purge of the top ranks.

On August 27, Fannie announced the departures of Robert Levin, a twenty-seven-year veteran who was chief business officer, and two executives who had joined within the past two years: Stephen Swad, who was chief financial officer, and Dallavecchia, the chief risk officer. Fannie promoted Peter Niculescu to chief business officer. Niculescu, a native of New Zealand who spoke with quiet authority, had joined Fannie in 1999 after working as a top bond-market analyst and strategist for Goldman Sachs. There was some concern he might jump ship if he wasn't promoted.

The decision to push out Levin, who was popular and respected within Fannie, was troubling to many people inside the company. Mudd regretted the bloodletting, which turned out to be a futile exercise: "I put bullets in three or four people I know and like," he told me long afterward.

But there was no allowance for such sentiment at the end of August. After announcing the management changes, Mudd, in marine mode, wrote in a memo to employees: "Now it is time to pull on our boots and march out of this mess."

Shortly after the new management lineup was announced, Fannie Chairman Ashley paid a visit to Lockhart at the FHFA. Ashley came away with the sense that the regulator was comfortable with Fannie's management. On August 22, the FHFA issued a letter stating that Fannie and Freddie had adequate levels of capital. The Treasury—furious about this contradiction with the already advanced plans to declare the companies financial disaster areas in need of a government rescue—demanded a retraction. On September 1, the regulator informed Fannie and Freddie that it had suspended that August 22 letter.

The FHFA told the companies it was taking another look at the adequacy of their reserves. Three days later, on September 4, the FHFA sent Fannie and Freddie letters containing the long lists of their failings that it had quickly compiled. Those letters did not mention conservatorship and left Mudd and his colleagues baffled about what was up.

That same day, Paulson informed President Bush of the plan to take over Fannie and Freddie. "We're going to move quickly and take them by surprise," Paulson later recalled telling the president. "The first sound they'll hear is their heads hitting the floor." The Treasury secretary believed he had to keep the companies in the dark. If they had been given advance word, "the news would leak, and they'd fight. They'd go to their many powerful friends on Capitol Hill or to the courts, and the resulting delays would cause panic in the markets."

Though many in the Bush administration would have liked to use this occasion to give Fannie and Freddie a death sentence with no appeal, Paulson was pragmatic. He didn't want an ideological fight with Congress just then about how the government should support housing over the long run. "The last thing we want to start right now is a holy war," he told the president. Instead, he would describe the conservatorship as "a time-out," leaving it to future administrations and Congresses to sort out the ultimate fate of Fannie and Freddie. This call for a time-out implied that the children had been naughty while the adults weren't looking. In reality, the adults had been negligent for most of the previous seven decades.

Finally, on September 5, a Friday, the top executives of Fannie and Freddie were summoned to the FHFA's headquarters for separate meetings. The Fannie executives were seated in a conference room across from Paulson, Bernanke and Lockhart. Lockhart was the first to speak. He presented the case for taking management control of Fannie through conservatorship, as summarized in the FHFA memo. The balding, dark-haired regulator, his face stern and gaunt, seemed nervous as he read a script, and his hands trembled, according to several people who were at the meeting. Lockhart made clear that the services of Mudd and most of the Fannie board would no longer be needed.

Paulson, reading from notes on a yellow pad, was cordial. He explained that the Treasury would provide capital, as much as $100 billion, to allow Fannie to cope with growing, and unpredictable, losses. The credibility of the U.S. government with foreign investors was at stake. Bernanke chimed in briefly to say the takeover was for the good of the economy.

Mudd put his head between his hands. Paulson later recalled him as "scowling and sneering" and shaking his head. When he was able to speak, Mudd protested that Fannie had been cooperating with the Treasury and Fed in trying to support the housing market and that his team had done everything that had been asked of it. Paulson felt sympathy for Mudd and agreed that he had been cooperative. But the Treasury secretary refused to negotiate. There were two choices, he explained. Fannie's board could accept government control within twenty-four hours or the government would impose it anyway.

"We have the grounds to do this on an involuntary basis," Paulson said, "and we will go that course if needed." Paulson insisted that the government's seizure of Fannie and Freddie wasn't "political" and that the fault lay with the hybrid public-private nature of the companies, not with their executives.

Mudd still wasn't quite ready to surrender. "Our board will want to take a close look at this," he said. Richard Alexander, an outside legal counsel for the FHFA, replied, "I need you to understand that when these gentlemen [Lockhart and Paulson] come to your board meeting tomorrow, it's not to have a dialogue."

ON SATURDAY, SEPTEMBER 6, Fannie's board met to hear the ultimatum directly from Paulson and Lockhart. After some debate about what would be an appropriate place for such a meeting, the organizers arranged to use a dreary, windowless basement room in a building that had housed part of the FHFA.

Ashley, the Fannie board chairman, asked what Paulson and Lockhart had expected the board and management to do beyond what they had done.

He got no clear answer, Ashley told me later. Some of the Fannie directors and executives believed that the conservatorship wasn't necessary and that they were being dragged into it because of Freddie's problems.

In the afternoon, after Paulson and Lockhart had left, the board debated how it should address its fiduciary responsibilities to shareholders.

Bart Harvey, former CEO of the Enterprise Foundation, a nonprofit organization that supported housing projects for low-income people, had joined Fannie's board just two weeks before. He understood the bind that the government was in. As Harvey later put it, "when the Chinese say, 'We're going to be net sellers [of your debt securities],' you're cooked."

But cooked exactly how? The board members went through the motions of considering every conceivable way of avoiding conservatorship. The meeting extended into the late afternoon. An aide to Lockhart called to press for quicker action. The board sputtered on. Directors raised the possibility of going to court and seeking a temporary restraining order against the regulators. But there was a consensus that trying to fight the federal government in court was futile. How could Fannie continue to borrow money in the debt markets in such a situation? Who would lend to a company that was defying Uncle Sam? "It would have been a nightmare," Ashley said later. The board capitulated. It let Secretary Paulson have things his way. There was really no other choice.

The mood was somber, Harvey said. Fannie, he believed, had been "a good soldier, trying to do the right thing" to support a collapsing real estate market. But, he said, buying the Alt-A loans in large quantities had been a "bad management decision."

After the Saturday board meetings, Mudd told his secretary to pack up the personal effects in his office, which included a framed cartoon from the *Wall Street Journal* depicting Mudd as a besieged marine defending the Fannie Mae headquarters from its enemies. He went home and had two or three glasses of wine with his wife.

Sometimes even a marine has no option other than retreat. Mudd said in a 2009 speech that "we were given 24 hours to accede to a government takeover—or else the government would effectively go to war against the company." In the same speech, he noted that he was promoted to CEO in late 2004 "with a mandate to restate the financials and change the political tone. We got that done—just in time for the housing crisis of the century."

ON SUNDAY, SEPTEMBER 7, the Treasury and FHFA publicly announced the details of the conservatorship. The Treasury agreed to provide as much as $100 billion of capital to each company. In return, the Treasury would acquire senior preferred stock paying dividends at a 10.0 percent annual rate. The companies also gave the Treasury warrants allowing it to acquire for a nominal sum as much as 79.9 percent of their common shares. The figure of 79.9 percent was chosen because at 80.0 percent, accounting rules would have put Fannie and Freddie obligations onto the government balance sheet.

These provisions effectively wiped out all or nearly all the value of common shares already issued. For years, any profits Fannie or Freddie might make would have to be turned over to the Treasury in the form of dividends; there was little hope that any crumbs would be left over for common shareholders. The common shares soon dropped to less than one dollar. Fannie and Freddie, once blue chips, had become penny stocks, the ultimate humiliation.

The selection of $100 billion as the maximum amount of Treasury investment in each company was little more than a guess of what they might require. Within about six months, in February 2009, the Obama administration had raised the limit to $200 billion for each company. Then, on December 24, 2009, the administration announced that the two companies would have unlimited access to bailout money through 2012. The belief in the markets was that the total cost of bailing out the two companies probably would not exceed $200 billion apiece—already a staggering sum— but that holders of their debt would be reassured by the knowledge that Uncle Sam would make sure Fannie and Freddie could pay off their debts no matter how immense their losses became.

The timing of this adjustment to the bailout was important. A provision in the September 2008 conservatorship agreement allowed the Treasury to make amendments in the agreement until December 31, 2009. After that, the Treasury would have had to seek Congressional approval. That might have ignited a fight in Congress over whether to limit the bailout and, if so, how.

There were predictable, and futile, fulminations from Congress. "The timing of this executive order giving Fannie and Freddie a blank check is no coincidence," said Representative Spencer Bachus of Alabama, then the ranking Republican on the House Financial Services Committee. He said the Christmas Eve announcement was designed "to prevent the general public from taking note."

For its part, the Treasury said the removal of the limits on the bailout was "necessary for preserving the continued strength and stability of the mortgage market."

The ultimate cost of the bailout is uncertain as of this writing and will depend on how much money Fannie and Freddie lose on the worst wave of mortgage defaults since the 1930s. As of mid-2012, the Treasury had injected about $93.5 billion into Fannie and $53 billion into Freddie through purchases of preferred stock to keep them solvent. (Those numbers are net of dividends paid by the companies to the Treasury.)

ON THE MONDAY MORNING after the Sunday announcement of the government's takeover, Allison arrived for work as the new CEO of Fannie. Unlike his predecessors, he did not have to worry about producing ever-higher earnings for shareholders. His mission was to keep money flowing into mortgages in a way that would help revive the housing market and the entire U.S. economy, by now in a severe recession that pushed the unemployment

Realtors hired young people to tout cheap homes along a highway in Maricopa, Arizona, in early 2009. *Photo by James R. Hagerty.*

rate about 10 percent. Another challenge was to recruit people to work at a company whose future was deeply uncertain.

As Allison explained it to me in an interview a few months later, Fannie's role was no longer "about maximizing returns on equity or profits. It's really about being of use to the country during a very difficult period."

Defining the mission remained tricky. How could Fannie be of most use to the nation? By extending mortgage credit to more people to fuel demand for housing, even at the risk of creating further losses? By forgiving principal for people whose homes were no longer worth anything near what they owed? Or by enforcing strict standards for mortgage lending to hold losses—and the taxpayer-funded bailout—to a minimum? In 2012, regulators and members of Congress were still bickering over the extent to which Fannie and Freddie should reduce loan balances to help struggling borrowers.

THE RESCUE OF FANNIE and Freddie announced on September 7, 2008, was supposed to be a bold government stroke that restored calm and order to the financial markets. It did not work out that way. Within days, Lehman Brothers, a major Wall Street investment bank that had gambled on mortgages and real estate, collapsed into bankruptcy. The government then felt compelled to rescue a giant insurance company, American International Group, which had a hideously complex web of financial obligations to companies and investors around the world and was deemed too big and important to fail. By the end of the year, the government had also agreed to provide bailout funds to General Motors, Chrysler and the country's biggest banks. Fannie and Freddie were part of a general crisis of confidence.

The conservatorship failed to persuade investors in the debt of Fannie and Freddie that they were certain to be repaid in full. One problem was that the Treasury agreement to provide capital specified that this rescue was "not intended and shall not be deemed to constitute a guarantee" by the U.S. government of those debts. Unlike a Treasury bond, a bond issued by Fannie or Freddie still was not legally backed by the full faith and credit of the U.S. government.

Investors and investment analysts generally believed that the government would never let Fannie or Freddie default. Yet the new conservatorship arrangement left a sliver of ambiguity over the degree of financial backing they had. As a result, their borrowing costs remained higher than usual. That meant they had less ability than the government had hoped to provide money to U.S. mortgage borrowers at low interest rates.

Interest costs for mortgage borrowers depended partly on how much Fannie and Freddie had to pay to their creditors. In the initial days after imposition of the conservatorships, the average cost for thirty-year fixed-rate mortgages fell below 6.0 percent, making home purchases more affordable. Then markets grew jittery again, pushing up borrowing costs for Fannie and Freddie and in turn raising costs for mortgage borrowers. By mid-October, the average mortgage rate was around 6.6 percent. Government officials began to fear that the takeover of Fannie and Freddie wouldn't meet one of the biggest objectives: keeping mortgage credit cheap.

Lockhart, the regulator, tried to reassure investors that they could buy Fannie and Freddie debt with no fear of loss. At a mortgage bankers' convention in San Francisco in October, he said the government *effectively* had guaranteed the companies' debts. After his speech, he told me, "The U.S. government will be behind them short, medium and long term."

Later in October, Lockhart said during testimony in Congress that there was an "explicit" government guarantee on the debt of Fannie and Freddie. He then was forced to issue a clarification, saying there was only an "effective" guarantee. Amid the confusion, Fannie and Freddie had to pay more for their debt again.

Finally, money talked. The Federal Reserve announced in late November that it would buy as much as $600 billion of debt issued by Fannie, Freddie and the Federal Home Loan Banks to drive down their borrowing costs. Mortgage rates for consumers soon fell below 6 percent again.

Yet even $600 billion can only speak so loud. The housing market still did not recover. No matter how low mortgage rates were, many people who would have liked to buy homes could not do so; they were unemployed or so burdened by debt that they couldn't qualify for mortgages. Meanwhile, banks were throwing more foreclosed homes back onto the market every day.

Uncle Sam had shot all his bullets, and it still wasn't enough. Years later, the housing market remained depressed. On average across the United States, home prices as of March 2012 were 35 percent down from the peak level of mid-2006, according to the S&P/Case-Shiller composite price index. The declines were steepest in areas such as Florida, Arizona, Nevada and California, where prices had soared the highest during the boom. By March 2012, average prices had dropped about 49 percent in the Miami metro area, 53 percent in Phoenix and 62 percent in Las Vegas, where they were back to 1996 levels.

More than half of the real estate wealth of American households was gone. They had about $6.2 trillion of equity in their homes at the end of

2011, down from $13.2 trillion six years earlier, according to Federal Reserve data. That left most people feeling poorer and disinclined to spend.

Nearly 1.0 million households lost their homes to foreclosure or related actions in 2008, up from 430,000 in 2007, according to an estimate by Mark Zandi, chief economist at Moody's Analytics. (Those related actions were mostly short sales, in which homes are sold for less than the loan balance due, leaving the former owner to walk away with nothing.) The number of lost homes was 1.5 million in 2009 and 1.4 million in 2010, Zandi estimated.

About 23 percent of all households with mortgages were under water, owing more than the current value of their homes at the end of 2011, according to an estimate by CoreLogic, a mortgage data firm. That meant many people couldn't sell their homes and move without taking crippling losses. This predicament marooned homeowners who might otherwise have decamped to areas with better job markets.

With a glut of foreclosed homes on the market, construction of new homes fell to the lowest levels since the 1950s. Construction was started on just 445,000 new single-family houses in 2009, about a quarter of the peak level in 2005.

As disastrous as the results were for Fannie and Freddie, the loans financed by Wall Street did even worse. Fannie and Freddie had a lock on loans to the better-quality or "prime" borrowers, so Wall Street focused mainly on loans to riskier borrowers. The FHFA found that 16 percent of single-family mortgages acquired by Fannie and Freddie from 2001 through 2008 were made to borrowers with credit scores below 660 (on the scale of 300 to 850). For the so-called private label market, in which Wall Street firms packaged loans into securities, 53 percent of the loans had credit scores below 660. The Fannie and Freddie loans also tended to involve larger down payments.

About 10 percent of the adjustable-rate loans financed by Fannie and Freddie during this period were ninety days or more delinquent at some point before the end of 2009, the FHFA found. For the Wall Street loans, that figure was 30 percent.

Fannie and Freddie were heavily exposed to the Wall Street poison, however, because they had been avid buyers of the mortgage securities packaged by Wall Street. In September 2011, the FHFA filed lawsuits against seventeen investment banks and other financial institutions involved in creating those securities, alleging that they had failed to disclose the risks adequately. The suits alleged, among other things, that the banks creating these securities routinely included in them loans that had been identified by independent monitoring firms as failing to meet quality standards.

Heavy job losses during the 2008–09 recession left about one in five homes vacant in Muncie, Indiana. *Photo by Lisa Xing.*

In any case, the government ended up holding most of the risk. By mid-2010, Fannie, Freddie and the FHA were responsible for the credit risk on 68 percent of all U.S. home mortgages outstanding. They had become "the mortgage industry's wastebasket for toxic mortgage debt," noted a report from *Canfield Press*.

Their share of this rotten pie kept growing. In the years immediately following the financial panic of 2008, Fannie, Freddie and the FHA were carrying the default risk on around 90 percent of all newly granted home-mortgage loans—a level of government involvement that was hard to reconcile with America's vision of itself as a free-enterprise society with minimal government involvement in business. Effectively, the United States had nationalized the business of providing funds and insurance for mortgage lending.

There was one sign of progress: fewer people in Washington still thought the U.S. system of mortgage finance was the envy of the world.

Mudd went on to become chief executive of a fund-management company in New York but could not escape the Fannie quagmire. In December 2011, the SEC filed a civil lawsuit against Mudd. The suit accused him and others of misleading investors by vastly understating the amount of high-risk subprime and Alt-A loans Fannie acquired. Fannie's holdings of subprime mortgages at the end of 2007 were about twelve times what the company disclosed to investors, the SEC said, and exposure to low-doc loans was about twice the level that Fannie acknowledged. Mudd vehemently denied that he had sought to mislead investors. "The SEC's case is purely political and entirely fictional," he said. "Contrary to their tortured retrospective rewrite of the facts, we did our very best to disclose all the information investors might find relevant."

Chapter 10

Fannie on Trial

Pending difficult decisions by Congress on how the country should remake its mortgage market and how much of a role the government should keep, Fannie and Freddie lived on as zombies, under the thumb of their regulator and the U.S. Treasury.

Before looking forward, it is helpful to glance back: Who was to blame for the failures of Fannie and Freddie? To what degree were Fannie and Freddie to blame for the crash of the housing market? What did they accomplish before they failed?

The first two questions were among many considered by the Financial Crisis Inquiry Commission. Created by Congress in May 2009, the commission was assigned to "examine the causes, domestic and global, of the current financial and economic crisis." Phil Angelides, a former California state treasurer, was chairman of the ten-person panel.

The commission interviewed hundreds of people, examined thousands of documents and held public hearings. One such hearing, on April 9, 2010, in the Rayburn House Office Building in Washington, focused on what went wrong at Fannie and Freddie.

First up at the witness table were Daniel Mudd, who by then had become chief executive officer of Fortress Investment Group, a fund management company, and Robert Levin, Fannie's former chief business officer, who was ousted in August 2008 by Mudd as part of a management shakeup shortly before the government took over and in turn ousted Mudd. Levin, who had spent twenty-seven years working for Fannie, embodied much of the institutional memory of the company. In 2007, his last full year at Fannie, Levin's compensation totaled $7 million. (That included about $2.3 million in salary and cash bonuses; most of the rest was in awards of stock and stock options, whose value was effectively wiped out in 2008.)

If Levin still felt any resentment over his sudden ouster, he did not let it show as he sat next to Mudd and gave his account of Fannie's downfall. Levin depicted Fannie as a victim of events: "From my perspective, Fannie Mae was engulfed by an unprecedented decline in home prices and resulting dislocations in the housing markets. And these were truly catastrophic. While some people foresaw a correction, few, if any, predicted the unusually rapid and devastating destruction of real estate values that occurred."

Should Fannie have been better prepared for a storm? "In hindsight, if we, and the industry as a whole, had been able to anticipate the nature and extent of the crisis that engulfed the market, it is clear that we all would have conducted our business differently....But we, like everyone else, were surprised by the unprecedented extent of the economic crisis."

MUDD ADMITTED THAT THE standards Fannie set for Alt-A mortgages "weren't tight enough," though he said that was clear only in retrospect. Mudd, still the stoical ex-marine, was willing to accept some blame: "I was the CEO of the company and I accept responsibility for everything that happened on my watch." Yet he described Fannie's move into riskier loans not so much as an error but as something that seemed to make a lot of sense based on what he knew at that time: "We found ourselves...basically not being able to imagine how bad reality would be."

A member of the commission, Keith Hennessey, former senior economic adviser to President George W. Bush, quizzed Mudd about the extent to which Fannie had worsened the housing bubble by backing riskier types of loans: "Do you think that Fannie Mae's increased participation in subprime and Alt-A markets contributed to these homeownership rates rising too high?" Hennessey asked Mudd.

"Contributed?" Mudd replied. "I would say so."

Mudd argued that the company's dual role of pleasing shareholders while serving a public mission ended up being untenable in turbulent times: "So many decisions were a choice between unsavory alternatives." He added, "I did the best that I knew how to consider alternatives, develop processes, to listen to critical voices and ultimately to try to predict the perilous path of the housing market."

Fannie had one line of business—mortgages—and they were at the center of the crisis. "I could not do what a private firm could do, leave the market, close the window, or short mortgages," he said. Fannie and Freddie had "to stay in the market, provide liquidity....Virtually every other housing sector investor fled the market, and the GSEs were specifically required to take up the slack....I sought to balance the fine points of mission and business, insofar as I could understand them....That was no longer possible by September 6th, 2008, and I am sorry for that."

It was a hedged and limited apology. In essence, Mudd was saying he was sorry that he couldn't do the impossible. As he told it, the disaster was inevitable: "A monoline GSE, asked to perform multiple tasks, cannot withstand a multi-year 30% home-price decline, on a national scale, even had it been without the accompanying global financial turmoil." The threat of further legal action, of course, may have inhibited Mudd and others from speaking more frankly about their errors.

HEATHER MURREN, A MEMBER of the commission, was a former equity analyst at Merrill Lynch who later served as chief executive of the nonprofit Nevada Cancer Institute. She knew both the nonprofit world and Wall Street. She zeroed in on compensation.

"So let's talk a little bit about the numbers," she began, addressing Mudd and Levin. "You were, over the course of your tenure at Fannie Mae, extremely well paid, both of you were, correct?"

Mudd replied, "I think so." He said compensation "was set to a level, to the best of my knowledge, about 70% of the total compensation for comparable positions in the marketplace."

The company's proxy statements, legal filings to the SEC, for 2006 and 2007 state that the company's board used as a guideline for pay the median amount paid by a "comparator group" of seventeen major financial companies, including the giant banks Citigroup and Wells Fargo and the country's largest mortgage lender, Countrywide. That meant Fannie compensation *could* be set at the typical level, the midpoint, of this group of companies, not 70 percent of the typical level. It would depend on decisions by the board.

Mudd's total compensation was $12.2 million for 2007. About $3.2 million of that came in base salary and bonus. The remaining $9 million was in stock awards whose value collapsed before Mudd could cash in on them.

Even if compensation was 70 percent of the going rate, Murren would not have been assuaged. "I would say that 70% of a huge amount of money is still a huge amount of money," she said at the hearing.

Murren pointed to the list of seventeen financial companies whose pay was used to determine what Fannie would offer its executives. "There is not one single company there that is a mission-driven company," Murren said. "And I would wonder if you could explain to me, please, why you did not compare your compensation to, say, someone like the director of the Homeless Coalition."

Mudd replied that Fannie was competing for talent with major financial companies, not nonprofits.

"But what you're talking about," Murren persisted, "is comparability and motivation." People at Fannie had "an opportunity to cloak yourself in the public-service mission," she said, so the decision on pay should "span the waterfront of all of what it is that you do and motivates you. And you just told us that you were motivated by a public purpose. But I don't see that reflected anywhere in how you actually got paid, which, to me, suggests that maybe your motivation for doing what you did was not related necessarily in that great of a part to the public mission but really rather to achieving financial goals."

Mudd hesitated. "Well, I...I...I have a different opinion. And my opinion is that we had...to recruit people or try to retain people. And the places that they were going tended to be on the business side of the equation."

COMMISSIONER HENNESSEY CHALLENGED MUDD's depiction of the company as a victim of an unforeseeable crisis. In Hennessey's view, Fannie helped shape the circumstances that made it vulnerable.

"We've heard several times that Fannie Mae was in compliance with the regulatory capital standards," Hennessey said, "but if Fannie or its proxies were at the same time trying to keep those capital standards from being raised to something more like what a national bank or another large financial institution would have used, then there's a problem." He added, "I just think we need to understand...to what extent were these firms trying to influence both legislative and executive branch policy makers to not just keep the funding for the regulator low, but to prevent stricter capital standards and to prevent the regulator from having stronger authority over the size of the portfolios."

Regulators also gave their verdicts to the commission. Armando Falcon, who had been in charge of regulating Fannie and Freddie from 1999 to

2005, declared, "Ultimately, the companies were not unwitting victims of an economic down cycle or a flawed product or service of theirs. Their failure was deeply rooted in a culture of arrogance and greed." He added, "I should be clear that this was a failure of leadership. There were and are many good people in the ranks of both companies."

Lockhart, another former regulator, testified, "The companies' opposition to legislation for so long was a major mistake. The boards focused on maximizing shareholder profitability. In the end, they failed both the shareholders and the taxpayers."

The biggest failing was "the legislative framework, especially the capital rules," Lockhart said. "The GSE structure allowed them to be so politically strong that they resisted the very legislation that might have saved them."

Even under that flawed legislative structure, regulators "could have done more," Lockhart said. There was so much emphasis on fixing operational problems at the company (such as those that led to the accounting misdeeds) and on monitoring the companies' risks from fluctuations in interest rates that "the credit risk was not emphasized as much as it should have been in 2006," at the top of the housing bubble.

ALMOST EVERYONE BY NOW agreed that the ambiguous quasi-private, quasi-government nature of Fannie and Freddie had been a mistake and that their executives had made bad choices in financing too many high-risk mortgages. But how much blame should Fannie and Freddie bear for the housing-market crash?

That question, impossible to answer with precision, was more than academic. Verdicts on the causes of the crash would help shape U.S. government policy in the decades to come. Many Republicans wanted the historical narrative to show that Fannie, Freddie and other government programs to promote affordable housing were the biggest contributors to the debacle, or "the match that started this forest fire," as Senator McCain put it. The implication of that view was that government meddling in the economy was the main problem and must be reduced or eliminated to prevent future crises.

Democrats tended to agree, belatedly, that Fannie and Freddie were part of the problem, but they put more blame on Wall Street greed, deregulation and market forces that spurred risky mortgage lending outside the Fannie-Freddie world. If their view prevailed, the answer would be more regulation of financial companies, as embodied in the

Dodd-Frank legislation, enacted in 2010. That law gave the government powers to take over and liquidate failing financial institutions and restricted the amount of risk banks could take with their capital, among many other things. Even after the Dodd-Frank Act took effect, Democrats and Republicans continued to bicker over whether regulation was the problem or the solution.

AFTER INTERVIEWING MORE THAN seven hundred people and holding nineteen days of public hearings, the Financial Crisis Inquiry Commission was unable to resolve this debate. Its January 2011 report, approved by only six of the ten commissioners, concluded that a wide variety of failures caused the financial panic of 2008. Among them:

- Regulators failed to crack down on risky practices. They "had ample power in many arenas but chose not to use it."
- Banks and other companies fell down on corporate governance and risk management, partly because compensation plans rewarded short-term profits rather than long-term consequences.
- Financial institutions and households "borrowed to the hilt, leaving them vulnerable to financial distress or ruin if the value of their investments declined even modestly."
- There was a "systematic breakdown" in accountability and ethics. "Lenders made loans they knew borrowers could not afford." Mortgage brokers sometimes offered the loans that would generate the biggest fees rather than the ones that were most appropriate for the borrower. Some borrowers "likely took out loans they never had the capacity or intention to repay."
- The government was ill prepared to manage a financial crisis.

The report also concluded that the government, while promoting homeownership for poor people, "failed to ensure that the philosophy of opportunity was being matched by the practical realities on the ground.... The talk of opportunity was tragically at odds with the reality of a financial disaster in the making."

Fannie and Freddie "contributed to the crisis, but were not a primary cause," the majority concluded.

Fannie on Trial

Peter Wallison blamed federal housing programs for causing a wave of foreclosures. *Courtesy of Peter Wallison.*

PETER WALLISON, A FORMER Reagan administration official and long-standing critic of Fannie and Freddie, disagreed vehemently. As a member of the commission, he published a ninety-five-page "dissenting statement," blaming the financial crisis almost entirely on U.S. government policies to increase homeownership by encouraging looser mortgage-lending standards, notably through smaller down payments. Without these policies, "the great financial crisis of 2008 would never have occurred," he wrote.

Wallison blamed the housing goals established for Fannie and Freddie under the 1992 regulatory act. These and other federal housing policies, Wallison wrote, led to a "gradual degrading of traditional mortgage underwriting standards." Easier credit, in turn, helped inflate housing prices to unsustainable levels.

Wallison based his indictment of those policies partly on research by Edward Pinto, who was chief credit officer of Fannie in the late 1980s. (Pinto told me that he was pushed out of Fannie and was never given a reason for that.) Pinto later worked as a financial consultant and then became a fellow at the American Enterprise Institute, a conservative think tank where Wallison also worked.

Pinto calculated that in 2008 about 26.7 million home mortgages then outstanding, or 49 percent of all home loans in the United States, had "high-risk characteristics, making them far more likely to default." He called these loans "nontraditional mortgages" and included under that term his own definitions of subprime and Alt-A loans.

About two-thirds of these high-risk loans were made as a result of government policies, Wallison estimated. (Not all of these loans were equally risky, however. The default data from the FHFA, discussed in chapter nine, showed that Fannie and Freddie loans performed better than loans packaged into securities by Wall Street.)

Pinto defined his terms broadly, in a way that produced a larger number of high-risk loans than some others would find. Nonetheless, his findings showed that the number of high-risk loans backed by Fannie and Freddie was much higher than generally believed. He also argued that their embrace in the 1990s of low down payments (as a way to meet their affordable housing goals) made that practice legitimate for the mortgage-lending industry as a whole.

In his dissent, Wallison stressed the damage done by government housing policies, rather than other possible culprits, including market forces and human folly outside of the government. But, contrary to Wallison's suggestion, it wasn't a matter of one or the other—the government's fault or everyone else's fault. It was both. The share to be assigned to each actor is impossible to calculate. By their own admission, Fannie executives loosened their mortgage standards to regain market share (the profit motive), as well as to meet government housing mandates (the government-policy motive). If it had been all the government's fault, Fannie executives could more convincingly excuse themselves from blame.

The other dissenting statement to the commission's majority report came from three Republican commission members: Hennessey, Douglas Holtz-Eakin and Bill Thomas. They found a wide array of causes for the financial crisis, including a "credit bubble" caused by huge surpluses of dollars held by China and other fast-growing nations, leading to large flows of money into U.S. mortgages and real estate. They found that "poorly designed government housing policies" distorted the market, but they rejected Wallison's idea that these policies were the main cause of the crisis.

In any case, Wallison's dissent neatly summed up the psychology of bubbles: "Human beings have a tendency to believe that things will continue to go in the direction they are going, and are good at explaining why this must be so. Blaming the crisis on the failure to foresee it is facile and of little value for policy makers, who cannot legislate prescience."

WHAT WENT WRONG WITH Fannie Mae? A program that started out as a minor policy gambit in the late 1930s was allowed to grow and mutate indefinitely. A sunset clause in the initial charter could have set a time limit on this experiment before it got out of control. President Eisenhower and Congress tried to bring down the curtain in the early 1950s but failed to set a timetable. The Johnson administration pretended to pluck Fannie out of the public sphere but left its true status in a muddle.

A few quirky politicians and assorted economists piped up in the 1980s, 1990s and the first decade of the 2000s to deplore the dangers of leaving

Fannie and Freddie as rapidly expanding contingent liabilities for the unsuspecting American taxpayer. Yet there was never enough political will to face down the Realtors, home builders, affordable-housing advocates and other interested parties determined to preserve one of their favorite subsidies. No one could say exactly how the mortgage market would manage without Fannie and Freddie; to many people in the industry, it seemed safer to stick with the devils we knew.

Fannie and Freddie defeated efforts by Congress to constrain their growth and subject them to strict regulation and higher capital requirements. They accepted, as a price for their privileges, unrealistically steep "goals," or quotas, for the portion of their financing that flowed to the poor.

On the plus side, Fannie and Freddie helped create a national market for mortgages to replace the local or regional markets of old. As a result, money could flow more easily from regions with plenty of savings to those without enough.

Yet they may have been too good at attracting "the money bees," as Joseph Califano put it. Because the bonds they issued suited the needs of central banks and other investors around the world, Fannie and Freddie funneled vast amounts of foreign money into U.S. housing, helping to inflate a bubble. (Some of that money otherwise would have flowed into U.S. Treasury bonds, reducing borrowing costs for Uncle Sam.)

Fannie and Freddie's low borrowing costs helped reduce interest rates for home buyers, though academics debated whether the savings were more than negligible. In any case, lower interest rates are not always an advantage for home buyers. When interest rates fall, borrowers can afford to spend more on housing and so tend to bid up prices. Higher home prices can negate the savings on interest. In their 1958 book *Federal Lending and Loan Insurance*, R.J. Saulnier and his coauthors found that, during the housing boom after World War II, Fannie and other federal credit programs helped raise home prices "above the levels that would otherwise have prevailed." Much of the government-backed lending was "dissipated" in the form of inflation, they wrote.

To promote homeownership, government authorities could have pursued a more effective policy: making more land available for housing. At the local level, that can be done through more flexible zoning, including provisions for greater density of housing—more homes per acre.

Defenders of Fannie and Freddie argued that the companies' continual presence in the mortgage market ensured that home loans were available even at times of financial panic or national crisis, such as the days after the

September 11, 2001 terrorist attacks. But there was a cost for this constant availability of mortgage funding: the U.S. government became the main guarantor of home loans, a costly proposition for taxpayers.

The willingness of Fannie and Freddie to finance thirty-year fixed-rate mortgages ensured that Americans would have access to that type of loan, rarely available in other parts of the world, where mortgage rates normally have adjustable rates. However, it isn't clear that thirty-year fixed-rate mortgages are possible only via entities like Fannie and Freddie; such loans are common in Denmark, which has no government-sponsored mortgage companies.

Does America need thirty-year fixed-rate loans? Americans are accustomed to these loans, and many would squawk if suddenly deprived of them. What many Americans do not realize is that they pay dearly for fixed rates. Interest on thirty-year fixed-rate loans is much higher than on adjustable-rate loans. Home buyers in many other countries, including Canada, cope quite easily with the uncertainties of adjustable rates. In any case, very few Americans keep their loans for thirty years; the vast majority move long before paying off their loans, and so face the risk of higher rates.

Fannie and Freddie contributed to a rise in the percentage of Americans who owned homes during the late 1990s and early 2000s, but that proved untenable. U.S. homeownership was steady from the mid-1960s to mid-1990s at around 63.0 to 66.0 percent of households. It began climbing in the late 1990s and peaked at around 69.0 percent in 2004, 2005 and 2006. (When he was CEO of Fannie, James Johnson said the goal should be 75.0 percent.) Then foreclosures dislodged millions from homes they couldn't afford. The rate had dropped back to 65.4 percent by the first quarter of 2012, within the norm of the past few decades.

FANNIE AND FREDDIE GREW too large and powerful for their own good or the good of the nation. As they bloated, the attacks on them—both from jealous rivals among financial firms and from politicians opposed to government involvement in the housing market—grew fiercer. To fend off those attacks, they had to finance more and more questionable loans in the quest to show they were serving the nation.

"It just got too big," Doug Bibby, a former senior vice-president at Fannie, told me after the company's fall into conservatorship. At such a scale, the business model wasn't sustainable. Fannie and Freddie "got caught up in the mortgage-feeding frenzy," he said. "You look back on it and you say, 'Whoa!'"

Chapter 11

Now What?

After the financial crisis of 2008 tipped the nation into the worst economic slump since the 1930s, Congress strove to legislate away the risk of a rerun. The Dodd-Frank Wall Street Reform and Consumer Protection Act, enacted in 2010, included an attempt to reduce the risk of future excesses in mortgage lending. Under that law, firms that sell mortgage-backed securities were required to retain 5 percent of the credit risk unless the mortgages met certain safety standards. Sellers of mortgage securities were required to make more disclosures about the loans that underlay those securities.

The Dodd-Frank law required lenders to ensure borrowers had the ability to repay mortgage loans—something that might seem obvious but wasn't always standard practice during the boom years. The law prohibited lenders from giving loan officers or brokers incentive payments to steer borrowers into more costly types of loans. The law also created an agency, the Consumer Financial Protection Bureau, charged with protecting Americans from deceptive practices by lenders and other financial firms. (No means had been discovered to protect Americans from their own foolishness.)

One benefit of the housing crash was that it forced a rethinking of government support for housing. By 2010, there was serious discussion in Washington of abolishing or reducing the tax deduction for mortgage interest—long thought to be too popular for any politician to touch.

Congress did not move swiftly, however, in deciding what to do about Fannie and Freddie. They hobbled along as the main U.S. providers of funding for home loans, putting their guarantees on three out of every four mortgage loans made in 2011. Lawmakers still saw them as convenient pots of money. When Congress was unable to agree on spending cuts or tax increases in late 2011 to cover the cost of a two-month extension of a payroll tax break, it opted to increase the guarantee fees Fannie and Freddie charge lenders. Those extra fees were funneled to the Treasury to offset the cost of the tax cuts.

The companies' regulator, the FHFA, was seeking to reduce their role in the mortgage market, gradually, while waiting for Congress to make up its mind on their future. Though the Fannie-Freddie system was now almost universally scorned as a huge mistake, it was hard to decide exactly what should replace them.

One of the few areas of agreement was that any government backing for the mortgage market should be explicitly stated rather than merely implied, as it was with Fannie and Freddie. Any kind of ambiguity over the government's obligations could lead to trouble, Congress now realized. At a hearing of the House Financial Services Committee in October 2008, Representative Maxine Waters, a California Democrat who was among the most fervid defenders of Fannie and Freddie in the days when they were quasi-government agencies, said Congress would have to think carefully about how to remake them. "Clearly," Waters said, "the word 'quasi' is an adjective that should probably not be applicable to the new structure."

In February 2011, the Obama administration released a report to Congress that amounted to a death sentence for Fannie and Freddie. It left plenty of time for a reprieve. The administration said it would develop a plan "to responsibly reduce the role" of Fannie and Freddie in the mortgage market "and, ultimately, wind down both institutions." It would not do that immediately, however, because the housing market remained "fragile" and needed protection from sudden jolts. The administration described its thirty-one-page report as a "plan to reform America's housing finance market." In fact, it was only a set of three options to serve as a basis for discussion:

- The government's role could be limited to programs—such as those of the FHA and the Department of Veterans Affairs—helping "narrowly targeted groups of borrowers." That would leave "the vast majority of the mortgage market" to fend for itself. While such an approach would reduce the risk of taxpayer-funded bailouts, mortgage costs for most Americans "would likely increase." Smaller lenders and community banks might have trouble competing as big banks grew more dominant.

- The government could develop a "backstop mechanism" to ensure a flow of credit during housing crises. This backstop might be in the form of a government guarantee on mortgages that would be priced high enough so that lenders would use it only in times when private capital is scarce. The report noted that it might be difficult to design and manage "an organization that can remain small during normal economic times, yet has the capacity to take on much more business quickly during these times of need."
- The government could offer a form of guarantee for securities backed by certain kinds of approved mortgages. Private mortgage insurance companies would provide guarantees that the securities would be repaid, and the government, for a fee, would stand ready to cover any "catastrophic" losses that remained if the private mortgage insurers were wiped out. This system "likely provides the lowest-cost access to mortgage credit" of the three options, the report said. Still, the government's promise to pay for losses beyond a certain level "exposes the government to risk and moral hazard." If the cost of the government's insurance is too low, "then private actors in the market may take on excessive risk and the taxpayer could again bear the cost."

Another problem with the third option is that the cost of the insurance might become a matter for political debate. Realtors and builders would be likely to resist substantial fees to the government on the ground that they would raise mortgage costs and slow the housing market.

A striking feature of this report is that it mentions rental housing as a desirable option in the second paragraph, before mentioning homeownership: "Our plan champions the belief that Americans should have choices in housing that make sense for them and their families. This means rental options near good schools and good jobs. It means access to credit for those Americans who want to own their own home." Washington was no longer exalting homeownership for all.

The plan envisioned a much smaller role for government in housing finance, saying private markets would become the "primary" source of mortgage credit and "bear the burden of losses." The government's main role was to be "limited to robust oversight and consumer protection, targeted assistance for low- and moderate-income homeowners and renters, and carefully designed support for market stability and crisis response."

For many people, the American dream ended in ruin, as was the case with this vacant house near Pittsburgh in 2012. *Photo by James R. Hagerty.*

THE HOUSING INTERESTS ALREADY were gearing up to defend government backing for their industry. The Realtors ran an advertisement in the *Washington Post* on February 13, 2011, declaring, "Jobs and Home Ownership. You can't have one without the other." The ad, aimed at Congress, stated, "Strong federal government support for home ownership equals strong support for American jobs." Another Realtor ad, in *Roll Call* the same month, warned that "eliminating all federal involvement would harm economic recovery and put the housing market at greater risk." It added, "Home buyers need a steady, reliable flow of mortgage funding."

At a hearing in the House of Representatives on March 1, 2011, the Obama administration also seemed wary of withdrawing the federal government from the mortgage market. Treasury Secretary Timothy Geithner warned against limiting federal involvement to programs like the FHA. That approach, he said, might merely shift the risks borne by Fannie and Freddie onto federally insured banks.

Two days later, the *New York Times* ran a page-one story warning about the possible consequences of abolishing Fannie and Freddie. "The 30-year fixed-rate mortgage loan, the steady favorite of American borrowers since the 1950s, could become a luxury product," the *Times* wrote, adding, "Interest rates would rise for most borrowers, but urban and rural residents could see sharper increases than the coveted customers in the suburbs. Lenders could charge fees for popular features now taken for granted, like the ability to 'lock in' an interest rate weeks or months before taking out a loan." The Realtors distributed that story nationwide through e-mail blasts.

EVEN IF THE IMMENSE lobbying power of the Realtors can be turned back, it may be impossible to get Uncle Sam out of housing finance. Phillip Swagel, who was Treasury assistant secretary for economic policy under Henry Paulson, in a commentary published by the Bloomberg news service on July 18, 2011, drew "one clear lesson" from his experience with the rescue of Fannie and Freddie: the U.S. government always "will be compelled to step in if it becomes concerned that American families cannot obtain mortgages," even though "market purists might not like it."

Because "the government will always be part of the housing market," he wrote, "let's make sure we keep its role as small and contained as possible." Swagel advocated a legislative plan similar to one of the Obama administration's stated options: at least five private companies would provide funding for mortgages by issuing securities backed by high-quality mortgages. These firms would pay insurance premiums to the government, which would guarantee the mortgage securities (but not the survival of the firms issuing those securities). Swagel acknowledged the difficulty of finding the right price to pay the government for providing that insurance. Still, he said, "any price it charges will be better than zero, which was the de facto rate in the Fannie-Freddie system."

A different proposal came from the American Enterprise Institute, or AEI, a think tank that long housed some of the most determined critics of Fannie and Freddie. In a paper released in January 2011, Wallison, Pinto and Alex J. Pollock of the AEI rejected the idea that a healthy U.S. mortgage market requires some sort of government backing for mortgage securities. Instead of providing such a government guarantee, they said, the government should require that only prime-quality mortgages can be used to back mortgage securities. Defaults on such mortgages should always be rare, making the securities sufficiently attractive without government backing, they argued.

To be considered prime, they wrote, mortgages would need to meet these standards, among others:

- The loan would have to be on a home occupied as a primary or secondary residence (thus excluding investor-owned rental properties, which tend to have higher default rates).
- The amount borrowed could be no more than 90 percent of the estimated value of the home.
- The borrower would need a credit score of 660 or more.
- The lender would have to verify the income, assets and credit situation of the borrower.

Any government support or subsidy to help poor people afford housing would be treated as an expense on the government budget. Fannie and Freddie would be wound down gradually.

Loans of less than prime quality would still be made, but these loans would have to be held individually by banks, insurers or other investors rather than placed into securities for public sale.

LET'S CONSIDER THE VIEWS of some of the prime actors in this drama.

David Maxwell, the former Fannie CEO, remained convinced that banks could not be relied on to provide a steady source of funding for mortgages. But he agreed that the Fannie/Freddie structure "needs to be rethought and reworked." Any new version of Fannie and Freddie would need "defined earning power and compensation arrangements, as well as close and effective regulation," he told me. "Lobbying Congress," he added, "could be banned."

Daniel Mudd declared in an August 2009 speech that "policies that aim to increase homeownership without limit are unwise....When the economy is strong, homeownership will rise, and when it is weaker, and families have less certainty about the future, they will be less inclined to buy. Using the capital markets as the tool to force [up] the homeownership rate is dangerous." Rather than treating a low-cost mortgage loan as a right for all Americans, he suggested, the policy ought to be, "You have the right to own a home, if you can afford it."

Writing in the *Washington Post* in July 2010, former Treasury Secretary Paulson questioned "the combined weight" of government support for housing, including Fannie and Freddie, the FHA, the Federal Home Loan Banks, the tax deduction for mortgage interest and state housing programs. "Homeownership was overstimulated to the point that it was unsustainable and dangerous for the broader economy," he wrote.

Now What?

For the future, Paulson suggested turning Fannie and Freddie into "one or two private-sector entities that would purchase and securitize mortgages with a credit guarantee explicitly backed by the federal government and paid for by the new entity. These privately owned entities would be set up like public utilities and governed by a rate-setting commission that would establish a targeted rate of return."

FINALLY, MY OWN VIEW. Seven decades of growing federal support for home mortgages have ended in a collapse of the housing market that has crippled the finances of millions of Americans and helped drag our economy into the worst slump since the Great Depression—the cataclysm that was the original pretext for this experiment in housing finance.

America still has a housing problem. Millions live in squalor or on the streets. The solutions lie mainly in policies that encourage job creation and improve education. Any government spending to spur investment in housing should be on the books, not conjured via an implied guarantee. Any government intervention should be subject to limits in scope and duration. There is no need for Uncle Sam to favor homeownership over renting—a choice Americans can make for themselves.

Bibliography

Acharya, Viral V., Matthew Richardson, Stijn Van Nieuwerburgh and Lawrence J. White. *Guaranteed to Fail.* Princeton, NJ: Princeton University Press, 2011.

Department of Housing and Urban Development. "The National Homeownership Strategy: Partners in the American Dream." May 1995.

———. "Report of the Office of Inspector General." October 5, 2004.

Financial Crisis Inquiry Commission. "The Financial Crisis Inquiry Report." 2011.

Fish, Gertrude S., ed. *The Story of Housing.* New York: Macmillan Publishing, 1979.

Frame, W. Scott, and Larry D. Wall. "Financing Housing Through Government-Sponsored Enterprises." *Federal Reserve Bank of Atlanta Economic Review* (First Quarter 2002).

Hutchison, Janet. "Building for Babbitt: The State and the Suburban Home Ideal." *Journal of Policy History* 9, no. 2 (1997).

Johnson, James A. *Showing America a New Way Home.* San Francisco: Jossey-Bass, 1996.

Keith, Nathaniel S. *Politics and the Housing Crisis Since 1930*. New York: Universe Books, 1973.

Lehnert, Andreas, Wayne Passmore and Shane M. Sherlund. "GSEs, Mortgage Rates and Secondary Market Activities." Federal Reserve Board, 2005.

McCarthy, Jonathan, and Richard W. Peach. "Are Home Prices the Next 'Bubble'?" *Federal Reserve Board of New York Economic Policy Review* (December 2004).

McLean, Bethany, and Joseph Nocera. *All the Devils Are Here: The Hidden History of the Financial Crisis*. New York: Portfolio, 2010.

Morgenson, Gretchen, and Joshua Rosner. *Reckless Endangerment*. New York: Times Books, 2011.

Muolo, Paul, and Mathew Padilla. *Chain of Blame*. Hoboken, NJ: John Wiley & Sons, 2008.

Musolf, Lloyd D. *Uncle Sam's Private, Profitseeking Corporations*. Lexington, MA: Lexington Books, 1983.

Office of Federal Housing Enterprise Oversight. "Report of the Special Examination of Fannie Mae." 2006.

Paul, Weiss, Rifkind, Wharton & Garrison LLP. "A Report to the Special Review Committee of the Board of Directors of Fannie Mae." 2006.

Paulson, Henry M., Jr. *On the Brink*. New York: Hachette, 2010.

Pollock, Alex J. *Boom & Bust*. Washington, D.C.: AEI Press, 2010.

Rossi, Clifford V. "Anatomy of Risk Management Practices in the Mortgage Industry." Research Institute for Housing America, May 2010.

Saulnier, R.J., Harold G. Halcrow and Neil H. Jacoby. *Federal Lending and Loan Insurance*. Princeton, NJ: Princeton University Press, 1958.

Stanton, Thomas H. *Government-Sponsored Enterprises: Mercantalist Companies in the Modern World*. Washington, D.C.: AEI Press, 2002.

———. *A State of Risk: Will Government-Sponsored Enterprises Be the Next Financial Crisis?* New York: HarperCollins, 1991.

Stiglitz, Joseph E., Jonathan M. Orszag and Peter R. Orszag. "Implications of the New Fannie Mae and Freddie Mac Risk-Based Capital Standard." *Fannie Mae Papers* 1, no. 2 (March 2002).

Wallison, Peter J., ed. *Serving Two Masters Yet Out of Control*. Washington, D.C.: AEI Press, 2001.

Wallison, Peter J., Thomas H. Stanton and Bert Ely. *Privatizing Fannie Mae, Freddie Mac and the Federal Home Loan Banks*. Washington, D.C.: AEI Press, 2004.

Index